PERGAMON INTERNATIONAL LIBRARY
of Science, Technology, Engineering and Social Studies
*The 1000-volume original paperback library in aid of education,
industrial training and the enjoyment of leisure*
Publisher: Robert Maxwell, M.C.

Disarmament and World Development

THE PERGAMON TEXTBOOK
INSPECTION COPY SERVICE

An inspection copy of any book published in the Pergamon International Library will
gladly be sent to academic staff without obligation for their consideration for course
adoption or recommendation. Copies may be retained for a period of 60 days from
receipt and returned if not suitable. When a particular title is adopted or recommended for
adoption for class use and the recommendation results in a sale of 12 or more copies, the
inspection copy may be retained with our compliments. The Publishers will be pleased to
receive suggestions for revised editions and new titles to be published in this important
International Library.

Other Titles of Interest:

Disarmament and World Development

Edited by

RICHARD JOLLY

Institute of Development Studies
University of Sussex

PERGAMON PRESS

OXFORD · NEW YORK · TORONTO · SYDNEY · PARIS · FRANKFURT

U.K.	Pergamon Press Ltd., Headington Hill Hall, Oxford OX3 0BW, England
U.S.A.	Pergamon Press Inc., Maxwell House, Fairview Park, Elmsford, New York 10523, U.S.A.
CANADA	Pergamon of Canada Ltd., 75 The East Mall, Toronto, Ontario, Canada
AUSTRALIA	Pergamon Press (Aust.) Pty. Ltd., 19a Boundary Street, Rushcutters Bay, N.S.W. 2011, Australia
FRANCE	Pergamon Press SARL, 24 rue des Ecoles, 75240 Paris, Cedex 05, France
FEDERAL REPUBLIC OF GERMANY	Pergamon Press GmbH, 6242 Kronberg-Taunus, Pferdstrasse 1, Federal Republic of Germany

First edition 1978

British Library Cataloguing in Publication Data

Disarmament and world development.
(Pergamon international library).
1. Underdeveloped areas - Social conditions
2. Disarmament
I. Jolly, Richard
309.2`3`091724   HN980   77-30757
ISBN 0-08-023019-9 (Hardcover)
ISBN 0-08-023018-0 (Flexicover)

In order to make this volume available as economically and as rapidly as possible the author's typescript has been reproduced in its original form. This method unfortunately has its typographical limitations but it is hoped that they in no way distract the reader.

Printed in Great Britain by A. Wheaton & Co. Ltd., Exeter.

Contents

v

List of Tables, Figures, Charts and Resolutions

FIGURES

CHARTS   (Centre Section)

RESOLUTIONS ON DISARMAMENT AND DEVELOPMENT

Preface

The idea of this volume and a number of the papers within it have their origins
in a conference arranged by the UK section of the United Nations Association
and the Society for International Development, organizations primarily interested in promoting world economic and social development. The topic, armaments
and development, arose from the growing awareness, based on past experience,
that the motivations and resources necessary for development will not be forthcoming as long as they continue to be tapped and drained away to fuel the psy-
chosis, institutions and industries of war.

The persistent expansion of defence expenditure, totalling some $350 billion
in 1976, consuming scarce resources of many kinds, including those most precious ones of science and technology, may be likened to a vast cancer in the
world body politic. Armaments are growing, development is faltering. These
two facts are not unconnected, as the papers in this volume will make clear.
Somewhere along the line, unless this process can be arrested and reversed,
humanity will destroy itself.

The belief underlying the convening of the initial conference is that the
present fatal order of priorities must and can be transposed. It is a call to
all mankind, especially those who are young, to exert themselves creatively to
visualize the kind of world community based on the full observance of human
rights to which humanity is capable of moving and to work unremittingly towards
its realization. The challenge is to people and countries in all parts of the
world, East and West, North and South, for the logic of the situation is
equally binding upon all.

In 1978, the United Nations will be holding a special session of the General
Assembly on Disarmament. In parallel, it will be preparing a new International
Strategy for economic and social development for the Third UN Development Decade to be proclaimed in 1980. Progress in Disarmament will be a condition of
success in the Development Decade, as has now been recognized by the latest
report of the UN Committee for Development Planning, which stated:

> "The single and most massive (obstacle to development) is
> the world-wide expenditure on national defence activity".

It called for "unflagging emphasis" on the global need for re-allocation of
resources from defence to development.

The papers in this volume document the enormity of the waste and danger involved in the present scale of armaments activities, which have reached unprecedented levels in both developed and developing countries and in the arms trade
between them. A summary of Philip Noel Baker's eloquent opening address to
the conference on disarmament and development states with passionate simplicity
the real costs of these military excesses: they are a theft from the millions
who hunger and are not fed, from those who are cold and are not clothed.

Frank Barnaby draws on the research of SIPRI to document authoritatively the
current scale of world military expenditures, and their thirty-fold growth
since the beginning of the century.

In addition to unprecedented waste, the worldwide deployment of armaments,
especially nuclear weapons, also involves risks of unprecedented danger. One
is apt to forget the extent of human suffering and destruction which even the
detonation of two "small" atom bombs at Hiroshima and Nagasaki caused in 1945
and afterwards: the deaths of at least 250,000 people and the injuring of
many others. Yet the world now contains more than 60,000 nuclear weapons —
including 12,500 independently targetable warheads on bombers and missiles —
mostly much more powerful than the two which obliterated Hiroshima and Nagasaki in 1945.

The scale of current military and armament activity throughout the world is
such that any ordinary imagination finds it hard, if not impossible, to grasp.
Even more difficult, with activities so enormous and far ranging, is to establish the broad outlines of the causes and connections which sustain these
activities and the impact they have on world development. The two major
pieces by Robin Luckham and Mary Kaldor attempt this. Robin Luckham provides
an overview of world armaments production and trade, showing their intimate
links with the whole structure of industrial production and particularly to
the technological heart which provides the life-blood of so much of the indus-
trial-military-academic complex. The international arms economy is thus not
simply an unwanted outgrowth, surplus and blood-sucking to the main structure.
It is, to continue the metaphor, a cancer in a fairly advanced stage, in which
a large part of the whole body economic and politic is using its energy and
resources to support this life-killing growth. Not surprisingly, disarmament
involves a much more complex operation than simply cutting out or cutting down
on military activities.

Mary Kaldor provides a parallel view of the military in the Third World, foc-
ussing on the twin-roles of the military as organized force and as a consumer
of resources. Mary Kaldor reviews some 100 key works on the military, contras-
ting the easy optimism of the "modernists", who suggest the military will have
a positive modernizing impact on Third World development, with the impatient
pessimism of the Marxists and others who see the military as serving as an
instrument for maintaining the dominance of a repressive state acting in the
interests of a rich elite and against the poor majority.

These articles reveal only too clearly, one could add depressingly, the complex
set of mutual dependences between the military and armaments sectors and the
structures of economic production and political power in both the industrialized and less developed parts of the world. Scarce wonder that disarmament
should have proved so complex and intractable a concern.

Nevertheless, for two simple but fundamental reasons, disarmament, in part or
in whole, is still the path of sanity, which on both moral and rational grounds
must tirelessly be pursued. The first reason, as Alva Myrdal so succinctly
states in her extract from The Game of Disarmament, is "that the building up
of the giant military establishments has gone, and is going, right against
what would be rational from the point of view of every nation. This applies
as well to the super powers' policy of increasing armaments. It is beyond all
reason".

The second argument is set out in the piece by Inga Thorsson on "Ways to Gen-

erate the Political Will". In the words of the UN Planning Committee, this is
that the scale and pattern of resource use in the current armaments race is
now the single and most massive obstacle to development. Put in human terms,
one can say that the poverty in which half mankind must live is directly related to the absurdities under which the world military establishment has stored
up the equivalent of 15 tons of TNT for every man, woman and child on the globe
and spends annually on armaments more than the poorest half of mankind spends
on everything.

Even when the moral and rational imperative is so clear, precisely what to do
is not. This is not due to lack of suggestions. The pieces by Alva Myrdal,
Inga Thorsson and Robert Neild explore a number of proposals, based on their
long experience with practical negotiation in international arenas. But as
Richard Jolly emphasizes, significant progress towards disarmament is increasingly likely to depend on making changes in the internal economic structures
of the major industrial powers. Without serious steps to restructure their
domestic patterns of production, technology, employment and international trade
over the long run, the various interests tending to maintain these patterns in
the short run are likely to undermine international negotiations for reducing
the scale of armaments and military activities.

Extracts from three pieces prepared by the United Nations are also included:
the expert report of August 1977, prepared as a background document for the
1978 Special Session on Disarmament and Development of the General Assembly;
the 1975 proposal for linking a measure of disarmament with an increase in
resource transfers for Third World development; and the famous 1972 report of
a UN expert group on disarmament and development which shows how disarmament
and development could be combined in ways which would increase employment in
both the developed and developing countries. Finally, the conclusions of the
UNA/SID conference and the formal resolutions on disarmament and development
of the UNA Annual General Meeting are included, in order to make the implications for policy specific in the context of Britain today. Although these are
focussed on the conclusions for British policy, it will be clear that their
broad thrust is also applicable to other countries, particularly to others
with large armaments and military activities.

Both disarmament and development have been continuing preoccupations in international and national debate for several decades. Unfortunately they have
rarely been analyzed together — and the mutually reinforcing opportunities
emphasized, if only some measure of disarmament could be combined with a new
thrust for development. The Special Assembly of the United Nations to be held
in 1978 provides one opportunity for this simple but politically enormous idea
to be pursued. There will be others.

One hopes that the documents in this book may serve to underline the size of
the gains which could be achieved and help to convince policy makers and ordinary people alike that a measure of disarmament for development is infinitely
more sensible and desirable than the continuation of the current military mad-
ness.

Acknowledgements

On behalf of the Society for International Development and the United Nations
Association I would like to thank

— the Edith Ellis Charitable Trust whose generous assistance
enabled the original conference to be held;

— the United Nations, the Dag Hammarskjold Foundation, the
New Internationalist, the New Scientist and World Development
for permission to reprint sections of reports or articles
earlier appearing in their own publications;

— Ruth Leger Sivard for permission to include selections
from World Military and Social Expenditures 1977;

— Kevin Brown, Helen Rees, Pamela Smith and Barbara Taylor
of the Institute of Development Studies for assistance
with typing and the preparation of the manuscript.

PART I

Disarmament and Development:
The Need for Action

Disarmament and Development

Philip Noel Baker

[handwritten annotations: good; poverty – armament]

"Every gun that is made, every warship launched, every rocket fired, signifies, in a final sense, a *theft* from those who hunger and are not fed, from those who are cold and are not clothed." *[handwritten: money loss or a potential death.]*

It was President Eisenhower of the United States who said this, while he was still in the White House. He also said while he was President that "war in our time has become an anachronism. Whatever the case in the past, war in the future can serve no useful purpose".

And he said that nothing in the world is as important and urgent as world disarmament. "The alternative is so terrible that any risks there might be in advancing to disarmament are as nothing" — "nothing" is Eisenhower's word — compared to the risks of *not* disarming, the risks of "sitting on your hands," of drifting on with the arms race and the so-called balance of power.

Eisenhower was a life-long soldier, devoted to the study of war, and to the build-up of US military strength. He was chosen, among all the generals of the western world, to command the greatest armed forces in the greatest battle in the history of war. With the elements against him, storm in the Channel, his invasion of Normandy was victoriously achieved, and the Nazi-Fascist aggression finally defeated.

In the speeches I have quoted, Eisenhower provides the final answer to any militarist who tries to argue that wars are still "inevitable", and may be useful; or that armaments are a source of security, influence or prestige; or that defence should have priority over aid to the poor.

And Eisenhower says that war is out-of-date; that disarmament is supremely urgent, if mankind is to survive, and that the present world armaments are the *cause* of the scandalous and tragic poverty that now afflicts a great proportion of the human race. The development of the arms race in the last twenty years has only reinforced everything he said.

But are world armaments the *cause* of world poverty? Yes, Eisenhower's "*theft*" means precisely that.

Sir Edward Grey (Lord Grey of Falloden) tried his utmost as British Foreign Secretary to prevent the First World War. When it was over, he wrote:

"The increase of armaments that is intended in each nation to produce consciousness of strength and a sense of security, does not produce these effects. On the contrary, it produces a consciousness of the strength of other nations and a sense of fear. Fear begets suspicion and distrust and evil imaginings of all sorts, till each government feels it would be criminal and a betrayal of its own country not to take every precaution, while every government regards every precaution of every other government as evidence of hostile intent."

D.W.D.— B

3

That is how the arms race works. Since 1945 it has led governments to spend vast resources on armaments, resources which ought, on grounds of morality, on grounds of equal human justice, on grounds of enlightened self-interest, to have been given instead to ending world poverty. That is how world armaments are the cause of world poverty.

Few people in the West have grasped the scale and the intensity of this poverty. The President of the World Bank, Mr. Robert MacNamara, told his Board of Governors in October 1976 that: "No statistics could illustrate the inhuman degradation to which the vast majority of the citizens of the Third World are condemned by poverty."

"Malnutrition", he said, "saps their energy, stunts their bodies, and shortens their lives. Illiteracy darkens their minds, and forecloses their futures. Simple, preventable diseases maim and kill their children. Squalor and ugliness pollute and poison their surroundings. The miraculous gift of life itself, and all its intrinsic potential — so promising and rewarding for us — is eroded and reduced for them to a desperate effort to survive."

There are more than a thousand million men and women in the world who cannot read or write or do the simplest sums. Their illiteracy helps all too powerfully to keep them poor. It prevents the rural proletariat from learning and applying the known agricultural techniques which would double their crops and change their lives. Illiteracy bars their path to social, cultural and political progress.

Yet if UNESCO were given a fund of $200 million for a worldwide literacy campaign, it could free every nation from this evil handicap. $200 million is approximately the price of two strategic bombers of the latest type.

The nations of the Third World suffer grievously from diseases which have disappeared from the "developed" West. Malaria still kills great numbers, and weakens millions more so that their productive output is reduced. Trachoma is very simple to cure, but, if untreated, it makes the victim blind, his life a burden to himself, and him a burden to society. Leprosy makes its victims segregated social outcasts. Yaws, a diet deficiency disease, covers the body with running sores, makes a man unfit for work or play, and allows him no real rest.

These four diseases impose a heavy annual load of economic loss and human suffering on the Third World. Yet all of them are easily preventable. The World Health Organisation could eliminate them — wipe them out now and for the future — for an expenditure of $500 million — about the cost of an aircraft carrier.

And this is not all, for the world hungers. The 1200 million individuals who have to live on incomes of less than 150 dollars a year are hungry from the cradle to the grave. They never know what it is to have a solid meal.

Less than two years ago the great Sahelian drought brought famine on an unprecedented scale to many countries in Africa. In those bad times, many thousands of starving children looked to Britain and we answered roughly: "No, we cannot help you. We can't afford the paltry millions of our precious sterling that would save you all. We must spend £5 500 million on armaments instead."

Spokesmen of the Third World have made extremely plain their demand for an end to world poverty. It is a demand for more equal distribution of the world's

wealth; a demand for more money from the UN and International Banks, for more
money for the UN Development Plans, for more favourable terms of trade for
third world exports in the markets of the rich.

The triumph of the oil producing countries, in their action through OPEC to
raise the world price of petroleum products, was a first successful venture in
the revolution of the exploited and the poor. It wrought havoc for the richer
industrialized nations and it was hard on some third world countries, too.
The revolt of OPEC against the rich nations' exploitation of their oil was not
immoral or unjust.

The result has certainly encouraged the Third World's spirit of revolt against
their poverty. That spirit is not going to "go away". Sooner or later, after
greater or lesser disasters of different kinds, after a longer or shorter period of loss and misery for the poor, the revolt will be successful, and the
shame of world poverty will be removed.

But that will only happen when nations have begun the world disarmament which
has for so long been overdue. It is only from the reduction of military expenditure that the vast resources needed for development can be obtained.

Thus Disarmament and Development are not two problems; they are one. They
must be solved together, or neither of them will be solved at all.

Just as many people in the advanced countries of the West have not really
understood what world poverty is like, so they have not understood the almost
incredible world expenditure for armaments and they do not know that more than
70 million men and women are now engaged full-time in the armed forces of the
world, in arms factories, in scientific research, in preparing for new wars to
come.

They do not know that in 1976 three hundred and fifty thousand million dollars
was the world expenditure on armaments — nearly a thousand million dollars a
day, nearly forty million dollars an hour.

They do not realise that the world society of states has been so militarized
that the greater part of almost all the major governments' foreign policy is
concerned with military alliances or with other issues relating to past, present and future wars.

The time has come for action. Action to provide public understanding of the
twin dangers of World Armament and World Poverty. Every individual has a part
to play in this, however small. Talk to others about the need for disarmament,
write letters to the press, to your head of government, to the Minister or
Secretary of Defence and to your political representative. Not one letter but
a letter every month to each of them. The postage stamp can, in time, silence
the reactionary bureaucrat in the government department and make the people's
will prevail.

Write letters, march, demonstrate and always remember that Pascal was right:
"Opinion is the sovereign of the world".

It is what men and women believe, what they accept as natural or necessary or
right, that determines the events that actually occur — *not* the trends of history, *not* the forces of nature, *not* the traditions of the past, but the thoughts,
convictions, surrenders or resolves that germinate in human minds today.

Only a veritable tide of world opinion, of new resolves, can overwhelm the
vested interests, and ensure the survival of mankind.

Note:

A slightly fuller version of this summary of Philip Noel-Baker's address for
the UNA/SID Conference at Goldsmith's College was originally printed in the
New Internationalist, No. 51, May 1977, pp. 25-26.

The Scale of World Military Expenditures

Frank Barnaby

p 21 - nuclear

"Military expenditures undoubtedly absorb resources which are substantial enough to make a considerable difference both in the level of investment for civil purposes and in the volume of resources which can be devoted to improving man's lot through social and other services. There is no doubt that a transfer of resources from military to civil uses would provide further possibilities for an increase in the rate of economic growth." This judgement is made in a 1972 UN report entitled Economic and Social Consequences of the Arms Race and of Military Expenditures. "If there were no arms race", the report concludes, "trade and other exchanges would almost certainly be easier. One major effect of the arms race and military expenditure has been to reduce the priority given to aid in the policies of donor countries."

The resources absorbed by military activities are indeed substantial. Annual military outlays equal the entire GNP of a typical highly industrialized country with a population of about 50 million and are about 25 times the funds given in foreign aid to Third World countries.[2] Governments spend on the military more than twice as much as they spend on health and about the same as they spend on education. Military research and development consumes about six times more money than does medical research. There are about the same number of persons in military uniform as there are teaching in our schools. Even in the under-developed regions troops are nearly fifteen times as numerous as doctors.

Before considering why Third World countries use scarce resources for military purposes, and participate in arms races, it is helpful to know the extent and regional distribution of military spending, the development of defence industries in the Third World, and the volume and scope of the arms trade with the third world.

World and regional military expenditures

The quantity of resources devoted to military use is usually measured by the level of military expenditure. Estimating world military expenditure is, however, very difficult and, for a variety of reasons, the results are inevitably inaccurate. One main reason for inaccuracy is the absence of a generally agreed definition of the term "military expenditure". Another is that many countries fail to include in their official military budgets significant categories of military spending. This problem is compounded by the difficulty of estimating realistic exchange rates so that military expenditures can be converted into a common currency (traditionally US dollars) for summation. For example, the difficulty of realistically expressing the Soviet military budget in US dollars is well known. A third reason for the inaccuracy of military expenditure figures is the underestimation of the real value of some of the resources employed by the military — a particularly gross example being the undervaluation of conscripted manpower. But despite these, and other, sources

7

F. Barnaby

of error, military expenditures are perhaps the most useful indicators we have
of the social and economic implications of armaments.

Throughout this century, world military expenditure has increased steadily
(Fig. 2.1). According to estimates of the Stockholm International Peace Research Institute (SIPRI), in 1976 it exceeded $300 000 million, at least thirty
times more than it was in 1900 (in constant prices).

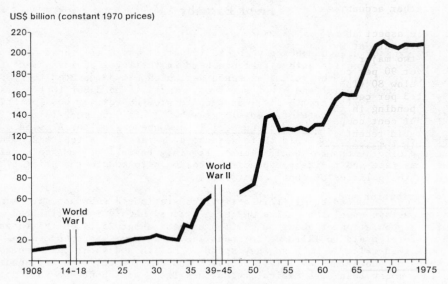

Fig. 2.1. World military expenditure, 1908-1975.
Source: SIPRI data.

In the twenty years between 1956 and 1975 the world spent about $5 000 000
million, in constant 1976 dollars, on the military.[3] Of this total the Third
World spent about $390 000 million, or 7 per cent (Table 2.1). The Middle
East contributed about 29 per cent of total third world expenditures, the Far
East 26 per cent, South Asia and South America each 15 per cent, Africa 10 per
cent, and Central America 4 per cent.

TABLE 2.1
Total World and Regional Military Expenditures, 1956-1975.
(US$ million at constant 1976 prices and exchange rates)

Region	Total expenditure	Percentage of world total	Percentage of third world total
Middle East	98 900		29
Far East (excl. China)	89 500		26
South Asia	52 200		15
South America	51 200		15
Africa (excl. Egypt)	32 800		10
Central America	13 800		4
Total Third World	388 400	7	100
China	234 200	5	
Total World	4 900 300	100	

Source: SIPRI data

Military spending by individual Third World countries varies greatly. In 1974, for example, 2 out of 93 Third World countries[4] each spent more than $2 000 million. These countries (Iran and Egypt) accounted for 23 per cent of Third World military expenditure. Four more countries (Israel, India, Saudi Arabia, and North Korea) each spent between $1 000 and $2 000 million. The six together accounted for 51 per cent of Third World expenditure. Each of another seven countries (Brazil, South Viet-Nam, South Africa, Pakistan, Taiwan, Iraq, and Kuwait) spent between $500 and $1 000 million. These top thirteen countries together accounted for 70 per cent of Third World military expenditure.

One notable aspect about military spending over the past 20 years is the relatively rapid rate at which it has increased in the Third World (Fig. 2.2). In 1955, the two major alliances of industrialized countries, NATO and WTO, accounted for over 90 per cent of total military expenditure. In 1975, this percentage was below 80 (Table 2.2). The Third World share over this period rose from about 3 per cent in 1955 to 12 per cent in 1975. Over these two decades, military spending in the Third World increased at an average annual rate of about 10 per cent compared with a world increase of just under 3 per cent. The most rapid recent rise was in the Middle East (Fig. 2.3). Since 1965 expenditure in this region has increased at an average annual rate of 22 per cent.

TABLE 2.2
Distribution and Growth Rate of Military Expenditures, 1955-1975.

	Average annual per cent change[a]	Percentage distribution (per cent)				
		1955	1960	1965	1970	1975
World total	2.7	100	100	100	100	100
NATO	1	62	62	55	49	45
WTO	3	29	27	31	33	33
Other developed	4	3	3	3	3	3
China	6.5	3	3	5	6	6
Third World	10	3	5	6	8	12

Source: SIPRI data   [a] Constant prices

The smallest relative regional increase was in South America where military expenditure (in constant 1970 prices) has increased from $1 200 million in 1955 to $2 200 million in 1975 (Table 2.3), which represents a rate of increase of about 3 per cent. In Africa (excluding Egypt) expenditure rose from $150 million in 1955 to $2 750 million in 1975, giving an annual growth rate of 16 per cent.

Over the past two decades, annual military spending in the Third World has increased (in constant dollars) by over six times (Figure 2.2). In the developed world, military spending over this period has increased by 1.5 times and in the world as a whole it has increased 1.7 times. It is true that the underdeveloped countries started off at a relatively low base but the trend has nevertheless been for a rapid militarization of the whole globe.

Military expenditure as a percentage of gross domestic product varies considerably throughout the Third World (Table 2.4). In each of seven underdeveloped countries, all in the Middle East, apart from South Viet-Nam, the average

10   F. Barnaby

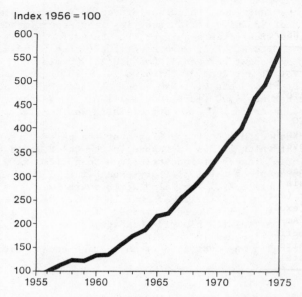

Fig. 2.2. Rate of increase of Third World military expenditure,
1956-1975 (constant prices). Source: SIPRI data.

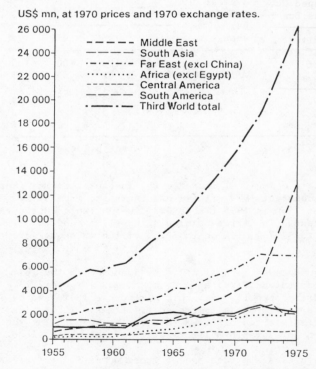

Fig. 2.3. Third World military expenditure, 1955-1975.
Source: SIPRI data.

TABLE 2.3
Military Expenditures
(US$ mn, at 1970 prices and 1970 exchange rates)

	1955	1965	1975
USA	58 850	63 748	64 178
Total NATO	78 605	89 523	95 813
USSR	34 900	44 900	61 100
Total WTO	37 500	49 498	71 313
Other developed countries	3 522	5 026	7 321
Total developed countries	119 627	144 047	174 447
China	3 700	7 900	13 100
Middle East	595	1 785	13 140
South Asia	935	2 166	2 545
Far East (excl. China and Japan)	975	3 136	4 944
Africa (excl. Egypt)	150	970	2 750
Central America	210	466	700
South America	1 200	1 699	2 220
Total Third World	4 065	10 222	26 299
World total	127 392	162 169	213 846

Source: SIPRI data

TABLE 2.4
Underdeveloped Countries Classed by Military Expenditure as Percentage
of Gross Domestic Product, Averaged Over the Years 1970 to 1975

Military expenditure as percentage of gross domestic product (1970-1975)	Number of countries	Names of countries
Over 10	7	Egypt, Iraq, Israel, Jordan, Syria, Yemen Democratic, South Viet-Nam
5 to 10	11	Burma, Cuba, Iran, Libya, North Korea, Pakistan, Saudi Arabia, Singapore, Somalia, Sudan, Taiwan
2.5 to 4.9	18	Chad, Chile, Congo, Guinea, India, Indonesia, Kuwait, Lebanon, Malaysia, Morocco, Nigeria, Peru, South Korea, Thailand, Yemen, Uganda, Zaire, Zambia
Less than 2.5	48	Afghanistan, Algeria, Argentina, Benin, Bolivia, Brazil, Burundi, Cameroon, Central Africa Republic, Colombia, Cyprus, Dominican Republic, Ecuador, El Salvador, Ethiopia, Gabon, Ghana, Guatemala, Guyana, Haiti, Honduras, Ivory Coast, Jamaica, Kenya, Liberia, Malagasy Republic, Malawi, Mauritania, Mauritius, Mexico, Nepal, Nicaragua, Niger, Paraguay, Philippines, South Rhodesia, Rwanda, Senegal, Sierra Leone, South Africa, Sri Lanka, Tanzania, Togo, Trinidad and Tobago, Tunisia, Upper Volta, Uruguay, Venezuela
Total	84	

Source: SIPRI data

percentage in the 1970s exceeded 10, the overall average for these countries
being 16 per cent. In another 11 Third World countries the average was between
5 and 10 per cent, and in 18 it was between 2.5 and 4.9. But in 48 out of 84
underdeveloped countries, mostly in Africa and South America, the average percentage was less than 2.5. In the Third World as a whole, military expenditure
in the 1970s averaged about 4 per cent of gross domestic product. For the developed countries this average was about 6 per cent.

An impression of the burden of military spending in some Third World countries
may be gleaned by the fact that Israel's average gross domestic product per
capita in the 1970s was about $2 000 out of which about $650 was spent on the
military (the amount spent in 1973 was twice this). For Egypt the figures are
$200 and $50 respectively. In comparison, the United States per capita military expenditure (the highest of all developed countries) in the 1970s averaged
about $350.

Third World defence industries

A country normally obtains arms in peacetime by making them, buying them or
acquiring them as gifts. An increasing number of Third World countries are
establishing significant defence industries to develop and produce weapons
indigenously, to produce weapons or parts of weapons under licensing arrangements with other countries and to participate in joint production projects
with foreign companies. Military aircraft, guided missiles and armoured fighting vehicles are mostly produced under licences whereas warships, military
electronics and aero-engines are more often produced indigenously (Table 2.5).
Codevelopment projects, comparatively rare at present and mainly confined to
aircraft, are increasing steadily in number.

A number of Third World countries, notably Argentina, Brazil, China, India,
Israel and South Africa, have well established and extensive defence industries
able to produce complex weapons-systems. Others are in the process of building
up such industries. Egypt, for example, has established the Arab States Military Industrial Organization, initially funded to the extent of $1 000 million
by a four-country agreement signed in April 1975. In addition, Peru, the
Philippines and North Korea have recently set up aircraft-manufacturing plants.

Sophisticated missiles of various types — anti-tank, anti-ship, surface-to-
surface and air-to-surface — are being produced in Brazil, China, Israel, South
Africa and Taiwan and have been developed in India. Combat aircraft are in
production in Argentina, China, India and Israel. In 1975, Israel became the
first Third World country and the seventh country, after the USA, the USSR,
the UK, China, France and Sweden, to develop and produce indigenously an advanced, supersonic, combat aircraft. In less complex areas — such as trainer
aircraft, small arms, small ships — indigenous development and production is
widespread throughout the Third World. For example, about 30 Third World countries have ship-building industries.

A complex network of licensing arrangements exists between Third World countries and the industrialized countries (Table 2.6). Israel and China even
license weapons production in other third world countries. We can expect licensed production and codevelopment projects to increase in number at a relatively rapid rate.

Even though Third World defence industries are growing in size and becoming

TABLE 2.5
Production of Major Weapons and Components in the Third World, 1950-1975

Country	Military aircraft	Guided missiles	Armoured fighting vehicles	War- ships	Military elect- ronics	Aero engines
Argentina	*	*	*	*		*
Brazil	*	*	*	*	*	*
Burma				*		
Chile	*			*		
China, People's Republic	*	*	*	*	*	*
Colombia				*		
Dominican Republic				*		
Egypt	*	*				*
Gabon				*		
India	*	*	*	*	*	*
Indonesia	*			*		
Iran	*					
Israel	*	*	*	*	*	*
Korea, North				*		
Korea, South	*			*		
Libya	*					
Mexico	*			*		
Pakistan	*	*	*			
Philippines	*	*	*	*	*	
Rhodesia				*		
South Africa	*	*	*	*	*	*
Syria				*		
Taiwan	*			*		
Thailand	*			*		
Vietnam, South	*					

Source: SIPRI data

more widespread, the international trade in arms will remain the chief source
of major weapons for the Third World for some time to come.

The arms trade with the Third World

War is a very difficult activity to define. One definition, evolved by Istvan
Kende, regards war as any armed conflict in which the regular armed forces of
the government in power are engaged, in which there is a certain degree of
organization and organized fighting by both opposing sides, and in which there
is some continuity between the armed clashes.[5] Centrally organized guerilla
forces are regarded as making war if their activities extend over a considerable part of the country concerned. On the basis of this definition Kende
lists 119 wars between 1945 and 1975. The total duration of these conflicts
exceeded 350 years. The territory of 69 countries and the armed forces of 81
states were involved. Since September 1945 there was not one day in which one
or several wars were not being fought somewhere in the world. On an average
day 12 wars were fought. Since 1945, war casualties number tens of millions.

The bulk of these wars were fought in the Third World. And most of the weapons

TABLE 2.6

Licensed Production of Major Weapons in Underdeveloped Countries in 1975

Licenser Licensee	USA	USSR	France	UK	Italy	FR Germany	Czecho-slovakia	Switz-erland	Spain	Israel	China
Argentina	1,2			5		6		4			
Brazil	1			5	1,2	3					
Colombia	1										
Egypt				1,2							
India		1,3	2,3,5	1,4,5			4	7			
Indonesia						2			1		
Korea, North		1,6									
Korea, South	1,6										
Pakistan	1,2		1,2			3					3
Peru					5						
Philippines				1	1	2					
Singapore						6					
South Africa			1,4		1	4				6	
Taiwan	1,2										
Venezuela					5						

Source: SIPRI data

Code:
1   Aircraft
2   Helicopters
3   Missiles
4   Tanks or armoured cars
5   Major warships
6   Other ships
7   Electronic systems

used in them have been supplied by the developed countries. There is no reason
to believe that this appalling record of violence will soon improve.

Like military expenditure, the arms trade has grown rapidly, both in volume
and in scope, since World War II. The annual value of the global arms trade
in 1976 was probably about $10 billion, with new orders running at about $20
billion. If there were no arms trade, participants in arms races — at least
so far as acquiring evermore sophisticated weapons was concerned — would be
limited to that small number of industrialized countries able to support sufficient military research and development activities to develop new weapons.
As it is, participation in arms races is almost worldwide. In 1976, a total
of 95 countries imported major weapons — tanks, ships, missiles or aircraft.
In almost all of these countries there was no other feasible way of obtaining
these weapons.

Estimating the value of traded arms is not a straightforward operation. Official prices for arms deals cannot be relied upon for comparative purposes because these prices are frequently adjusted for political considerations and do
not, therefore, represent the market values of the weapons involved.[6] To overcome these difficulties, SIPRI makes its own valuations of arms deals, based
on its arms trade registers and using a list of comparable cost prices for the
different types of major weapons supplied. SIPRI figures do not, therefore,
show the actual monetary value of the major weapon transactions. Nor do they
show the size of the cash flow between suppliers and recipients. Most transactions in any case involve credit arrangements of some kind and others are on
a grant basis. What the figures do is to provide an index of the quantity of
resources involved in the arms trade.

About two-thirds of the current global arms trade is to Third World countries.
Major weapons probably account for about one-half of the total trade in weapons
and equipment with the Third World. The remaining items traded — spare parts,
small arms, ammunition, support equipment, etc. — are very difficult to trace.
But it is unlikely that the basic trend in the arms trade would be much affected if these components were included.

Over the past few years the arms trade with the Third World has escalated
alarmingly (Fig. 2.4). Between 1970 and 1975 alone the value of major weapons
supplied to the Third World was, in constant dollars, nearly as much as that
of the major weapons supplied over the entire period between 1950 and 1969
(Table 2.7).

As might be expected, the four major arms producers — the USA, the USSR, the
UK and France — dominate the weapons trade. Over the period 1950 to 1975 these
four countries supplied 92 per cent of the major weapons sold to the Third
World. The USSR and the USA accounted for about 34 per cent each, and the UK
and France for about 12 per cent each. During the 1950s, however, the USA and
the UK were the main suppliers, supplying 33 and 24 per cent respectively.
The USSR followed with 15 per cent and France with 8 per cent. During the
1970s, the USSR and the USA each supplied about 36 per cent of the major weapons sold to the Third World, and France and the UK each supplied 10 per cent.
In the 1950s China was a significant supplier of arms to the rest of the Third
World, accounting for about 6 per cent of the total supplied. Although China
supplied about the same absolute value of arms in the 1970s, its percentage
share had dropped to about 2 per cent. The pattern has been for the smaller
suppliers to provide less in relative terms, if not absolutely. Nevertheless,
the number of suppliers is, in fact, increasing as the capacity to produce
weapons spreads.

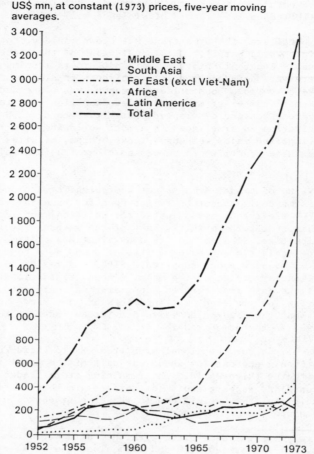

US$ mn, at constant (1973) prices, five-year moving averages.

Fig. 2.4.   The arms trade in major weapons with the Third World,
1952-1973. Source: SIPRI data.

The regional distribution of Third World importers has also changed over the period 1950 to 1975. In the 1950s the Far East accounted for 34 per cent of the major weapons imported by the Third World, with South Asia and the Middle East accounting for 51 per cent of the major weapons imported, followed by the Far East with 17 per cent (Table 2.7). Over the whole period, 1950-1975, the Middle East accounted for 40 per cent of the major weapons imported by the Third World, the Far East accounted for 25 per cent, South Asia for 12 per cent, and South America for 9 per cent (Fig. 2.5).

The Israel-Arab war of October 1973 and its consequences — particularly the increased wealth of the oil-producing countries — led to an astonishing increase in the arms trade. Between 1974 and 1975, the value of resources transferred to the Third World in the form of major weapons increased by as much as 65 per cent, which comprised a 40 per cent increase in 1974 and a near 25 per cent increase in 1975. The value of the major weapons sold to the Middle East

TABLE 2.7
SIPRI Valuations of Imports of Major Weapons by Third World Regions.
US$ mn at constant (1973) prices.
Figures in brackets are percentages of totals.

	1950-1959	1960-1969	1970-1975	1950-1975
Far East (excl. Viet-Nam)	2 301 (34)	2 988 (21)	1 561 (8)	6 850 (17)
South Asia	1 453 (21)	1 935 (14)	1 565 (8)	4 953 (12)
Middle East	1 576 (23)	4 684 (33)	9 959 (51)	16 219 (40)
North Africa	21 (-)	496 (3)	1 181 (6)	1 698 (4)
Sub-Saharan Africa	106 (2)	496 (3)	883 (5)	1 485 (4)
South Africa	182 (3)	517 (4)	515 (3)	1 214 (3)
Central America	124 (2)	592 (4)	305 (2)	1 021 (2)
South America	962 (14)	1 040 (7)	1 775 (9)	3 777 (9)
Total (excl. Viet-Nam)	6 725 (99)	12 748 (90)	17 744 (91)	37 217 (92)
Viet-Nam	93 (1)	1 456 (10)	1 801 (9)	3 350 (8)
Total	6 818 (100)	14 204 (100)	19 545 (100)	40 567 (100)

Source: SIPRI data

during these two years equals about 44 per cent of the value of those sold to the region throughout the preceding 25 years. Significant increases in arms imports also occurred during these two years in the Far East (excluding Viet-Nam), in Africa, and in Latin America (Table 2.9).

The twelve countries which spent the most on importing major weapons between 1965 and 1975 are listed in Table 2.10. The value of the weapons imported by these countries over this period was 70 per cent of the total value of major weapons supplied to the Third World. Six of the twelve countries are in the Middle East. A consequence of this huge inflow of arms is that there are as many combat aircraft and tanks in the Middle East as there are in NATO forces. Not only are Middle Eastern arsenals quantitatively very large but the weapons are very modern and include, for example, the Soviet MiG-23 and the US F-14 and F-15 fighters, the Soviet T-62, the American M-60 and AMX-30 and British Chieftain main battle tanks. In fact, in terms of major conventional weapons systems, the Middle East arsenals are among the world's most modern.

F. Barnaby

TABLE 2.8
SIPRI Valuations of Major Weapons Supplied to Third World Countries
by the Four Major Suppliers, 1950-1975.
US$ mn at constant (1973) prices.
Figures in brackets are percentages of totals.

	1950-1959	1960-1969	1970-1975	1950-1975
USSR	1 058 (15)	5 749 (41)	7 381 (38)	14 188 (35)
USA	2 272 (33)	4 506 (32)	6 690 (34)	13 468 (33)
UK	1 631 (24)	1 745 (12)	1 951 (10)	5 327 (13)
France	561 (8)	1 877 (13)	1 881 (10)	4 319 (11)
Total of four major suppliers	5 522 (80)	13 877 (98)	17 903 (92)	37 302 (92)
Total value of major weapons supplied to Third World countries	6 850 (100)	14 205 (100)	19 577 (100)	40 632 (100)

Source: SIPRI data

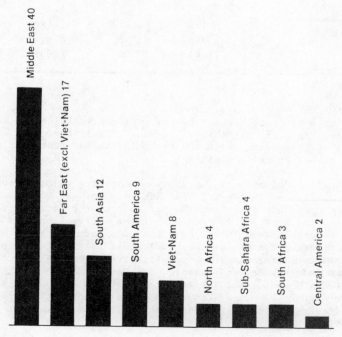

Fig. 2.5. Regional distribution of imports of major weapons
by underdeveloped regions according to SIPRI valuations,
1950-75 (in percentage). Source: SIPRI data.

TABLE 2.9
Distribution of the Value of Imports of Major Weapons by the Third World,
1970-75
(Per cent)

Region	1970	1971	1972	1973	1974	1975
Middle East	50	48	31	59	56	56
Far East (excl. Viet-Nam)	9	11	5	8	5	10
Viet-Nam	15	12	34	2	3	-
South Asia	10	13	12	8	7	3
South America	5	6	9	13	10	10
Central America	1	1	1	2	2	2
North Africa	4	3	5	4	4	12
Sub-Saharan Africa	4	4	3	5	7	4
South Africa	3	2	1	1	5	3
OPEC	15	21	16	19	29	48

Source: SIPRI data

TABLE 2.10
The Twelve Leading Importers of Major Weapons in the Third World, 1965-1975.
Over this period Iran bought about $12 000 million worth of arms
and military equipment from the US government.

Country	Cumulative imports 1965-1975 (US$ mn at constant 1973 prices)	Percentage of total arms trade with third world
Iran	3 200	11
Egypt	3 000	11
Syria	2 200	8
Israel	2 100	7
India	1 900	7
Viet-Nam, North	1 500	5
Viet-Nam, South	1 500	5
South Africa	1 100	4
Iraq	1 100	4
Libya	1 100	4
North Korea	650	2
Saudi Arabia	600	2
Total percentage		70

Source: SIPRI data

Many other Third World countries have relatively large numbers of the most
sophisticated weapons in their arsenals (Figs. 2.6 and 2.7). This is because
of the willingness of some governments of developed countries (particularly
the USA, the USSR, the UK, and France) to sell these weapons in bulk, often
even before they enter the supplier's own arsenal.

F. Barnaby

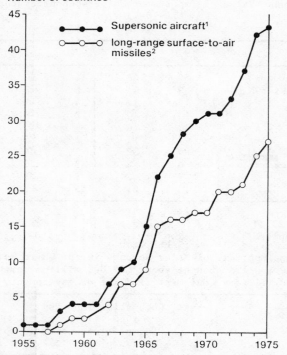

Fig. 2.6. Proliferation of sophisticated weapons
to Third World countries. Source: SIPRI data.

[1] The 43 Third World countries with supersonic aircraft are:

Abu Dhabi*	Israel*	Singapore*
Afghanistan*	Jordan	Somalia*
Algeria*	Korea, North*	South Africa*
Argentina	Korea, South*	Sudan*
Bangladesh	Kuwait	Syria*
Brazil*	Lebanon	Taiwan*
China*	Libya*	Tanzania
Colombia	Malaysia	Thailand*
Cuba*	Morocco	Venezuela
Egypt*	Nigeria	Vietnam, North*
Ethiopia	Pakistan*	Vietnam, South
India*	Paraguay	Uganda*
Indonesia*	Philippines	Yemen
Iran*	Saudi Arabia*	Zaire
Iraq*		

[2] The Third World countries with long-range surface-to-air
missiles are those marked * in Note 1 above, plus Zambia.

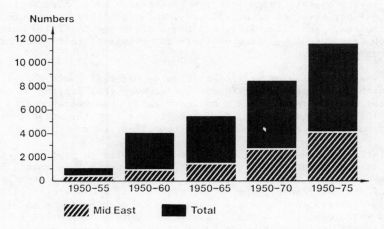

Fig. 2.7a. Cumulative numbers of jet combat aircraft
supplied to underdeveloped countries, 1950-1975.

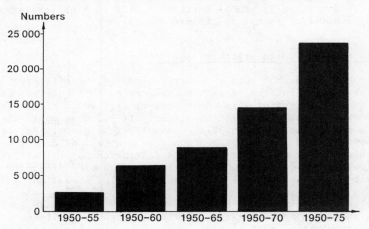

Fig. 2.7b. Cumulative numbers of medium and light tanks
supplied to underdeveloped countries, 1950-1975.
Source: SIPRI data.

Third world nuclear proliferation

Countries with significant peaceful nuclear-power programmes have the capability to produce the fissile material for atomic bombs. In today's world, where
the technical knowledge and expertise required to construct atomic bombs are
widely available, acquiring the capability to produce these weapons is politically as important as acquiring the weapons themselves.

Nuclear technology is spreading rapidly throughout the Third World. At present,
Argentina, India, and Pakistan operate nuclear-power reactors. Brazil, Iran,
South Africa, South Korea, Mexico and Taiwan are constructing power reactors.

Egypt and Israel operate large research reactors. These Third World countries,
therefore, either have, or scon will have, the capability to produce plutonium
for atomic bombs. And Cuba, Iraq, and Libya are among the Third World countries which have recently announced their intentions of initiating nuclear-
power programmes.

Moreover, the production of sufficient fissile material for a modest nuclear
force is within the reach of virtually any country that decides to do so, on
a small scale and secretly, once a nuclear reactor has been acquired specifically for this purpose. Israel, for example, has kept the world guessing about
whether or not it has atomic bombs for a number of years.

Even a relatively crudely designed atomic bomb having an explosive yield equivalent to that of about 20 000 tons of TNT should weigh less than 1 000 kilo-
grams. Several types of combat aircraft — such as the US A-4 Skyhawk, F-104
Starfighter and F-4 Phantom, the French Mirage III, the Soviet Ilyushin-28 and
the British Canberra and Buccaneer — are capable of carrying such a payload.
Most Third World countries already have one or more of these types of nuclear-
capable aircraft in their arsenals. For these reasons many regard the proliferation of nuclear forces to Third World countries as a virtual certainty.
Such proliferation would have considerable consequences for the stability of
the region concerned and is almost certain to lead to a nuclear arms race as
neighbouring countries attempt to restore the balance.

Determinants of third world military expenditures

Which factors determine how much a country spends on the military? Why do some
countries participate in arms races? Do arms races in themselves cause wars?
Or do wars and the threat of wars cause arms races? Would significant disarmament be beneficial to Third World countries? If so, what would the benefits
be? Precise answers to these questions cannot yet be given. But it is clear
that the answers which apply to some countries and regions do not necessarily
apply to others. That each case has to be considered on its merits is especially true for the Third World which contains such a wide diversity of political, economic and social systems in various stages of evolution.

Many societies seem to demand "security" as much as they demand social services,
like health and education. Because security is seen to be linked with military
force, the psychological need to feel "secure" is normally (and, politically,
probably most conveniently) satisfied by military expenditure. This demand is
often present even if there is no direct threat to the country concerned.

A given society often seems to have a crude idea of the amount of resources
which have to be devoted to the military so that most of its citizens feel
"protected". In many European countries, for example, about 3 to 5 per cent
of the gross domestic product currently seems to be the required level of
military spending. If politicians spend a much higher proportion they are criticised for wasting resources and if they spend much less they are criticised
for "neglecting the country's defences". Perceptions such as these, rather
than any sound reasons, are powerful determinants of the size of many military
budgets, including those of some Third World countries.

Not surprisingly, military expenditure is high when countries feel directly
and imminently threatened or when political leaders deliberately pursue aggressive policies likely to lead to war. The tension produced by such policies,

which are most likely to be adopted by single-party dictatorships, will almost certainly lead to increasing levels of military spending — and often an arms race — within the region concerned.

Once a significant level of military spending has been reached, vested interests — military, industrial, bureaucratic, and even academic — in maintaining and increasing the size of the country's arsenal are likely to become more powerful. When such groups acquire political power, a process which usually occurs rather rapidly, the size of military budgets tends to be determined purely by lobbying pressures rather than security needs, even perceived ones.

In today's world, large and modern military establishments are often believed to provide status and influence. A political leader striving for hegemony within his region may, therefore, devote considerable resources to the military purely for this reason. Autocratic leaderships are once again the most likely to do so. Some may indulge in large military forces in an attempt to draw international attention to themselves.

Once money has been budgeted for the military it has to be spent. Just as is the case for the budget itself, the ways in which the money is used is often determined largely for reasons unrelated to the security interests of the country concerned. Interservice rivalries frequently determine which weapons-systems are acquired. Further, the most sophisticated weapons are often purchased, for reasons of prestige, when simpler ones would be more rational for the country's security needs. Large sums may be spent on, for example, supersonic aircraft even though a strong case can be made for investment in, say, helicopters.

Some countries demand that they gain and retain military superiority in their region, or even beyond it. This usually occurs when a country believes, perhaps almost as an article of faith, that the form of its society is such that it is better able to innovate, and therefore to keep ahead in military technology, than rival societies. Priority is then given to military research and development which normally leads to the establishment of a relatively large indigenous defence industry, and eventually to participation in the international arms trade. Such activity can, and often does, also lead to a local arms race in which neighbouring states either attempt to develop their own arms or purchase them from abroad. If a participant in such an arms race feels unable to keep abreast of the technological progress of its neighbour, quantity of armaments may be seen as a substitute for quality.

In summary, high levels of military spending and arms races — in both Third World and developed countries — are often related to internal (i.e. domestic) factors rather than international or regional ones. Countries do react to the size and nature of their neighbours' arsenals in a way which generates arms races but to a far lesser extent than is often assumed. The desire for prestige, influence or hegemony, a faith in military technological superiority, the pursuit of vested interests in armament production, the glamour of complex weapons in the eyes of influential military groups, and the pursuit of an aggressive foreign policy for party-political reasons (or because of the psychology of the leadership), are all significant factors. In any given country, it is often impossible to ascertain which factors operate, and to what extent. But it is certain that only rarely are military procurements, in men or machines, determined by rational assessments of security and strategic needs.

Great power involvement

The governments of the industrialized countries involve themselves in the military affairs of Third World countries mainly through the supply of weapons and
of technicians to operate the weapons or to train nationals to operate them.
The reasons for this involvement vary but include a desire for economic or political influence, the acquisition of military bases, or the temptation to sell
weapons to offset high research and development costs, to try to alleviate the
effects of an economic recession, or to achieve the economies of scale of
large-scale production. Commercial armament firms, anxious to maximise profits, are powerful lobbies applying continuous pressure on governments to
allow them to participate in the arms trade.

The dominant reasons of the largest arms suppliers, the USA and the USSR, are
probably associated with their desire to extend their political and economic
interests world-wide. This policy, however, carries with it grave dangers for
world security.

A future general nuclear war between the USA and the USSR is probably most
likely to come about through the escalation of a local war in an unstable region. Such a war may begin as a conventional war and escalate to a nuclear war
in which the nuclear weapons of one or more of the participants are used.
Subsequently the two great powers may come to the assistance of client states
threatened with destruction. This great power involvement may well end in a
general nuclear war which would have disastrous consequences for all mankind.
States become clients of the great powers mainly as a result of the arms trade.

Because modern war involves the use of vast quantitites of munitions, particularly missiles, the survival of the client state may depend on the willingness of the supplier to replace expended munitions during the period of fighting. In this sense, the great power becomes virtually the guarantor of the
smaller power. Both the development of first-strike strategic nuclear weapons
by the great powers and the proliferation of nuclear weapons to countries which
at present do not possess them are likely dangers, and would considerably increase the likelihood of this scenario. Inevitably, this danger would be compounded by a continuation of the arms trade at present or increased levels.
It is the increasing danger of general nuclear war which makes disarmament,
particularly nuclear disarmament, so necessary.

If disarmament comes about it could have far-reaching consequences for the
Third World. As the report quoted at the beginning of this article concluded:
"A halt in the arms race and a significant reduction in military expenditures
would help the social and economic development of all countries and would increase the possibilities of providing additional aid to developing countries".[7]
It is in fact difficult to see how the governments of developed countries could
find significantly greater funds for development aid than now provided, except
from those freed by reduced military budgets. In this sense, disarmament and
development are intimately linked.

Notes

1. The information in this article is based on data in: World Armaments and
    Disarmament, SIPRI Yearbook 1976 (Stockholm, Almquist & Wiksell, 1976,
    Stockholm International Peace Research Institute); The Arms Trade with
    the Third World (Stockholm, Almquist and Wiksell, 1971, Stockholm Inter-

national Peace Research Institute) and <u>Arms Trade Registers: The Arms Trade with the Third World</u> (Stockholm, Almquist & Wiksell, 1975, Stockholm International Peace Research Institute).

2. The industrialized countries are here taken to be the countries of NATO (the North Atlantic Treaty Organization), WTO (the Warsaw Treaty Organization) and the rest of Europe, and Australia, China, Japan, and New Zealand. The rest of the world's countries are taken to be the Third World countries. This division is not based on any general economic, political, or social criteria. It is simply a convenient division for the purposes of this paper.

3. World War II levels of forces lasted until 1948. Since 1948, the world has spent more than $6 000 000 million, in constant 1976 dollars, on military activities. This sum is equal to about $1 500 per head of today's world population or about 10 years' income for today's "average Indian".

4. Fourteen in the Middle East, 6 in South Asia, 14 in the Far East, 38 in Africa, 10 in Central America, and 11 in South America.

5. <u>Local Wars in Asia, Africa & Latin America 1945-'69</u>. Hungarian Academy of Sciences, Centre for Afro-Asian Research. Studies on developing countries, No. 60, p. 11.

6. According to official US figures, for example, the global arms trade between 1964 and 1973 totalled $58 000 million. The shares of the USA and the USSR were 51 per cent and 27 per cent respectively. Less than one-half of this sum was for weapons-systems (major and other). The rest was for the construction of air fields, roads, and communications systems, for training purposes and support equipment. In US Senate hearings, Senator Edward Kennedy said that "from a figure of only $300 million in 1952, the worldwide trade in arms has grown to more than $18 billion annually", and that total US arms sales increased from $900 million in fiscal year 1970 to nearly $11 billion in fiscal year 1974. Once again, these figures are for <u>all</u> military sales, not only weapons, and are for new orders rather than actual deliveries. The different ways of expressing figures on the arms trade cause much confusion.

7. <u>Economic and Social Consequences of the Arms Race and of Military Expenditure</u>, UN, 1972.

Hiroshima and Nagasaki: The Survivors

Frank Barnaby

Considerably less than one-half of the people now living remember the atomic bombing of Hiroshima and Nagasaki, 32 years ago. The two bombs, euphemistically called "Little Boy" and "Fat Man", dropped on the Japanese cities were all that then existed. But in the meantime the nuclear arsenals have been stocked with tens of thousands of nuclear weapons, most of them much more powerful than those that obliterated Hiroshima and Nagasaki. And the probability that all, or a major fraction of them will be used in a nuclear world war is steadily increasing. Prudence demands that we do not forget the awesome damage done and the terrible suffering caused by those early nuclear weapons.

A great deal of information on the physical, biological, medical, genetic, social and psychological effects of the atomic bombs was made specially available by Japanese scientists to the international team* which gathered in Japan in July 1977. It included the results of comprehensive surveys of the personal and social disabilities of the survivors.

Perhaps surprisingly after three decades, the investigation turned up new information. It also discovered serious and disturbing gaps in existing knowledge and research. But perhaps the most important conclusion of the investigation is that our knowledge of the long-term consequences of the atomic bombs will remain shockingly incomplete unless there is a massive injection of financial and scientific resources. In particular, the effort so far made to discover the social and psychological effects is pitiful. But very much remains to be done in the biological, genetic and medical areas. Given the urgent need for better data on the biological effects of ionising radiation on man, the paucity of the current research effort, the complacency of some of the relevant local authorities, and the lack of interest of international bodies is inexcusable.

In the words of the natural science experts: "While viewing with abhorrence the events that produced this type of experimental material, consideration of the well-being of present and future generations requires that full use be made of it. In a world still faced with the spectre of a nuclear war — in which radiation is now given the role of the main weapon of destruction — on the one hand, and with the possibility of large-scale utilization of nuclear energy on the other, it is imperative that the maximum information be obtained from the fate of the victims of the A-bombs."

The international experts worked mainly in two groups — a natural science group and a social science group. The documents they produced give a fairly comprehensive description of the events following the bombings.

The atomic bomb dropped on Hiroshima on 6 August 1945, is thought to have had an explosive yield equivalent to that of 12.5±1 kilotons of chemical explosive.

---

*The international team consisted of 44 scientists from 14 countries, assembled by the Geneva-based International Peace Bureau.

The yield of the Nagasaki bomb, dropped on 9 August 1945, is thought to have been 22±2 kilotons.

The Hiroshima bomb exploded 580±20 metres above the centre of the city, which lies on a flat delta with mountains to the north and west, and sea to the south. The entire city was damaged concentrically. The Nagasaki bomb exploded 500±20 metres above ground to the north of the city. Because the terrain is mountainous the damage in Nagasaki varied considerably according to direction.

Effects of fire, blast and radiation

About 35 per cent of the total energy generated by the bombs was given off as thermal radiation, about 50 per cent as blast, and about 15 per cent as ionising radiation. The fireballs produced by the explosions reached maximum temperatures of several million degrees Centigrade at the instant of detonation and grew to their maximum diameters of about 280 metres in about one second. At this time the surface temperature of the fireballs was about 5000°C. Two seconds later it was 1700°C; thereafter it fell more gradually.

The infra-red radiation emitted during the first three seconds after the explosion was a particularly powerful cause of burns on unclothed parts of the human body. Even at a distance of 4 kilometres from the hypocentre (the point on the ground directly below the centre of the explosion) of the Hiroshima bomb, the thermal radiation emitted in the first three seconds amounted to about 1.3 calories/sq. cm, about 20 times more than that from the Sun. At a distance of 500 metres from the hypocentre nearly 60 calories/sq. cm of thermal radiation were emitted in the first three seconds. The thermal radiation from the Nagasaki bomb was about twice as intense as that at Hiroshima.

The thermal radiation was intense enough to burn exposed human skin at distances as far as 3.5 kilometres from the hypocentre in Hiroshima and 4 kilometres in Nagasaki. At these distances, fabrics and wood were charred. People caught in the open air within about 1.2 kilometres from the hypocentres were often burnt to death.

A widespread fire storm raged in Hiroshima for six hours, completely burning every combustible object within a radius of 2 kilometres from the hypocentre. The fire-storm in Nagasaki, even though less general than that in Hiroshima, was severe in specific areas.

Moisture condensed around rising ash particles, produced by the intense fires, as they came into contact with the cold air above. Consequently, much rain fell on the two cities. But it was not clear rain. The highly radioactive and oily liquid that came down is known to this day as "black rain".

The atomic explosions produced exceedingly high pressures of several hundred million millibars at the detonation points. The explosive expansion of the surrounding air produced a great blast. The front of the blast moved as a shock wave — a wall of air at high pressure, transmitted like a sound wave and spreading outward at a speed equal to, or greater than, the speed of sound. The shock wave travelled nearly 4 kilometres in the first 10 seconds after the explosion. In 30 seconds it had travelled about 11 kilometres and still retained some destructive power. It was followed by an exceedingly strong wind. But as the shock wave spread outward, the pressure within fell below atmospheric pressure and eventually the air flowed in the inward direction. Thus,

at a given point from the hypocentre, a supersonic shock wave was followed by
a very powerful wind and then, after an instant of stillness, a strong wind
blew in the opposite direction.

At Hiroshima the maximum blast pressure at a distance of 2 kilometres from the
hypocentre was about 3 tons/sq. m and the maximum blast velocity was about
70 m/s. All buildings within this distance were damaged beyond repair. Casualties due to blast, caused mainly by collapsing buildings and flying debris,
were particularly severe within about 1.3 kilometres of the hypocentre. At
this distance the blast pressure reached 7 tons/sq. m and its velocity 120 m/s.

Because of the destruction of an extensive area by a single powerful blow, fire-
fighting facilities were all but completely destroyed. In any case, water
stopped running in both cities. And the damage was so extensive that fire-
fighting was impossible. In Hiroshima, about 76 000 buildings stood before
the bomb dropped. Of these, 63 per cent were totally destroyed and 11 per cent
seriously damaged. About 25 per cent of Nagasaki's 51 000 buildings were totally destroyed and 11 per cent seriously damaged.

Physical damage similar to that done to Hiroshima and Nagasaki by the atomic
bombs could, of course, have been produced by high-explosive and incendiary
bombs. Estimates show that, for Hiroshima, this would have taken about 290
tons of high-explosive bombs and 900 tons of incendiaries. But an atomic bomb
delivers its enormous destructive power in an instant. And it inevitably produces ionising radiation and radioactivity. People exposed to this radiation
may die of diseases which appear many years after exposure. And their off-
spring may be malformed because of genetic damage. The horrors of Hiroshima
and Nagasaki are qualitatively worse than the horrors produced by the bombing
of Tokyo, Coventry, Hamburg or Dresden.

About a third of the ionising radiation produced by the atomic bombs was emitted within one minute of the explosion. This is called initial radiation. The
remainder, called residual radiation, was emitted by fission products deposited
on the ground and by radioactive isotopes produced by neutrons in the soil and
elsewhere.

The main components of initial radiation are gamma rays and neutrons. The
initial radiation dose (air dose) 500 metres from the hypocentre at Hiroshima
is thought to have been about 6000 rads, 2800 from gamma rays and 3200 from
neutrons. At Nagasaki the dose at this distance was probably about 7700 rads,
7000 from gamma rays and 700 from neutrons. The neutron components of the
initial radiation differ because each bomb had a different fissile material:
uranium for Hiroshima, plutonium for Nagasaki.

It is generally reckoned that one-half of those receiving a whole-body radiation dose of 400 rads (air dose) will die, and that all those exposed to whole-
body radiation of 700 rads or more will die in a short time. Exposed people
within about 1 kilometre of the Hiroshima bomb, and 1.2 kilometres of the Nagasaki bomb, are thought to have received doses of about 400 rads.

Anyone coming within about a kilometre of the hypocentres in the first 100
hours after the explosions could have received substantial amounts of residual
radiation, and could have ingested or inhaled radioactive materials. Only
rough estimates of the doses of residual radiation received are available.
The maximum possible dose is thought to be about 130 rads in Hiroshima and 50
rads in Nagasaki. But people in the "black rain" area of Nagasaki could have
been exposed to doses of up to 150 rads.

Number killed

About 90 per cent of all those within 1 kilometre of the hypocentres when the atomic bombs exploded died by the end of 1945. About 60 per cent of those within 2 kilometres died: about three-quarters in the first 24 hours, and nearly 90 per cent within 10 days.

The number of people in Hiroshima at the time the bomb exploded is very uncertain, mainly because the number of troops there is unknown. But estimates indicate that about 350 000 people were directly exposed to the bomb. Considerable differences exist between the various estimates of the total number killed or injured. The international experts concluded that the most likely figure for the number of deaths up to the end of 1945 is 140 000, about 20 000 of whom were military servicemen. If anything, that may be an underestimate, as a large number of people are still unaccounted for in the 1950 national census. Many of those who survived the initial onslaught must have died within the next few years. And very little information is available about the fate of the 37 000 or so people who entered Hiroshima within the first week.

The number of persons directly exposed to the Nagasaki bomb is thought to be about 280 000, of whom approximately 74 000 died by the end of 1945. Again, the number who perished after 1945 is not known.

Large numbers of Korean forced labourers were in both cities during the bombings, and the fate of the majority of them is unclear. About 23 American prisoners-of-war are known to have died in Hiroshima. In Nagasaki about 450 Dutch, American and British prisoners were exposed but the number who died is not known.

All in all, the total number of people killed by the two atomic bombs is probably well over a quarter of a million, a death rate of about 40 per cent.

People killed instantly were mainly either crushed or burnt to death. The seriously burnt and injured suffered fever, intolerable thirst and vomiting. They went into a state of shock. Almost all of them died within a week. Such was the lack of doctors, nurses, medicines and even bandages that most died virtually without treatment.

Many of those exposed to large doses of radiation rapidly developed symptoms of radiation sickness. They became incapacitated, with nausea and vomiting. A few days later they typically vomited blood, developed a high fever, had severe diarrhoea and much bleeding from the bowels. They usually died within 10 days.

Those exposed to smaller doses of radiation suffered a wide variety of symptoms including nausea, vomiting, diarrhoea, bleeding from the bowels, gums, nose and genitals, and menstrual abnormalities. There was often a total loss of hair, fever and a feeling of great weakness. Resistance to infection was markedly decreased. And septicaemia was a frequent cause of death.

Delayed effects

The really unique, and perhaps the most terrifying, consequences of the atomic bombs are the delayed effects. Because of these, survivors, their children, and their grandchildren will live in fear for years to come.

Most of the survivors still alive at the end of 1945 appeared superficially to be in good health. But later a variety of medical effects — including diseases of the eye and blood, malignant tumours and psychoneurological disturbances — began to appear.

The incidence and mortality rate of leukaemia among survivors increased fast for about a decade and then reached a level about 30 times higher than that of non-exposed Japanese. Afterwards it started to decrease slowly but has still not reached the national average. An enhanced incidence of leukaemia occurred in those who received relatively low radiation doses, of well below 100 rads.

The incidence of other malignant tumours — thyroid, breast, lung, salivary gland, bone, prostate, and so on — has been, and still is, significantly enhanced among those exposed to radiation at Hiroshima and Nagasaki.

Tragically, children born to women survivors who were pregnant when the bombs exploded show an increase in some congenital malformations, particularly microcephaly (abnormally small size of the head) resulting in mental retardation. But no increase has been reported in the incidence of leukaemia among children exposed in utero.

Among explanations advanced for this absence are: that the number of survivors available for investigation, and the radiation dose received by them, are such that too few children show genetic effects — even though these may be present — to be statistically significant; the research methods used to search for effects are insufficiently sensitive; the mutations induced are predominantly recessive ones and so they will only show up in second, third or even later generations; many of the affected persons may have died from acute radiation effects; and there may have been a large number of undetected spontaneous abortions.

The absence of demonstrable genetic effects among the offpsring of the survivors of the Hiroshima and Nagasaki bombs does not, of course, mean that there is no genetic effect of radiation. On the contrary, the use of large numbers of modern nuclear weapons could, over a number of generations, decimate human life.

The social and psychological effects of the atomic bombings were extremely severe. In some ways they overshadow the other effects. The damage was so great that the communities totally disintegrated. So many firemen, doctors, nurses, policemen, teachers, and so on died or were injured that social services collapsed. Of those people that initially survived, many went mad or committed suicide. Thousands of children became orphans. Hiroshima and Nagasaki became ghost towns.

Thirty two years later, the effects of the bombs are still apparent. So many young people died that there is a disproportionate number of aged among the survivors. This imbalance is being increased by the widespread use of contraceptives among survivors who fear that their children would be malformed. Acute diseases and chronic after-effects do not allow the survivors to live normally. Fear of genetic damage often prevents marriage, and susceptibility to disease and fatigue often prevents employment.

The ratio of sick and injured among the survivors is about 40 per cent — almost twice the national average. The ratio of physically handicapped is over three times the national average. The vicious circle of disease and poverty among the survivors is continuously aggravated by ageing and failing health.

Academic discussions of nuclear strategies have lost sight of the human suffering caused by atomic bombs. Hiroshima and Nagasaki leave no doubt about the
immorality of strategies based on nuclear weapons.

AN EYE - WITNESS REMEMBERS

Futaba Kitayama, then a 33-year-old housewife, was 1.7 kilometres from the
hypocentre when the atomic bomb exploded over Hiroshima at 8.15 am on 6 August
1945. In her words, first published in a Japanese journal:

"Someone shouted, 'A parachute is coming down.' I responded by turning in the
direction she pointed. Just at that moment, the sky I was facing flashed. I
do not know how to describe that light. I wondered if a fire had been set in
my eyes.

"I don't remember which came first — the flash of light or the sound of an
explosion that roared down to my belly. Anyhow, the next moment I was knocked
down flat on the ground. Immediately, things started falling down around my
head and shoulders. I couldn't see anything; it seemed pitch dark. I managed
to crawl out of the debris.

"Soon I noticed that the air smelled terrible. Then I was shocked by the
feeling that the skin of my face had come off. Then, the hands and arms, too.
Starting from the elbow to the fingertips, all the skin of my right hand came
off and hung down grotesquely. The skin of my left hand, all five fingers,
also came off.

"What happened to the sky that had been such a clear blue one only a moment
ago? It was now dark, like dusk. I ran like mad toward the bridge, jumping
over the piles of debris.

"What I saw under the bridge was shocking: Hundreds of people were squirming
in the stream. I couldn't tell if they were men or women. They looked all
alike. Their faces were swollen and gray, their hair was standing up. Holding
their hands high, groaning, people were rushing to the river. I felt the same
urge because the pain was all over the body which had been exposed to a heat
ray strong enough to burn my pants to pieces. I was about to jump into the
river only to remember that I could not swim.

"I went back up to the bridge. There, school girls, like sleepwalkers, were
wandering about in confusion. Upon crossing it, I looked back and found that
the Takeyachō-Hatchōbori area suddenly had burst into flame. I had thought
that the bomb hit only the area where I was.

"When crossing the bridge, which I did not then recognize, I found all its
parapets of solid ferro-concrete had gone. The bridge looked terribly unsafe.
Under the bridge were floating, like dead dogs or cats, many corpses, barely
covered by tattered clothes. In the shallow water near the bank, a woman was
lying face upward, her breasts torn away and blood spurting. A horrifying
scene. How in the world could such a cruel thing happen? I wondered if the
Hell that my grandmother had told me so much about in my childhood had fallen
upon the Earth.

"I found myself squatting on the centre of the parade ground. It must not have taken me more than two hours to get to the parade ground. The darkness of the sky lessened somewhat. Still, the Sun, as if covered with a heavy cloud, was dim and gloomy.

"My burns started paining me. It was a kind of pain different from an ordinary burn which might be unbearable. Mine was a dull pain that was coming from somewhere far apart from my body. A yellow secretion oozed from my hands. I imagined that my face also must be in this dreadful shape. By my side, many junior high school students were squirming in agony.

"They were crying, insanely, 'Mother! Mother!' They were so severely burned and blood-stained that one could scarcely dare to look at them. I could do nothing for them but watch them die one by one, seeking their mothers in vain.

"As far as I could see with my declining eyesight was all in flames.

"Steadily, my face became stiffer. I put my hands carefully on my cheeks and felt my face. It seemed to have swollen to twice its size. Now I could see less and less. Soon I would not be able to see at all. I kept walking. I saw on the street many victims being carried away by stretcher. Carts and trucks, heavily loaded with corpses and wounded who looked like beasts, came and passed me. On both sides of the street, many people were wandering about like sleepwalkers."

Note

Frank Barnaby's summary (with minor amendments) and "An Eye-Witness Remembers" are reprinted from New Scientist, 25 August 1977, pp. 472-475.

Militarism and International Dependence

Robin Luckham

Introduction

The military and economic expansion of the central capitalist powers has irrevocably shaped the destinies of the countries of the Third World and moulded the international system. Yet the military dimension of this expansion and its continuing effects both in the underdeveloped regions and indeed in the advanced industrial countries themselves has received remarkably little serious discussion.

The basic facts of militarism are of such a scale as to make most of the subjects which preoccupy development experts and policy makers almost pale into insignificance by comparison. World military expenditures currently run at about $350 billion and are more than the gross national products of the countries of South Asia, the Far East and Africa combined. (Stockholm International Peace Research Institute, 1975 and 1976; UN, 1972; US Arms Control and Disarmament Agency 1976; Barnaby and Huisken, 1975; Marchetti and Marks, 1974). The military expenditures of the industrial countries are around 6 per cent of their total GNP, being more than twenty times greater than the resources they devote to official development assistance to the developing countries. The United States alone spends very nearly as much on intelligence, surveillance and espionage network (of which the CIA is only one part) as *all* the developed countries together spend on development assistance to the Third World.

Although the developing countries themselves spend much less on armaments than the advanced industrial countries (approximately $55 billion in 1974) the proportion of their GNP devoted to military spending is roughly similar. Moreover, their arms expenditures have risen faster than those of industrial countries, leading to substantial increases in their arms imports. Increases have taken place in most parts of the Third World, though they are by far the most dramatic in the Middle East which now imports substantially well over one-half of the weapons transferred to the Third World. The value of these arms imports (about $6.6 billion in 1974) has been fast overtaking the value of the development assistance from the industrial countries to the Third World. It is estimated that in the space of only two years, 1974 and 1975, the volume of resources transferred to the Third World in the form of major weapons has increased by over 60 per cent.

This rise in arms spending has occasioned considerable international concern. Unfortunately concern has not been matched by sufficient serious analysis. Is there any connection between arms spending and the fact that most countries in the Third World live under authoritarian or military governments, the number of which has greatly increased over the past ten years? To what extent does the arms trade reinforce economic dependence? What are the consequences for the distribution of wealth and power; both nationally within individual Third World countries and internationally between them and the advanced industrial countries?

Not only is militarism economically and socially wasteful but also it is accompanied by insecurity, violence and armed struggles on a world scale. For the past 30 years the major world powers have been locked in nuclear stalemate, restrained only by their fear of a holocaust made increasingly terrifying by the incessant arms race. The struggles between them have often been diverted to the periphery where violent upheavals — coups, revolutions, strikes, communal rioting civil wars and wars between rival states — are commonplace. This is a matter for concern if only because human beings in their thousands, tens of thousands, hundreds of thousands and millions have been slaughtered in the process: whether by their own compatriots or ruling classes, as in Uganda, Argentina, Indonesia or Cambodia; or by the direct intervention of imperial powers as in Vietnam. The social and economic costs of violence, social disruption, warfare and movements of population on the scale that they have taken place in the Third World over the past three decades are incalculable.

Peace is a realistic programme only if it is sought through an understanding of the political and economic forces which create struggles for domination. The military is a crucial instrument in such struggles: both as an agent of internal repression and international domination; and (on the whole less frequently) of radical social change and national liberation.

There are two ways of approaching the problems of peacekeeping. The first is more cautious and incremental: how, given *existing* forms of force, of class conflict, of state and international organization, can conflict be averted, arms races be kept under control and the human and material costs of international conflict minimised? The second tackles the issues more comprehensively: what transformations in class structure, military, state and international organization would be required to assure conditions of lasting peace, both nationally and internationally?

The arguments of this paper suggest that the patterns of accumulation which prevail in the world economy, the existing forms of force and the present organization of the international system of nation states, severely limit the scope for international agreement on arms control and conflict resolution along incremental lines. In addition, the present international system is based on a distribution of economic resources and of political and military power that systematically disadvantages the Third World. Its populations will not for long be able to accept this inequitable state of affairs.

These limits and conflicts are described below. It is a much more difficult task to suggest alternatives. What forms of force and of popular mobilization can negate the coercive power of professional military organizations? How can the nexus between armaments and international capital accumulation be broken? How can existing international institutions and the prevailing international distribution of power be changed without precipitating a nuclear holocaust? This paper does not pretend to give ready answers, although the chances of providing such answers are increased if we have some understanding of the interaction of the historical forces which have co-acted and still sustain the pattern of military expansion.

To understand the location of the Third World within this framework requires an historical understanding of the legacy of imperialism, in which military force played a critical role in opening up the countries of the periphery to the trade and capital of the advanced capitalist powers and in ensuring their political subordination to the latter. This historical legacy has, certainly, been greatly transformed since its zenith in the late nineteenth century. Most

countries of the Third World have gained their political independence, although
many of them remain extremely vulnerable to external political and military
pressures. New world centres — the USA and the USSR — have come to the fore-
front. The consolidation of a bloc of socialist countries means that the world
system is no longer dominated exclusively by the capitalist mode of production.
The effects on Third World countries are, however, two-edged. On the one hand,
they gain greater freedom to manoeuvre, allowing at least some of them to distance themselves from foreign domination. Yet at the same time the cold war
between capitalist and socialist powers adds to the external pressures on the
uncommitted to ally themselves to one side or the other.

The Technology of Force, 'Modernization' and Technological Dependence

The expansion of the advanced capitalist powers of Europe and North America
which took place between the sixteenth and early twentieth centuries was
achieved as much by force of arms as by trade and investment — or at least
they were two sides of the same coin. To put it crudely, better methods of
manufacture of industrial goods resulted in improved armaments and these in
turn made possible the conquests which opened up new markets for the factories
and workshops of the industrial powers.

Since the dismantling of the great colonial empires, the technological advantages of the central countries in terms of armaments have not merely remained,
they have greatly increased. This is largely the consequence of rapid technical progress. Military Research and Development has increased to around 10 to
15 per cent of total world military spending, compared with only one per cent
before World War II. For the developing countries the critical fact is that
virtually all of this R & D takes place in the advanced industrial countries,
85 per cent in the USA and the USSR alone and a further 10 per cent in the
four other most important arms producers, Britain, France, West Germany and
China. It is true, to be sure, that some of the more industrialized Third
World countries manufacture part of their own arms, one or two like Brazil or
India even having a certain amount of design capability. Yet the greater part
of this manufacture takes place under licence, makes use of components available only from the major arms suppliers, and is closely tied in with their
other economic and military links.

The implications of this technological dependence for the way Third World military organizations are structured and the role they play in their national
societies are far-reaching. Over the past one or two hundred years the peripheral countries have imported with their weapons a military division of labour
shaped by the technology of the advanced industrial countries from which the
weapons were obtained.

The countries of the Third World do not *have* to adopt the division of labour
established in the professional armies of the central countries to make use of
their imported weapons. But as a historical pattern the link between military
professionalism and the absorption of external technology is extremely powerful. Professional soldiers identify themselves with the organizations they
control and accordingly choose weapons which the latter can assimilate. By
the same process the increasingly complex hardware they import from abroad —
the tanks, the jet aircraft and missiles — tend to accentuate the complexity
of the military establishment. Once set in motion, this process of profession-
alization on the one hand and absorption of external technology on the other
tends to be self-generating. (It should be noted that this is largely indep-

endent of the particular source of technology imports: Soviet or Czechoslovak
military hardware reproduces military organizations just as well as American,
French or British.)

It has sometimes been contended that it is precisely its training in the use
of advanced technology which gives the military a special role to play in the
"modernization" of the less developed countries. The position is stated by
Lucien Pye in an article published in the 1950s which in some ways became a
self-fulfilling prophecy because of the way it was used to make the military
assistance programmes of the United States government seem respectable. As
Pye puts it:

> "Above all else . . . the revolution in military technology
> has caused the army leaders of the newly emergent countries
> to be extremely sensitive to the extent to which their
> countries are economically and technologically underdev-
> eloped. Called upon to perform roles basic to advanced
> societies, the more politically conscious officers can
> hardly avoid being aware of the need for more substantial
> changes in their own societies" (Pye 1962: 78).

But training in the use of sophisticated weapons does not mean that army officers are more skilled or progressive in their attitudes than any other elite
groups. The military has a special place in Third World societies not because
its technology is "modern", but because it is a particular kind of technology,
that of force. And force is never used in the abstract, but in the struggle
between different classes and groups. The functions of military force are
different in situations of revolutionary change (as in Cuba, Mozambique or
China); of broad social reform imposed by the military and other elite groups
from above (as in Peru from 1968-1975 or Nasser's Egypt); yet again where it
is used mainly to reproduce the existing regime and class structure (as in
Iran); to change the regime in the interests of local or international economically dominant classes (as in Chile); or merely to secure (as in Uganda)
the dominance of a parasitic military establishment.

The critical role of force in securing stability — or the power of dominant
political groups and classes — has led to increased research in so-called
"counter-insurgency". This has produced not only sophisticated technology
such as that of the "electronic battlefield" (Klare, 1972), but also greater
attention to the "software" of communications, propaganda and surveillance
over the civilian population. Its results are directly disseminated by the
military assistance programmes of the major powers, particularly the USA. Not
only do countries like Iran, Indonesia, Brazil, Chile or Zaire import large
quantities of equipment, they also receive technical assistance from the CIA
and similar agencies in organizing the intelligence and propaganda networks on
which the security of those who control the state apparatus depends.

Let us now look a little more closely at the international mechanisms by which
the techniques of force are proliferated. In the first place there is technological competition. Third World countries take part in it only as clients of
the greater powers willing to sell or donate them the necessary arms or production facilities. The precise form that the transferred technology takes is
therefore shaped by the dialectic of the arms races taking place between the
supplying (industrial) rather than the receiving (peripheral) countries. It
is distorted in the direction of military hardware — like advanced jet aircraft or tanks — which fits in with the existing production patterns of the
former rather than the latter.

Yet technical progress has a logic of its own which sometimes throws up consequences which the major industrial powers neither desire, nor are able, given
the intense competition for markets and spheres of influence, to keep fully
under their control. The new generations of portable anti-tank and anti-aircraft missiles, for example, have been put to very effective use against conventional forces by the liberation fighters of Vietnam, Palestine or Mozambique. The Americans can now produce small guided "cruise" missiles capable
of delivering nuclear warheads with great accuracy over long distances and at
a small fraction of the cost of the ICBMs which are now the mainstay of the
great powers' nuclear armouries. These have been the subject of heated arguments at the Strategic Arms Limitation Talks. The USA has thus far resisted
attempts to make a ban on the development and production of cruise missiles a
part of the arms limitation agreements, although it maintains that under no
circumstances will they be supplied to third countries, even close allies.
Yet it must surely be only a matter of time before they are more widely produced
and marketed. Nuclear technology itself is within reach of a number of the
larger or more advanced developing countries such as India, Brazil or Israel,
where despite the surveillance of the International Atomic Energy Authority
over international transactions in nuclear materials and technology, it is
becoming more and more difficult to prevent the development of nuclear energy
for peaceful purposes from spilling over into more warlike uses.

The Non-Proliferation Treaty attempts to deal with the very real danger of the
proliferation of the means of mass nuclear destruction. Yet it is easy to
understand the cynicism of countries like Argentina or Pakistan — or indeed of
producers and suppliers like France and China — about agreements which in their
nature create a cartel of the great powers in the means of destruction, thus
stabilizing the existing balance of power in the international system; particularly so when the major world powers themselves have made little serious
effort to limit their own technological competition.

But would the ability of the large powers to intervene militarily and politically in the Third World be any the less if some of the latter countries controlled their own means of mass destruction? How far would it on the other
hand increase the regional sub-imperialism of wealthier countries like Brazil,
Iran or India, at the expense of their less powerful neighbours? Would it
merely make the world a more dangerous place to live in by proliferating dangerous weapons whilst not fundamentally altering the dependence of peripheral
countries on the suppliers of their arms and technology?

Conversely, how far is the military ascendance of the major powers *actually*
increased by their enormous technological superiority? The peculiar feature
of nuclear arms is that there are almost no circumstances in which either side
in a conflict would dare to use them. The major powers continue to rely on
conventional forces to stabilize existing international arrangements like NATO
and the Warsaw Pact and to increase their spheres of influence (viz. the Soviet
Union's build-up of naval fleets in the Mediterranean and Indian Ocean). The
ability of the great powers to intervene with force in other parts of the world
depends on their vast stocks of conventional armaments. Indeed, the production, operation and development of nuclear weapons and their delivery systems
takes up only 10-15 per cent of total world military expenditures.

It is doubtful whether the acquisition of missiles and advanced nuclear technology by Third World countries would itself make up for their technical and
quantitative inferiority in terms of conventional weapons. This fact is well
appreciated by the few Third World countries which are in a good position to

build up their military forces. In a recent television interview with the
BBC, the Shah of Iran admitted that it was unrealistic for Iran to engage in
nuclear competition with the USA, USSR, France or Britain. But he said it was
his ambition to make the Iranian armed forces the largest and best equipped
(with non-nuclear arms) in the world.

Yet the greater sophistication and quantity of the conventional weapons available to large powers is not always militarily decisive. Technology, as already
noted, may be turned on its head by more effective ways of putting social organization and technology together. The Vietnam War illustrates perfectly the
difficulties of using capital intensive methods of warfare against a population
that is politically and militarily highly mobilized. To be sure, military R & D
has developed technical solutions to get around some of these limits — defol-
iants, for example, helicopters and gunships and the "electronic battlefield".
In Vietnam they merely contributed to the military stalemate from which the US
government was eventually forced to pull out its forces. But their transfer
to Latin America has undoubtedly made the repression of revolutionary guerilla
groups more effective.

At the same time, professional military establishments have consciously made
use of the lessons of revolutionary military organizations. As Regis Debray
puts it, "Socialist revolution revolutionizes the counterrevolution" (Debray,
1973: 150). Mao Tse Tung's doctrines of revolutionary war are taught in the
academies and staff colleges of the advanced capitalist countries as well as
in those countries like Brazil, Indonesia or indeed South Africa. Nevertheless
the basic limitations remain. Professional armies — be they those of the Western powers or those of Third World countries modelled upon them — can neither
fight "people's wars" nor always be certain of success against them by virtue
of their technological superiority.

Economic Dependence and the International Arms Economy

What are the main factors responsible for the growth in military expenditures
in the Third World? And what are the effects of the expansion of the military
upon patterns of national development?

To begin with, there are the pressures which arise from the logic of military
organizations themselves. In some ways modern armies are like industrial
firms. They are organized around a large physical plant of capital equipment,
employ a numerous labour force of men in uniform and coordinate their activities in a hierarchical structure controlled by military managers, the members
of the officer corps. Yet there are certain critical differences. In the
first place it is hard to say just what the "output" is: fighting wars, preparing for wars they never fight, national security, or violence and insecurity;
intervention when the police and civilian authorities are unable to deal with
internal disturbances, the mailed fist of the ruling class, making and breaking
regimes by military coups, symbolizing national sovereignty and independence?

It is peculiarly difficult, therefore, to apply criteria of economic cost-
effectiveness to military spending and activity. In a conflict-ridden nation
or in a volatile international situation the threats to security which exist
or can be invented are almost without limit. The situation is exacerbated
because technical progress makes weapons systems obsolete almost as soon as
they are introduced. Military men in developing countries usually complain
that their armies, navies and airforces are weak and badly equipped by inter-

national standards. The gap is indeed real, though the standards of judgement applied to it are influenced by the arms salesmen and military training prog- rammes of the rich countries.

Such pressure for military growth must be presumed to exist in most Third World countries which have professional armies. They do not, however, help explain the great variation in levels of military spending between different developing countries set forth in Table 4.1.

Armies are in a unique position to extract the resources they want by black- mailing, coercing or taking over governments. Yet a cursory glance at Table 4.1 confirms that military regimes spend little more on armaments than their civilian counterparts.*

Nor does it seem that authoritarian regimes spend much more on armaments than their neighbours. Some of the world's more repressive regimes — Haiti, for example, Malawi, Swaziland, Paraguay, Nicaragua, Uganda and Argentina — are proportionately low military spenders. This is partly because the financial costs of internal repression are not usually high since it is not capital in- tensive and is often underwritten by large powers. Low spending is possible, furthermore, because many such countries — particularly in Africa and Latin America — are relatively insulated from the major sources of international con- flict.

For it is the international influences on levels of military spending which make the most difference. In the first place, a good part of the variation can be accounted for by the concentration of hard currency earnings in the hands of particular Third World countries which control resources that are strategic for the economic expansion of the major powers. The heaviest inc- reases in military spending in recent years have taken place in the oil-rich countries of the Middle East, which (together with Egypt, Jordan and Syria whose military spending they subsidize) form the majority of countries devoting more than 10 per cent of their GNP to armaments (see Table 4.1).

The other major determinant of military spending is (not surprisingly) armed conflict itself — actual or threatened — both inside nations and between them. Almost all the countries shown in Table 4.1 whose military burden exceeded 10 per cent of GNP in 1974 were involved in the wars of liberation in Indo-China, the Arab-Israel conflict or are oil producers. The only exceptions are the USSR and North Korea which fit better with the next group, those which spend between five and ten per cent of their GNP, made up of: NATO and Warsaw Pact powers, China and Taiwan, Portugal (still at the time fighting revolutionary movements in its African colonies), Pakistan (conflict with India), Somalia (border conflicts with Ethiopia and Kenya), Nigeria and Chad (fighting or hav- ing recently fought civil wars), and two more oil producers (Libya and Qatar).

---

*This observation is on the whole confirmed by the detailed studies that have been made of the relation between military regimes, arms spending and econ- omic performance. See, for example, R.D. McKinlay and A.S. Cohan (1975), who found that developing countries under military regimes had armies no larger and spent no more of their national product on the military than countries under civilian regimes which had also experienced periods of military rule. Both categories, however, had larger armed forces and spent more of their GNP on the military than developing countries which had never been under military rule, though this difference was not statistically significant.

TABLE 4.1

Relative Burden of Military Expenditures, 1973.

Per capita GNP	Military Expenditures (as percentage of GNP)				
	More than 10%	5 to 10%	2 to 4.9%	1 to 1.9%	Less than 1%
Under $100	Cambodia Vietnam, N.	Chad Somalia Yemen (Sana)	Burma Burundi Ethiopia Mali	Afghanistan Rwanda Upper Volta	Bangladesh Nepal
$100-199	Vietnam, S. Aden Yemen	Pakistan	Central African Republic Guinea India Indonesia Laos Mauritania Sudan Tanzania Zaire	Dahomey Kenya Malagasy Rep. Togo Uganda	The Gambia Haiti Lesotho Malawi Niger Sierra Leone
$200-299	Egypt	China, People's Republic Nigeria	Bolivia Thailand	Cameroon Honduras Philippines Senegal	Liberia Sri Lanka
$300-499	Jordan Korea, N. Syria	Albania	Congo Ecuador Equatorial Guinea Korea, S. Morocco Rhodesia Zambia	Colombia El Salvador Guyana Paraguay Tunisia	Botswana Guatemala Mauritius Swaziland

$500-999	Iran Iraq Oman	Taiwan	Algeria Bahrain Brazil Chile Lebanon Malaysia Peru Turkey Uruguay	Dominican Rep. Ivory Coast Nicaragua	Costa Rica Jamaica Mexico Panama
$1000-1999	Saudi Arabia	Portugal	Cyprus Greece Romania South Africa Spain Venezuela Yugoslavia	Argentina Gabon	Malta Trinidad & Tobago
$2000-2999	Israel Soviet Union	Bulgaria Czechoslovakia Hungary Libya	Singapore	Ireland	
$3000 & up	German Democratic Republic Qatar United Kingdon United States	Australia Belgium Canada Denmark France Germany (FRG) Kuwait Netherlands Norway Sweden United Arab Emirates	Austria Finland New Zealand Switzerland	Iceland Japan Luxemburg	

Source: US Arms Control and Disarmament Agency, World Military Expenditures and the Arms Trade, 1964-1974, Washington, D.C., USA, 1976.

What are the effects of military spending on patterns of national development
—or underdevelopment— in the Third World? Unlike firms or production units,
armies do not create the surplus value which sustains their own expansion.
The resources have to be provided from taxation or by subsidies from international patrons and suppliers of arms. In the first place this puts the military
in a special position relative to the remainder of the state machinery through
which the necessary resources have to be raised internally or negotiated exter-
nally. Second, it implies a degree of integration in the international economy
from which internationally negotiable purchasing power has to be obtained in
order to acquire military hardware.

Yet the implications of this interrelation between military spending, state
appropriation of surpluses and the international economy are little touched on
in existing discussions, which the most part attempt to measure the overall
effect of military spending on aggregate measures of economic performance.
From one of the most comprehensive crossnational studies of the effects of arms
spending (Benoit, 1973), we learn that levels of military spending in developing countries are (contrary to expectation) positively associated with non-
military growth rates (i.e. rates of GNP growth, taking out the military expenditure component of GNP). But the causal direction of this correlation is not
established. It could occur merely because countries with high GNP growth
rates have more to spend on arms. Or the relationship could be spurious in
the sense that military spending and high measured growth in non-military GNP
may both be the product of other influences, such as the tendency of the major
powers to pump economic development assistance as well as military aid into
countries in which they have strategic interests.

Such discussions presuppose, furthermore, that we are mainly interested in
growth rates rather than development defined in terms of broader criteria including how GNP is distributed. An explanation sometimes offered for the association between arms spending and growth — or rather for why there is not a
negative association between them — is that the resources for armaments are
typically diverted from social welfare spending rather than from productive
investment. Statistical comparisons of developing countries (Schmitter, 1971)
on the whole support this explanation. But it is a serious matter to divert
resources from schools, hospitals and welfare services to guns, tanks and jet
aircraft, and most probably can only be done by governments which are prepared
in the final analysis to repress the discontent it brings about.

Even if one were to accept at face value the evidence that arms spending prom-
otes growth it is difficult to find a sensible explanation for it. Military
spending, to be sure, has some spin-offs, but it is hard to see how these could
offset more than a small proportion of the cost of maintaining a large military
establishment, except in those few countries like Brazil, Argentina or India
which have arms industries of their own, backed by a relatively diversified
industrial base. Even here, many of the multiplier effects of military equipment purchases are felt by the arms industries of international suppliers
rather than in the domestic economy, with consequent pressure on the balance
of payments.

Nevertheless there is a certain logic to military spending because it plays a
role in reproducing certain structural patterns commonly found in peripheral
economies. Armaments may facilitate growth *within* the constraints established
by such patterns, though at the same time tying up resources that could be put
to much better use under alternative structural arrangements. What are the
patterns that military spending supports and how does it do so? The main

ingredients are as follows, though I should emphasize that different developing countries share in them to a different extent, and what I describe is very
much a general case:

1. Role of military spending in concentrating the capital and resources required for fast GNP growth in peripheral capitalist economies. Put simplisti-
cally, growth under these conditions requires forced saving, increased social
inequality and the diversion of government spending from welfare to production
and/or subsidies for capital. There are strong inflationary pressures and re-
current crises in the balance of payments. These pressures can only be dealt
with, or so it is suggested, by governments which are prepared to hold down
wages and rural incomes and to use military force to put down trades unions,
strikes and peasant protest. This results in higher military expenditure,
less because internal repression itself is costly than because soldiers have
to be rewarded for carrying it out. High military expenditure in turn requires
extra forced saving and increases inflationary pressure and public unrest.

2. Role of the military in strengthening the state structure and its control
over the process of economic growth. The arguments just put forward about the
role of military force in resolving the crises to which peripheral economies
are prone assume that military force is effective in redistributing resources
for capital formation and in repressing the conflict created by inequality and
inflation. But the political pressures which build up in such situations often
make stability problematic. The syndrome of military expansion, inequality,
inflation, discontent, repression and further military expansion is all too
common. Perhaps all one can conclude is that military force allows a greater
concentration of resources in the hands of the state than would otherwise be
possible (without necessarily accepting that a powerful state structure is any
the better at handling the economic and political crises to which such societies are prone). The military establishment itself, of course, has a direct
interest in a powerful and centralized state, since it can extract through it
the resources for its own expansion.

3. A built-in alliance between armaments and the international expansion of
capital into peripheral countries. From the point of view of foreign capital
and Western governments a large and powerful military establishment often seems
to guarantee the conditions under which profits can be repatriated from peripheral countries. As Robert MacNamara once put it to a US Congress Subcommittee, "the essential role of the Latin American military as a stabilizing force
outweighs any risks involved in providing (US) military assistance for internal
security purposes" (quoted in Klare, 1972: 287).

4. The military usually has its own interests at stake in the alliance with
foreign capital, brought into being because arms spending adds to the pressure
to increase or conserve hard currency earnings and to attract foreign investment. The military's preference for state-managed development may actually
strengthen such tendencies rather than detract from them. The alliance of
state and international capital, created through central planning, licensing
and import control, joint ventures and management agreements, is a well-docu-
mented feature of many Third World countries. Military expansion supports this
tendency as much under civilian governments such as those of Malaysia, Kenya
or Venezuela as under military regimes like those of Indonesia, Nigeria or
Brazil (even though it may add to the pressures on the former to succumb to
military rule in the longer run).

Variations in Military's Class Project

Structure of Economy	Nature of State Project
1. <u>Petty capitalist commodity production</u> Agricultural and natural resource based commodities produced for export and/or local sale by indigenous producers under petty capitalist or pre-capitalist relations of production. Examples: most countries of sub-Saharan Africa, Bangladesh.	1. Minimum conditions of law and order. 2. Mediation between petty producers and world market, either (a) via foreign merchant capital, or (b) directly via state marketing monopolies. 3. Extraction of surplus from export-import trade and conversion into (a) increases in size, power and military spending of state apparatus or (b) industrialization programmes.
2. <u>Enclave commodity production</u> Agricultural commodities produced or natural resources extracted on large scale (a) by international capital or (b) by state capital incorporated in circuits of international capital through export of commodities and imports of technology. Examples: most oil-producing (OPEC) countries and copper-producing (CIPEC) countries.	1. Minimum conditions of law and order. 2. Mediation between capital and labour in enclave enterprises; ensuring stability and quiescence of labour, in the last resort by physical repression. 3. Either (a) State is directly coopted by foreign capital and serves its interests (e.g. Gabon, Central American banana republics), or (b) State expropriates foreign capital. The latter reorganizes itself and appropriates its share of mineral rents by sales of technology, management agreements, military sales, etc. 4. (Where State not mouthpiece of foreign capital) promotion of natural resource ideologies; maximization of mineral rents and of state's share therein; conversion of these surpluses into expansion of state apparatus and/or industrialization.

4.2
in Dependent Capitalist Countries

Nature of Crises	Nature of Military Project
1. Political crises brought on by reinvigoration of pre-capitalist formations and loyalties (tribe, religion, language, region, etc.) in response to competition for state power, jobs, economic resources and benefits.	1. (a) Holding fragile nation-state together and/or (b) using state machinery to establish hegemony of the particular tribal, religious, linguistic or regional groups who happen to control the military hierarchy.
2. Instability induced by fluctuations in commodity prices in world market, undermining regimes and their long-term economic plans.	2. Intervention to secure changes of regime in response to externally-induced economic and political crises.
	3. Reinforcement (through arms purchases) of pressure to earn foreign exchange in world market or to save it by engaging in import-substituting industrialization.
1. Conflicts between central regions/groups/towns sharing the benefits of economic activity and employment created by enclave and peripheral regions/groups/rural areas.	1. Establishment of physical control by centre over peripheral regions.
2. Conflicts between capital and labour in enclave.	2. Intervention in conflicts between foreign or state capital and labour.
3. (a) Instability induced by fluctuations in commodity prices in world market, undermining regimes and their long-term plans, precipitating conflict between states and foreign capitalists, except (b) when associations of producers (especially OPEC) exercise monopoly control in world market, minimizing direct effect of externally induced crises on state machinery.	3. (a) Direct physical repression on behalf of foreign capital, particularly in times of economic and political crisis (e.g. Chile) or (b) intervention against foreign capital on behalf of nationalist projects to assure state control over natural resources (or support for such interventions by other groups or governments).
	4. Reinforcement (through arms purchases) of pressures to maximize natural resource rents and to participate in international arms economy.

Table 4.2 continued

Structure of Economy	Nature of State Project
3. <u>Import-substituting industrializ-ation</u> Development of industrial base through either (a) foreign invest-ment or (b) state investment or both, replacing goods previously imported. Examples: Brazil, Mexico, Argentina, Philippines and (combined with 2 above) Indonesia, Iran, Venezuela, Chile and Nigeria.	1. Maintenance of political stability to assure smooth process of indus-trialization and to prevent flight of foreign capital. 2. Mediation between capital and labour; repression of latter to subsidize investment by the former. 3. State promotion of industrialization bringing about symbiosis of state, local and international capital. Variations in extent of penetration by international capital, in the mechanisms (e.g. direct investment versus sales of technology) by which it is achieved and in extent of state control over the process.
4. <u>Export-promoting industrialization</u> Examples: South Korea, Taiwan, Singapore and (combined with 3 above) Philippines.	As above except foreign capital (a) more footloose because not tied to domestic resources of markets, (b) tends to an even greater extent to be vertically integrated with pro-duction and markets in central coun-tries. For these reasons (a) poli-tical stability (and organized phys-ical repression) are even more vital, and (b) the bargaining power of the State is weaker relative to that of international capital.

Such is the paradigm. But few countries fit it in all respects. Some of the main variations in the military's class project brought about by differences in the structure and international links of the national economy are summarized in Table 4.2.

The first two patterns set forth in the Table arise in economies which are based on the production of raw materials for the world market, though it makes a considerable difference whether these are produced (like many agricultural commodities) by numerous indigenous petty producers, or are extracted (like most minerals) through large investments of foreign capital. The third and fourth patterns are determined by the nature of a country's process of indus-trialization — whether by import-substitution or by the export of cheap manu-factures produced by low-cost labour.

Nature of Crises	Nature of Military Project
1. Conflicts between industrial/urban centres and rural/agricultural peripheries, intensified to extent that the latter subsidize process of industrialization.	1. Establishment of physical control by centre over periphery. Repression of peasant movements, rural guerillas, etc.
2. Conflicts between capital and labour in industrial sector, intensified to the extent that profits and investment subsidized by low wages.	2. Intervention in conflict between foreign or state capital and labour, usually to repress the latter on behalf of the former, but not always (e.g. the Peronist alliance between the military and unions in Argentina).
3. Marginalization, creation of reserve army of unemployed by industrialization/urbanization processes.	3. Establishment of physical "security" in restive urban areas. Repression of crime, squatters, demonstrations, urban guerillas, etc.
4. Crises created by exhaustion of process of import-substitution. Cycle of foreign exchange shortages, inflation, unrest, repression, military spending and more shortages, inflation, etc.	4. Reinforcement (through arms purchases and sometimes arms manufacture) of import-substitution and of the crises induced by it.
As above except (a) low wages often essential to attract foreign capital and hence greater repression of labour force; (b) vulnerability to crises in international markets for manufactures rather than to constraints of narrowness of domestic market.	As above, except military involved to an even greater extent in establishment of physical security (particularly in urban centres), repression and counter-revolution.

Armies or military regimes are seldom directly subservient to foreign capital. Even in countries whose economies are based on primary products extracted and sold abroad by foreign corporations, soldiers often favour state expropriation of foreign capital to the extent this can be achieved (as by the oil producers) without serious damage to the economy's international earning power.

Even military elites committed — like that of Brazil — to an orthodox strategy of capitalist development in close association with foreign investment face internal struggles against officers who advocate economic nationalism and greater state control over the economy (Stepan, 1971). In countries like Peru, Ethiopia, Libya and Egypt (under Nasser) it is the military radicals who have prevailed and have effected quite sweeping changes, including nationalization of key sectors of the economy.

Not all countries, further, are equally constrained by a lack of international earning power. Indeed in the oil-rich countries military spending is about the fastest way of realizing surplus hard currency earnings. A cynic would say that the availability of such earnings in countries such as Iran, Saudi Arabia and more debatably Nigeria, merely removes all obstacles to the expansion of the state apparatus and makes it easier to buy off or suppress internal contradictions, without fundamental change in the structure of the economy or links with the international economic system. Nevertheless, oil surpluses give radical regimes like those of Algeria or Libya more room in which to manoeuvre, even if they expose them to the same temptations to buy arms and proliferate soldiers and bureaucrats as the more conservative countries.

Moreover, contradictions in the international system alleviate some of the obstacles to national development strategies created by international capital. Peru has been able to play the major capitalist powers off against each other, buying arms from Britain, France, and now the USSR while never completely breaking with the USA.

Most important of all, there are a number of Third World countries (Cuba, Iraq, Syria, Algeria, Somalia, Angola, Uganda, Tanzania, India) which are supplied very largely or entirely by countries within the socialist bloc. Not all these countries are socialist themselves, by any stretch of the imagination. Yet there is no doubt that socialist arms sales and assistance makes a real difference to the recipient countries, enabling them to arm themselves without having to earn large amounts of hard currency in the world market (though some of them find the economic conditions laid down by their socialist suppliers almost as onerous). In some the only effect of socialist, like Western, arms and military assistance is to allow an oppressive regime to survive (like Amin's in Uganda, now heavily dependent on Soviet military support). The tendency in most of them is toward state capitalism and military-bureaucratic control of the development process rather than full-scale socialist transformation, for which socialist military assistance is probably a necessary but not a sufficient condition.

Few countries therefore fit fair and square into any one of the categories in the Table. Indeed, the military often plays a critical role in the transition from one pattern to another. The crisis which led first to the rise to power of the Allende regime in Chile and then to its overthrow by the soldiers in 1974 was, for example, brought on by the exhaustion of the process of import-substitution and the international forces set in motion by the government's expropriation of the foreign copper monopolies. In response to these external forces the military government has adopted economic policies — economic liberalization, sale of state enterprises, the curtailment of import-substitution, withdrawal from the Andean Pact — which virtually amount to a reassertion of its traditional position in the international division of labour as a raw material producer.

Further, it is not necessary to assume that the class project the military finally takes up is necessarily agreed in advance by the officer corps, still less their men, nor that it will be stable. Periods of crisis bring major shifts in the way the military interposes itself in class conflict, which are usually accompanied by violent internal struggles. The social origins of the soldiers who win such struggles, their civilian allies and their original intentions will have some influence on the class project the military undertakes, but may be distorted by the circumstances with which they have to cope once they take power. Examples are not difficult to find: the Nigerian army intervened to establish national unity in 1966 but broke up into tribal and regional factions six months later; the Chilean military seized power with the active support of the national bourgeoisie in order to halt what was perceived as a process of national disintegration, and ended up restoring the dominance of foreign mono- poly capital; the soldiers who took power in Brazil in 1964 quickly dropped their programme of economic and political liberalization in favour of state- sponsored industrialization under an authoritarian regime.

Having reviewed the consequences of military spending in the Third World, let us now turn to the international mechanisms which sustain it. Broadly speak- ing, the accumulation of armaments in peripheral countries is linked to the accumulation of capital in the central capitalist countries: both directly in that military spending in the Third World creates markets for the arms indus- tries of the industrial countries, and indirectly in that it increases pres- sures on Third World countries to earn the hard currency for their military purchases by trading in the world market or encouraging the inflow of foreign investment. Nevertheless this international arms economy is itself riven by contradictory pressures which make its analysis extremely complex:

1. In the first place the flow of armaments internationally is partly deter- mined by the logic of accumulation and arms production in the major capitalist arms producing countries, especially the USA, Britain, France, West Germany, Canada and in recent years Japan. The impetus comes from three sources:

(a) The logic of arms production itself. Because R & D is a high proportion of total production costs, long production runs are required to justify the initial outlay, creating strong pressures to market armaments abroad. Such pressures have increased because of the escalation in the cost of major items of military equipment and have affected the European arms producers the most, because their national military forces absorb a smal- ler proportion of the total weapons output than those of the USA or USSR (Kaldor, 1972).

(b) Pressures from the interrelation between arms production and the process of capital accumulation in the central capitalist countries. Here we are on more controversial ground, the issue having been debated with particu- lar bitterness in the USA as a result of the Vietnam War.* There are those on the one hand who argue that the enormous increases of arms prod- uction have helped the US economy overcome the crises of over-production to which capitalist economies are prone. The Vietnam war in sum was good for American capitalism. But others argue that the military-industrial alliance between the arms producing firms and the Pentagon has to the contrary diverted resources away from productive investment and brought about inflation. Although the Vietnam War was good for the US arms prod- ucers, it is argued, it put great strain on the productive capacity of American capitalism. Whichever of these diagnoses of American capitalism is correct, however, they both imply pressure to market arms to the Third World, be it because of the search for markets to make use of spare industrial capacity, or to alleviate balance of payments difficulties arising from America's own military spending.

(c) Pressures arising from the relation between armaments and the international economy. In a general way capital will be invested in arms production so

---

*The literature on this debate is too large to cite in detail here. There are useful summaries in Rosen, 1970.

long as there is an international market for weapons. Arms exports, furthermore, play a critical role in resolving crises in the international
economy such as that created by the redistribution of international purchasing power towards the oil producing countries. One of the major
ironies of recent history is the way the Middle East war precipitated the
oil embargo, subsequent oil price increases, and eventually a major crisis in the international economy — which has been partly bought off by
the escalation of the arms race in the Middle East.

The pressures arising at these different levels — the specific requirements of
capital invested in arms production, the logic of capital accumulation in the
central capitalist economies, and the logic of world-wide capital accumulation
— may be in conflict, though no doubt their overall effect is to increase the
pressure on the industrial countries to export arms to the Third World. Politicians in Britain, for example, are under great pressure to subsidize the
production of armaments and to promote their export, rather than to permit the
curtailment of existing production or the postponement of new investment, however strong the case that large-scale arms production is bad for the British
economy in the long run. This is partly because of the presumed short-term
effects of redundancies in the economy, and partly a matter of the economics
of remaining a world power. Investment in arms production and the despatch of
arms salesmen to the Middle East makes sense — it is alleged — if it maintains
Britain's capacity to develop weapons for its own use. The contradictions inherent in this position were made particularly clear recently by the commitments to sell almost the entire production of the next generation of Chieftain
tanks protected by the revolutionary new Chobham armour to Iran, thereby postponing deliveries to the British army.

2. The economic forces sustaining the arms trade are modified by the fact that
it is also an instrument of the states and ruling classes of the powers which
exercise or aspire to hegemony within the international system. Just as the
main importers of arms are the governments and military establishments of developing countries, so the suppliers are either the governments of the supplying
countries themselves or large firms closely inter-linked with these governments.
The governments of the industrial countries either negotiate arms exports directly themselves, take a direct part in the promotion efforts of their main
domestic arms producers, or push them indirectly through arms exporting firms
which sometimes act (like certain British arms suppliers) in all respects as
cover for the governments' own arms sales. Exports are usually licensed to
ensure they reach the "approved" recipient and are not diverted elsewhere, and
above all, the supply of arms is consciously used by governments to enlarge
their spheres of political influence and to promote their non-military trade
and investment. It is common for arms sales and military assistance to form
part of a wider "package", including trade and investment agreements or political accords, which may either be spelt out openly like the Treaty of Friend-
ship between the Soviet Union and Egypt which Anwar Sadat recently repudiated,
or form part of a more subterranean framework of economic and political under-
standings. Finally, a large proportion of the trade is subsidized, increasing
the ability of Third World governments to absorb huge quantities of armaments.
Much of the arms sales and military assistance provided by the countries of
the socialist bloc is subsidized and some still is given free. In the 1950s
and 1960s the greater part of arms transfers from the USA were also subsidized
under the Military Assistance Program, though cash and credit sales now pre-
dominate over grants.

3. The competition in the world market for arms between societies based on

antagonistic — socialist and capitalist — modes of production has a distinctive
impact on both the economics and the politics of the arms trade. Even if the
overall effect of the cold war is to reduce the price of the arms supplied to
developing countries, it undoubtedly increases their volume and total value.
This has three major implications. First it increases the flow of resources
towards the arms industries of the arms suppliers and increases the power and
resources of their respective military-industrial complexes. Second, in so
doing it helps to maintain the pace of technological innovation, increasing
the complexity and cost of weapons in the long run. Third, subsidized arms
supplies often increase rather than decrease the military outlays of developing countries, both directly through added local costs such as wages and accom-
modation and through imports of non-military supplies required to support larger military forces, and indirectly by increasing the power of the military
establishment's claim on national resources. Finally, to the extent that
hegemonic powers like the USA or France are actually successful in using military links to keep particular countries like Chile or Gabon within their respective spheres of influence, the economic benefits they hope for may well exceed the costs of the subsidy.

4. The expansion in the international market for arms is greatly accentuated
by the presence in the Third World itself of nodal points of international political conflict such as the Arab-Israeli conflict; the border disputes between
India and Pakistan and India and China; the border conflicts between Ethiopia,
Somalia and Kenya; and the struggle for black rule in Southern Africa. Trends
in the international arms trade can to some extent be explained in terms of
the "demand" for armaments created by such conflicts, though competition between the major suppliers reacts back upon the political situation, tending to
accelerate local arms races.

The effect of this complex interaction between the arms trade and struggles for
political hegemony on the flow of armaments from the major suppliers to the
different regions of the Third World can be seen in Table 4.3. By far the big-
gest recipients of arms from 1965 to 1974 were the countries of East Asia and
the Middle East, the dozen leading importers being (in descending order of magnitude): South Vietnam, Israel, Iran, Egypt, South Korea, Syria, India, Taiwan,
Pakistan, North Korea and Saudi Arabia.

Transfers of arms to East Asia have declined because of the end of the Vietnam
war. US arms sales and military assistance have consistently exceeded transfers from the socialist countries by a factor of over three to one, mainly because the US supplied large quantities of armaments to its allies at the fringe
of the main conflict — Thailand, the Philippines, Indonesia, Malaysia, Taiwan,
South Korea — as well as to Vietnam, Cambodia and Laos.

In the Middle East military spending has grown at a staggering 19 per cent per
annum over the past ten years. The transfer of arms from the advanced capitalist powers has more or less kept pace with transfers from the socialist bloc.
But if one disaggregates within the region, Israel, Iran, Jordan and Saudi
Arabia were almost exclusively supplied by the USA, Britain, France and West
Germany; and Egypt, Syria and Iraq by the Soviet Union and Czechoslovakia.
The countries of the Persian Gulf have purchased the greater part of their
arms from capitalist suppliers at commercial rates, whereas those involved in
the Arab-Israeli conflict have been extensively subsidized: with the result
that the value of arms transferred to the former has been about half that of
those imported by the latter, despite a similar level and growth of military
expenditure in both sub-regions.

TABLE 4.3

Total Arms Transfers, By Suppliers and Recipient Regions 1965-1974.

($ million)

Recipient Regions	Major Capitalist Suppliers					Major Socialist Suppliers			Other Suppliers	Total
	USA	France	UK	West Germany	Canada	USSR	Czechoslovakia and Poland	China		
World Total	31 563	2 826	2 089	1 221	1 187	18 793	2 481	2 119	2 125	64 404
NATO	8 447	770	505	724	893	-	-	-	515	11 854
Warsaw Pact	-	-	-	-	-	5 674	1 888	5	35	7 602
OPEC	2 374	668	662	154	89	2 152	136	-	570	6 825
East Asia	14 640	40	145	23	32	4 049	15	1 616	321	20 881
South Asia	139	271	98	36	10	1 706	159	335	36	2 922
Middle East	5 628	461	603	181	45	5 733	337	2	465	13 455
Africa	341	669	258	73	17	711	68	81	263	2 481
Latin America	811	463	269	137	172	323	2	-	229	2 406

Source: US Arms Control and Disarmament Agency, World Military Expenditures and the Arms Trade 1964-1974, 1976.

The growth of military spending in Africa has also been fast, though relative to low starting levels. By far the heaviest spenders in the continent have been Libya, South Africa, Algeria and Nigeria. The import figures reflect the continuing influence of the former colonial powers in the region, particularly that of France in her former colonies; the relative absence of US arms supplies, except in one or two individual countries like Ethiopia and Zaire; and a degree of socialist penetration, especially by the USSR in Algeria, Libya, Uganda and Somalia and by China in Tanzania. Several countries, including most notably Nigeria and Libya, have diversified sources of supply, obtaining a substantial proportion of their arms from capitalist and socialist camps alike.

The countries of South Asia have moved away from the colonial metropolis, and are now largely supplied by the socialist bloc — India, Bangladesh and Afghanistan by the Soviet Union, Pakistan by China (as well as by the USA and France). After increasing during the 1960s due to border conflicts between India, Pakistan and China, arms imports are now declining.

Latin America (except Cuba) is the only world region which is exclusively dependent on the advanced capitalist powers for its arms supplies. Imports have increased, but at the same time there has been diversification away from the USA towards France, the UK and West Germany, brought about both by the US government's ban on exports of advanced weapons to the region (now lifted) and by the economic nationalism of Latin American regimes.

To sum up, the nexus between militarism and international capitalism is found in its pure form only in Latin America and in those countries in Africa, the Middle East and East Asia which buy all their arms from the West. Even so, many of them have diversified in order to escape the influence of a single previously dominant supplier, be it the USA in Latin America or the former colonial powers in the Caribbean or Africa. Yet their military expansion is still connected to the *system* of international capitalism inasmuch as they rely on international purchasing power earned in the world market to finance their armies.

Competition among the capitalist arms suppliers and the struggle for hegemony between them and socialist suppliers are both responsible for an increased transfer of military resources to the Third World. The powerful socialist presence in the Middle East and Asia is thus two-edged, permitting disengagement from the West to an extent that is seldom possible in Latin America; but simultaneously raising the stakes in local conflicts, reinforcing military and bureaucratic control over the state apparatus; increasing military outlays; and expanding the market for the arms of the capitalist countries in equal measure to the inflow of socialist-provided weapons.

The final outcome depends very much on the nature of the struggle and of the groups to which the support of the socialist countries is given. Socialist support for liberation movements with a genuine prospect of socialist transformation and disengagement from the capitalist world economy, as in the wars of Indo-China and in former Portuguese Africa, is one thing. But military assistance given by socialist countries to authoritarian military or one-party regimes for reasons of international power politics is quite another. The paradox is that the latter supports a superstructure of political links with Third World countries, while at the same time permitting many of them to remain internationally dependent on the world economy and to repress socialism internally. Such a situation is inherently unstable, for client states which

do not have strong internal reasons for associating with the socialist bloc
can, like Egypt, go elsewhere for arms if they do not like the conditions laid
down.

This is but one aspect of a pervasive contradiction between the economic logic
and the political functions of the arms trade. Socialist arms suppliers face
it because they transfer arms to peripheral countries incorporated in a world
market, which, both in general and for arms in particular, is still mainly organized on capitalist principles. For capitalist countries, on the other hand,
the contradiction arises even more directly because of the link between the
international arms trade and their own capital accumulation. When an arms
producer is obliged to sell arms abroad to absorb high R & D expenditures, to
sustain capital accumulation and to ease balance-of-payments difficulties, it
is that much harder to use the promise of arms supplies or the threat of with-
holding them to influence the political behaviour of purchasers. At the same
time competition between the main arms suppliers — socialist and capitalist
alike — has made it difficult for any one of them to secure a lasting monopoly
over transfers to any particular country or region, of the type which the USA
previously enjoyed in Latin America.

The events of the past ten years have seen a strengthening of the economic
forces increasing the arms trade including: accelerated technological progress
in arms production; strong economic pressure within capitalist arms producing
countries to sell abroad; an international shift in purchasing power to the
OPEC countries; and the concentration of production in and greater competition
between large arms-producing conglomerates like Lockheed, Dassault or the
British Aircraft Corporation. The growth of the international market for arms
has helped the major capitalist powers to avert the present crisis in the international economy. But this has been achieved at some cost to their ability
to guarantee the political conditions for the expansion of capital at the periphery, except in particular regions or sub-regions like Latin America or the
Persian Gulf less open to socialist diplomacy and military assistance than
other areas.

The countries of the Third World can only escape the hegemony of the major
powers if they make good use of such contradictions. Disarmament is a critical
element of any strategy of disengagement because of the way that arms races
increase the dependence of countries of the Third World upon their suppliers.
But it must be disarmament which takes account of the realities of international struggle. One could not, for instance, expect either governments or
guerrilla movements to put aside weapons if this left them defenceless before
a hegemonic power or unable as in Southern Africa to use armed force or the
threat of it to remove fundamental injustices. What kind of disarmament, for
whom and in what international political and economic conjuncture are questions
that cannot be shirked.

Note

An earlier version of this article appeared in the IDS Bulletin, Vol. 8, No. 3,
March 1977, pp. 38-50.

The Military in Third World Development

Mary Kaldor

All the wars since 1945 have taken place in the poorer parts of the world. The military coup has become the rule rather than the exception in Third World countries. Budgetary outlays by Third World governments are, in general, dominated by military expenditure while roughly half the technology imported by Third World countries is military-related.

These facts alone, and many more could be cited, indicate the importance of the military contribution to the process of economic and social change in the Third World. And yet the subject has received remarkably little scholarly attention. Most of the work was undertaken by apologists for the US military aid programme in the early 'sixties; the analysis tended to be scant and the substantiation anecdotal. There were a couple of more solid statistical studies but these did not reach very definite conclusions. A lot of information about the size of military spending, the size of armed forces, and the size and nature of military equipment has been collected at a number of research centres[1] but by and large this is not directed towards any specific analysis so that its usefulness is limited. Similarly, there have been a considerable number of historical studies of the armed forces in Third World countries but these have largely analyzed the role of the military in politics and in war, ignoring the implications for economic and social development. Finally, much of the classical Marxist literature on militarism is relevant to the subject but it is only recently that radical critics of the military have attempted to apply these ideas to the current situation in Third World countries.

This survey summarizes what has been or could be said about the military in development from a reading of this disparate literature. Inevitably, it tends to attribute a coherent body of thought where none exists. Inevitably, also, there are major gaps; for example, very little has been written about the role of irregular or guerilla forces and about post-revolutionary armies — the Red Army in the Soviet Union and the People's Liberation Army in China, both of which have contributed in fundamental ways to development processes.

The topic is examined in the light of two aspects of the military which are common to all societies. The first is the role of the military as organized force. The use of this force whether explicitly in war or implicitly through political intervention, can determine the balance of power, the complexion of government and the prevailing social and economic conditions. The second aspect of the military is its role in the allocation of resources, whether or not this is part of a conscious policy. The armed forces absorb resources — people, equipment, money — but they may also mobilize resources through the concentration of skills, infrastructures, etc. The interesting questions are about the various forms these aspects take in different societies and whether we can generalize about the forms taken in the Third World.

CONCEPTUAL ANALYSIS

In trying to answer these questions, it is useful to distinguish between different approaches to development and how they incorporate the role of institutions. In a sense, the very concept of development conceals a particular
school of thought. It presupposes the possibilities of transforming Third
World countries from a state of rural poverty to one of urban wealth and it
implies that this transformation can be engineered by the ruling institutions
and/or external agents. There are, of course, other schools of thought. For
Marxists, institutions are subordinate to class. Transformation and change,
the product of class conflict, are endemic to all societies and in general,
this is reflected in, rather than engineered by, the ruling institutions.
Further, Third World countries are inextricably linked to the international
system, dominated by a few rich nations. The possibility for development as
described above, is circumscribed by the interests of the ruling classes in
the dominant nations. And then there is the school of thought which might be
described as politically conservative or economically liberal. It is the
school which attributes primary importance to the individual, rather than to
the institution or class. This school would draw a rigid distinction between
society and the state and would judge the ruling institutions by their contribution to political stability and a liberal economy; the contribution to development would be considered largely irrelevant. In particular, the military
in advanced capitalist societies are seen as "professional", i.e. merely part
of the overall division of labour. Where the armed forces do play a political
role, this is seen either as an unfortunate hangover from the feudal period,
c.f. Alfred Wagts (1967), or as the consequence of weak political institutions,
c.f. Samuel Huntington (1968), often associated with periods of economic and
social change. This school of thought will not be discussed at length except
in so far as it merges into the development approach.

The development approach

The concept of development tends to be ahistorical. Despite the use of such
terms as pre-capitalist or feudal, change, in so far as it occurs, is often
treated as movement from one static situation to another. Likewise, the institutions, as primary agents in this movement, can be separated from the social
setting and treated as free-floating entities. It then becomes possible to
analyze the role of the military in development in terms of the internal characteristics of the military as an institution. Precisely because of the assumptions made about the nature of the institutions and of change, this way of
thinking gives rise to totally contradictory arguments. Moreover, the arguments can always be substantiated because of the many and varied forms that
military institutions take in different societies. In a sense it is possible
to choose an argument in the same way that it is theoretically possible to
choose a policy, according to your position on the spectrum of development
approaches. At one extreme are the "modernizers", who argue for the positive
impact of the military on development. They are closely related to the conser-
vatives described above. Paradoxically, they tend to emphasize the role of
private initiative in the development process; they see maximization of output, particularly industrial output, as the goal of development; and they
consider that the main impediment to development is the persistence of "backward" attitudes At the other extreme, typified by a series of UN reports,
are those who see the military as reactionary consumers of scarce resources.
They tend to denigrate the role of private initiative and apportion an even
greater importance to the State; they stress non-growth goals such as the re-

distribution of income, education and health care; and they see the main impediment to development as the shortage of resources. It is possible to trace the way in which these contradictory arguments arise from very similar premises.

The military as organized force

In considering the role of the military as organized force, analysts are concerned to define the characteristics of the soldier as politician, the qualities which would lead the armed forces towards a particular set of policies. There are two ways in which this has been attempted. One looks at the nature of the military as an organization. The other, in a curiously undefined sense, looks at the military as a class.

Of "modernizers" who look at the characteristics of the military as an organization the most well known are Lucien Pye and Morris Janowitz. Indeed, it was Pye's original article on "Armies in the process of political modernization" that helped to initiate the debate and to influence US military assistance policies. Pye argues, with qualifications here and there, that the military represent the institution most likely to induce "modernizing" attitudes and encourage foreign aid. This contention is supported with a number of arguments. First, in the colonial attempts to create modern institutions, military organizations were much the most successful. This, he speculates, is due to the "paradoxical relationship between ritualized and rationalized modes of behaviour ... viewed from one perspective, a military establishment comes as close as any human organization can to the ideal type for an industrialized and secularized enterprise. Yet from another point of view, the great stress placed on professionalism and the extreme explicit standards for individual behaviour make the military appear to be a more sacred than secular institution. If discipline is needed to minimize random and unpredictable behaviour, it is also consonant with all the demands that custom and ritual make in the most tradition-bound organization". The military can be variously characterized as a modern institution. It is an "industrial-type" entity "typical of and peculiar to the most highly industrialized civilization yet known — instinct with rapid industrial change". It provides a "training in citizenship" and may lead to "responsible nationalism. Indeed, the recruit may be impressed that he must make sacrifices to achieve the goals of nationalism and that the process of nation-building involves more than just the shouting of slogans". It is a vehicle for upward mobility and provides the opportunity for teaching people the relationship between effort and reward.

A second explanation for the special role of the military is the fact that "the process of acculturation" to modern life is more successful in the army than elsewhere. This is not simply because the army is the most modern institution but also because army life is more secure than the civilian sector. The villager who moves to the town often finds himself in "a psychologically threatening position. These are the people who turn to extremist politics...".

Thirdly, Pye argues that the military find it easier to accept foreign aid. "Military leaders are often far less suspicious of the West than are civilian leaders because they themselves are more emotionally secure. This sense of security makes it possible for army leaders to look more realistically at their countries. All of these considerations make it easier for the military leaders to accept the fact that their countries are weak and the West is strong without becoming emotionally disturbed or hostile towards the West. Since these leaders seem to have less need to avoid realities, they are in fact easier people with whom to deal and to carry on straightforward relations".

To these arguments, Morris Janowitz adds two more. First, he argues that because social recruitment to the army is middle class or lower middle class,
"the military profession does not have strong allegiance to an integrated upper
class which it accepts as political leader nor does it have a pervasive conservative outlook". Secondly, where political institutions are weak, military
officers "develop a sense of public service and national guardianship as a result of their military training and experience. Their politics is the politics
of the 'suprapolitical' because they are suspicious of professional politicians
and of the bargaining process" (Janowitz, 1964).

The other version of the "modernization" theory treats the military as part of
a new middle class. The main exponent of this view is Manfred Halpern. He
argues that the new middle class, characteristic of Middle Eastern countries,
is salaried, "clustered around a core of civilian and military politicians and
administrators, seemingly capable of leading the quest for status, power and
prosperity, by taking control of the state apparatus". This class has a
"driving interest in ideas, action and careers", is committed to nationalism,
social reform, and modern technology, and is composed of individuals rather
than families. "It is therefore also the first class for which the choice
between democracy, authoritarianism and totalitarianism is a real and open
choice". Because there is unemployment in this class, it has penetrated the
military establishment. Because kings, landlords and traders are on the decline,
while workers and peasants have not yet entered politics, this class has become
the "principal actor" in politics. Halpern waxes enthusiastic about the abil-
ities of this class:

> The more the army was modernized, the more its composition,
> organization, spirit, capabilities and purpose constituted
> a radical criticism of the existing political system. Within
> the army, modern technology was eagerly welcomed and its
> usefulness and power appreciated. By contrast, the political
> system showed greater inertia, inefficiency, scepticism and
> greed in utilizing the products of modern science.
> They have served as a national standard bearer when others
> who claimed that role proved irresponsible and ineffective.
> They have supplied an education in modern technology when
> industry was too scant to provide it, a disciplined organ-
> ization without peer, a unity in the face of the corrupt
> and unprincipled competition of domestic interests and
> foreign imperialism" (Halpern, 1963).

In fact the class argument seems to be merely confusing. If a class is not
defined in terms of its participation in the production process, there is really
very little in the concept of class, distinct from the concept of community,
institution or organization. The salaried middle class is, by its nature,
parasitic or dependent on other classes. To argue that the army is middle
class because it stands between landed property on the one hand, and the lab-
ouring classes on the other, is tautological. It tells us nothing about why
this is so. We are better off with arguments about the organizational characteristics of the army.

Both kinds of modernizing arguments have been criticized from exactly opposed
standpoints. Nordlinger (1970) argues that the organizational characteristics
of the military make them likely to oppose all forms of change. He allows
that the military might support industrialization "both for its symbolic indication of military might and its presumed guarantee of national self-sufficiency

in the event of an improbable war". But he argues that, in general, the "near-universal military values" hinder economic change. These values include "normative attachments to order, dignity, hierarchy", "overwhelming concern for political stability", and "a keen sensitivity to any divergence from the status quo that contains the potential for unwieldy change". He also argues that the lower classes threaten the military "corporate self-interest" because they may want to reduce military spending or the political power of the military.

Uma O. Eleazu (1973) takes a similar line, in the African context. He criticizes the idea that the army is the most modern institution, pointing to the longer experience of civil administrations in West Africa. He rejects arguments about the social background of soldiers, pointing to colonial methods of recruitment from educationally backward tribes. And he suggests that it is not nationalism but loyalty to the imperialist power that motivates the soldier. He quotes the Ghanaian General Afrika in his accusation that Nkrumah broke "the bond that binds us in this great union (the Commonwealth) of all races, colour and creed". A similar point is made by Alain Rouquié concerning Latin America: "The theory of 'ideological frontiers', elaborated jointly by the Argentine and Brazilian staffs in 1965, is the logical conclusion to such a process of 'denationalization'. The nebulous 'Western Christian World' seems to have replaced the Nation-State in the hierarchy of loyalties to which the officer is professionally subject." (Rouquié, 1973).

Finally, Nordlinger also stands the middle class argument on its head, by suggesting that membership of the middle class is precisely what makes officers oppose economic and social change. Although such change is "in accord with the interests and prestige-seeking identities of the middle class officers — since they themselves have already achieved many of the prerequisites of middle class life there is not sufficient motivation for them to undertake strenuous programmes of modernization" (Nordlinger, 1970).

The point about these arguments is not that they constitute a criticism of the modernizing arguments. Indeed, the latter could be used to criticize the view of the military as a reactionary consumer of scarce resources. Rather they indicate how impossible it is to generalize about the military as an independent static institution, without careful analysis of different types of armed forces and of their relationship to the particular society in which they operate. To do Nordlinger justice, he points out, along with Samuel Huntington and Needler (1968) that the role of the military depends on the position of the middle class: "In oligarchic societies, the soldier is a radical; in societies dominated by the middle class the officers act as arbiters among middle class groups; and when mass political participation is in sight the soldier protects the existing order" (Nordlinger, 1970).[2] But this does not go far enough. Why should the soldier behave in this way? What of the soldier who protects the existing order in oligarchic societies? And what of the revolutionary soldier in Portugal or Peru?

The military in the allocation of resources
The same kind of contradictory arguments can be found about the role of the military in the allocation of resources. However, much less has been written about the subject. The main work is the study by Emile Benoit, entitled "Defense and Economic Growth in Developing Countries" (1973).

Professor Benoit's most significant finding is a positive correlation between the burden of defence spending, the share of Gross Domestic Product (GDP) devoted to defence, and the rate of growth of non-military output or civilian GDP.

This relationship could be spurious because it is also correlated with high foreign aid and, to a lesser extent, high investment. But Professor Benoit argues that, in addition to the indirect effect of defence in attracting high levels of foreign aid and encouraging investment, defence spending has direct growth stimulating effects and that both direct and indirect effects are greater than the adverse effects of defence in withdrawing resources from pottentially productive uses.

In particular he aruges that defence is not directly competitive with investment, since the resources which go into defence might otherwise have been devoted to consumption, welfare or imports.

He allows that defence absorbs more industrial-type resources than other kinds of expenditure, and calculates the adverse effects of defence, on the assumption that the share of resources going to defence which might otherwise have gone into investment is twice the share of total national resources devoted to investment.[3] When he adds to this the loss of productivity and civilian income as a result of military spending, he finds that a rise in the burden of defence of 1% of GDP would involve a loss of growth of one quarter of 1%.

Professor Benoit's direct growth stimulating effects are less susceptible to measurement. He is a development theorist who places more emphasis on attitudes than on resources. First of all he mentions the "primary economic contribution of the defence programme in assuring a minimum of physical security in the absence of which the political structure and hence also the civilian economy would falter and ultimately disintegrate". Secondly, he argues that defence spending boosts aggregate demand and utilizes idle capacity which is to be found in the manufacturing sector of many underdeveloped countries. His evidence suggests that, had it not been for military spending, a number of countries, most notably India, would have pursued more restrictive fiscal and monetary policies. Thirdly, defence programmes provide direct inputs into the civilian economy, such things as communications networks, roads, disaster relief and rehabilitation, and various other scientific and technical functions. In addition, Professor Benoit emphasizes the importance of defence spending in inducing "modernizing" attitudes. Soldiers learn such useful Western skills as "following and transmitting precise instructions; living and working by the clock; noticing and reading signs; spending and saving money; using transportation (bicycles, motorcycles, autos, buses, boats, planes, etc.); listening to radio". The military experience helps to break up traditional patterns of life which are a "vastly important impediment to development. The shaking-up experience involved in transforming tradition-bound peoples into modern urban types is unpleasant and difficult and usually resisted. Military discipline provides a mechanism for speeding up the process". Finally, defence spending may contribute to nation-building and help to overcome tribal or regional divisions. Military stress may "become a symbolic expression of national crisis, releasing psychological energies helpful to growth, such as willingness to work harder, curtail or postpone consumption, cooperate better with fellow citizens and the government, etc.".

A similar kind of analysis may be drawn from Gavin Kennedy's descriptions of the impact of war on development (Kennedy, 1974). War may provide access to new resources — oil, in the case of Nigeria, or foreign aid in the case of Vietnam's Asian neighbours. It may also provide the conditions for making use of those resources, by restricting private consumption and increasing the market for domestic industry (as a result of import controls, military spending or captive territory). According to Kennedy, the Nigerian War "imposed econ-

omic discipline and gave an impetus to local manufacturing and the emergency
provided the kind of stimulus to economic nation-building that seven years of
independence failed to produce. The result was a cumulative force that provided the right conditions for the oil revenues to be used to push development
positively. A report in 1972 (by UNECA) considered that the transfer from the
war economy generated by the secession to development activity was a major
contributor to high post-war growth rates".

Kennedy also analyzes arms production and makes much of the arguments about
demand stimulation and direct inputs into the civilian economy. He suggests
that military production is more likely to succeed than other industrial sectors because it has a ready and assured market, it is protected from foreign
competition, and is not subject to normal competitive criteria. (He does not
define what he means by "success".) Having succeeded, it will have a substantial impact on the rest of the economy. It provides a market for domestic
industry: "Large numbers of men have to be fed and clothed, sheltered, trained
and supervised. The administrative systems required just to control their location and their movement will require all kinds of inputs from the economy."
It creates a demand for training programmes and other kinds of infrastructure:
"This is probably the most important dimension in domestic arms production.
Because the government gives priority to arms production it also has to face
up to the shortage of human resources. To meet its military ambitions it has
to tackle some of the social barriers to development".

Other writers have stressed the importance of direct inputs into the civilian
economy. Many, including President Kennedy, have recalled the role of US Army
Engineers in opening up the West and some, like Lucien Pye, have referred to
the role of the Brazilian Army in "opening up the interior, in promoting natural
sciences and protecting the Indian population (*sic*)" (Pye, 1964). These views
have been echoed in official US reports and have powerfully influenced the US
military assistance programme. Because, in the words of the Draper Report,
"the military in many under-developed countries are closely related to domestic
affairs on all levels, from the man in the ranks who brings a scarce skill
learned in the military forces back to his village, to responsible leaders who
may be an important element contributing to successful opposition to communist
subversion" (USG, 1959), there has been an increasing emphasis on the non-military aspects of training programmes Also, particularly in the early 1960s,
the US government encouraged civic action programmes, defined by the Joint
Chiefs of Staff as "the use of preponderantly indigenous military forces on
projects useful to the local populations at all levels in such fields as education, training, public works, agriculture, transportation, communications,
health, sanitation, and others contributing to economic and social development,
which would also serve to improve the standing of the military forces with the
local population".[4]

Curiously enough, the views which led to these policies have received very
little serious criticism. A number of international reports have pointed out
that the military absorb scarce resources which might otherwise have contributed to economic and social development (UN, 1972a, b). But they do not deal
with the argument put forward by Benoit and others, that defence is not directly competitive with investment or welfare spending or that the resources,
whether derived from foreign aid, revenues from captured territories or restric-
ted domestic consumption might not be available in the absence of military spending. A few authors have criticized the emphasis on military inputs into the
civilian economy. Roads are built in remote areas where nobody wants to go;
skills are often too sophisticated for civilian use. Hurewitz (1969) makes the

point that the skills and infrastructure developed for the army may not be
transferred at all. In career armies, which account for two out of every three
Middle Eastern armies, soldiers do not return to their villages. The use of
airfields or communications systems may be exclusively confined to the military.
No one appears to have criticized the argument about modernizing and nation-
building attitudes, but it would be easy to do so on the basis of counter arguments about the military as a conservative institution.

Like the debate about the soldier as politician, the growth stimulating versus
resource absorbing debate is susceptible to example and counter example. As
we shall see, other evidence does seem to support Professor Benoit's findings
about the relationship between growth, military spending and foreign aid. But
this does not prove anything about the nature of the relationship, nor about
the impact of the military on the non-growth goals of development. Further,
it is possible to find exceptions that disprove the generalization precisely
because the military as an institution differs from society to society and so
does its behaviour. Like the debate about the soldier as politician, this debate is necessarily inconclusive because it fails to distinguish characteristics
of military institutions that are universally valid from those that are specific to their social setting.

Marxist approaches

In recent times, very little has been written about the role of the military in
the process of historical change from a Marxist perspective. However, two general approaches can be distinguished. The one, representing the polar opposite
of the development approach, would view institutions as replicas of the social
formation, or mode of production, and would confine the analysis to structural
changes in society. The other would view instutions as the historical product
of social conditions always one step ahead or one step behind the current
social structure and therefore always behaving in a relatively autonomous
fashion. This second approach, which was the one implied by Marx himself in
"The Eighteenth Brumaire of Louis Bonaparte", might be described as a synthesis
of the institutional line, taken by the development theorists, and the structural line, taken by one group of Marxists.

The military as organized force
One of the foremost classical writers on militarism was Karl Liebknecht. He
wrote that: "A history of militarism in the deepest sense discloses the very
essence of human development and of its motive force and a dissection of capitalist militarism involves the disclosure of the most secret and least obvious
roots of capitalism. The history of militarism is at the same time the history
of the class struggles within individual states and national units."

The importance of Liebknecht's work lay in this recognition that force plays
an essential role in the process of economic and social change and that the
form of force reflects its social setting. But in identifying the history of
militarism with the history of class struggles, he tended to obscure the differences between these two topics and thus to limit the possibilities for anal-
yzing the distinctive features of the military institutions as an agent in
"development or underdevelopment".

This difficulty arises from Liebknecht's assumptions about the nature of organized force. Liebknecht argues that "the basis of every social relation of
power is the superiority of physical force ...". But this is not simply the

physical strength of individuals; it depends on the armaments carried by men,
the "technique of arms". "An armed man increases his physical strength many
times through his possession of a weapon. The degree of the increase depends
on the development of the technique of arms including fortifications and strategy (whose form is essentially a consequence of the technique of arms). The
intellectual and economic superiority of one interest group over another is
turned into a simple physical superiority through the possession of arms, or
better arms, on the part of the ruling class." Engels said much the same
thing: "The producer of more perfect tools, *vulgo* arms, beats the producer of
more imperfect ones" (Engels, 1970).

In this there is a strong element of technological determinism. Military organization is also important. It took the introduction of a market for soldiers,
i.e. mercenaries, before guns, the product of bourgeois technology, were fully
accepted into the armed forces. They were unsuitable for feudal formations of
knights. Similarly, North Vietnam and the Vietnamese Liberation Movement had
capitalist arms (or imitations of them) but their organization enabled them to
use their weapons more effectively than could the Americans.[5]

The emphasis on techniques as opposed to organization implies that the army is
more or less a neutral instrument of the ruling class. It can be defeated
through the development of better techniques on the part of a more progressive
class or it can be dissolved through rebellion in the ranks in alliance with
other members of oppressed classes. On such assumptions, the main interest of
a study of militarism is exposure of the brutality of the ruling class. The
possibility of political manoeuvre by the army is not excluded but it is not
susceptible to abstract analysis.

Perhaps the main modern study of the military in development, from a Marxist
perspective, is that undertaken by a research group, under the auspices of the
German Federation of Scientists (VDW) in Hamburg (hereafter known as the Hamburg group) (Albrecht et al. 1974, 1975). Implicit in their work are similar
assumptions about the subordinate character of military institutions. Armaments
are seen to have had a decisive role in the process of capitalist accumulation
and in the absorption of peripheral economies into the world capitalist system.
They take, for example, the case of Meiji Japan as an "industrialization-late-
comer". They stress the importance of the State as a direct agent in industrialization and the development of its military apparatus for internal repression. They also consider that external war had a significant impact on industrialization; Japan's war with China, 1894-95, and with Tzarist Russia, 1904,
resulted in the occupation of Formosa, Korea and Southern Manchuria and these
territories provided important sources of raw materials and protected markets
for Japanese industrial products. In addition to its role as organized force,
the military had an allocative function for the Japanese economy. The wars
resulted "in positive effects for the rapid development of communications infrastructure (especially the establishment of the navy), the financial institutions and the technologically decisive branches of industry". The expansion
of military orders by the State was considered to be crucial for the development of Japan's heavy industry.

The Hamburg group argue that this model cannot be imitated by modern Third
World countries because their economies are too tightly integrated into the
world market to allow for independent action by local ruling classes. This is
reflected in the dependence of their armed forces on the metropolis and, indeed, in the role of the military as agents of underdevelopment, as opposed to
development. This force is currently essential to maintain the *unevenness* of

the world capitalist system either directly, as in Vietnam, or indirectly
through the arms transfer process. The relationship of the Third World to the
industrialized North can be likened to the relationship between Formosa, Korea
and Southern Manchuria on the one hand, and Japan on the other.

On the basis of this framework, two avenues of interesting research are re-
vealed. The one, which will be discussed below, is the role of the military
in the worldwide allocation of resources, as a mechanism for extracting surplus
product in the periphery in order to support capitalist accumulation in the
metropolis. The other concerns the development of new doctrines and new techniques for the suppression of revolt in the Third World. (This last falls outside the scope of this paper.)

Both are important issues. But there is another, equally deserving of attention. This is the political behaviour of the armed forces in Third World countries and how, in concrete cases, this influences the process of development
or underdevelopment. The Hamburg group consider that it is largely irrelevant
whether a regime is dominated by the military or democratically legitimized.
"To the manifold contradictions occurring in the process of drawing peripheral
societies into the world market, the military take-over appears to be the only
solution from the point of view of the dominant metropolitan interests and
their local counterparts. We therefore suggest to reject the heading 'military
regime' and propose rather to attempt classifying peripheral countries on the
basis of the socio-economic relations with the world market and the prevailing
mode of production" (Albrecht et al. 1974). This is surely correct as far as
it goes. But if the military are not an exact replica of the social formation,
then the conditions of military takeover become very significant. The current
situation in Ethiopia where the military appear to be leading an anti-imper-
ialist bourgeois revolution in a very backward society might be a worthy example.

An analysis of the military as an organization and its friction with society
is implicit in Marx's treatment of Louis Bonaparte's military coup in 1851, and
some of his conclusions are highly relevant for modern underdeveloped societies
(Marx, 1973). Marx explains why the revolution of 1848 which replaced the bourgeois monarchy with the bourgeois republic ended in the seizure of state power
by a stupid, greedy adventurer and what this seizure meant for the economic and
social condition of France. On the one hand he analyzes the social contradictions which undermined the potential for bourgeois democracy; the divisions
within the bourgeoisie, the strength of the social-democratic party, a coalition of petty bourgeois and proletariat, and the break-up of the alliance between the bourgeoisie and the peasantry which had provided the basis for the
French revolution. On the other hand, he analyzes the nature of the vast state
machinery which, under Louis Bonaparte, was apparently independent, so much so
that "all classes, equally impotent and equally mute, fall on their knees before the rifle butt".

This state machinery is an answer, albeit an unsuitable one, to the contradictions of French society. Its instability explains its perpetual growth. It
was created by the absolute monarchy in opposition to feudalism. It was perfected by Napoleon, when it became the ideological expression of the alliance
between bourgeoisie and small-holding peasant. Under the restoration, it became the instrument of the ruling class. And, under Louis Bonaparte, it
achieved a relative autonomy and could be bought with "champagne and cigars,
cold poultry and garlic sausage". "This executive power", says Marx, "with
its enormous bureaucratic and military organization, with its ingenious state
machinery, embracing wide strata, with a host of officials numbering half a

million, besides an army of another half million, this appalling parasitic body, which enmeshes the body of French society like a net and chokes all its pores, sprang up in the days of the absolute monarchy, with the decay of the feudal system, which it helped to hasten. The seignorial privileges of the landowners and towns became transformed into so many attributes of the state power, the feudal dignitaries into paid officials and the motley pattern of conflicting medieval plenary powers into the regulated plan of a state authority whose work is divided and centralized as in a factory — all revolutions perfected this machine instead of smashing it. The parties that contended in turn for domin- ation regarded the possession of the huge state edifice as the principal spoils of the victor."

The military-bureaucratic organization became the most important "*idée Napoleo- nienne*". Napoleon created the small-holding peasant out of the feudal peasant who joined the middle classes in opposition of the feudal overlords. Once this aim was achieved, the common interest of the bourgeoisie and the peasantry vanished. Indeed, in the course of the nineteenth century, as the condition of the small-holding peasantry deteriorated, "the feudal landlords were re- placed by urban usurers; the feudal obligation that went with the land was replaced by the mortgage; aristocratic landed property was replaced by bour- geois capital". Further, the peasants themselves shared no community of inter- ests, other than the similarity of their economic condition; Marx likens them to "potatoes in a sack" forming "a sack of potatoes". They were thus incapable of enforcing their class interest. Instead, Napoleon's state machinery appeared as their representative. "By its very nature, small-holding property forms a suitable basis for an all-powerful and innumerable bureaucracy. It creates a uniform level of relationships and persons over the whole surface of the land. Hence, it also permits of uniform action from a supreme centre on all points of this uniform mass. It annihilates the aristocratic intermediate grades bet- ween the mass of the people and the state power." The state machinery absorbed surplus population squeezed off the land. The taxes it levied on the peasantry were repaid with interest by the new markets, opened by Napoleon "at the point of the bayonet". And finally, the army was "the *point d'honneur* of the small- holding peasants; it was they themselves transformed into heroes, defending their new possessions against the outer world, glorifying their recently-won nationhood, plundering and revolutionizing the world. The uniform was their own state dress; war was their poetry; the small-holding, extended and roun- ded off in imagination, was their fatherland, and patriotism the ideal form of their sense of property."

Louis Bonaparte represented the peasantry. They believed "that a man named Napoleon would bring all the glory back to them". Yet his army had become their oppressor, enforcing the mortgage debt and the taxes, no longer repaid with new markets. "The parody of empire" was necessary to install Bonaparte's despotism. Once installed, he could do no more than play off one class against another and maintain his position by extending the sway of the state and by plying his "drunken soldiery — with sausages anew". Yet this was sufficient for the time being to create the stability required by capital. For all his absurdity, he had achieved the "centralization of the state that modern society requires"; the conditions, which he himself could not build on, for continued capitalist accumulation.

Some of the conclusions that can be drawn from this analysis have already been discussed. Marx emphasizes the need for a strong State, including its repres- sive apparata, as social contradictions intensify. He mentions the role of war in primitive accumulation and the allocative function of the army in absor-

bing surplus labour. In addition, there are two other important conclusions.
One concerns the relative autonomy of the State; its ability to support capitalist accumulation in general without apparently favouring any particular
class. The other concerns the specific characteristics of the internal state
organization, which, in effect, determine its political significance. In this
instance, the State appeared as the ideological expression of one particular
class or mode of production, the small-holding peasant, but acted on behalf of
another class, the bourgeoisie. In this way, it suppressed the contradictions
between these two classes.

One way to draw out the political role of the military institutions is to distinguish between the techniques of force and the relations of force. As we
have seen, the techniques of force are the weapons and the way they are used.
The relations of force are the organization of men, the nature of the military
hierarchy, the methods of recruitment. Together, they comprise the form of
force. The techniques of force are at once the product of the level of technology in society and the appropriate tool for a particular set of military
relations. The relations of force are those most convenient for organizing a
body of men, in a given society, and those most likely to generate loyalty to
the social formation.[6]

The form of force is thus a reflection of the social formation, or prevailing
mode of production. But it can also alter the social formation and it is this
contention which is important for an understanding of the military in development. Most obviously this can occur through war — through victory in a war
between different types of armed forces, as Cromwell's victory in the English
revolution, or through the experience of such wars. The German response to
the Napoleonic wars contributed to the democratization of Germany. Equally,
the counterinsurgency operations of the Portuguese and Peruvian armies might be
termed a radicalizing experience. But it might also occur through the import
of the form of force, through the adoption of a foreign form of force which
is alien to local society. In other words, the import of Western-type armies
into modern Third World countries could have very important political implications for the transformation of the prevailing social formation.

To understand these implications certain assumptions have to be made about the
form of force that is prevalent in advanced capitalist society. I argue in a
forthcoming paper that this form of force, which might be called the permanent
arms race, is decadent, reflecting decaying industrial structures, to be found
predominantly in Britain and America. Its roots can be traced to the Anglo-
German naval arms race before World War I, initiated in the depression of the
1800s and based on the need to protect specific industries, namely, ship-building and engineering, from the effects of that depression. Today, the permanent arms race guarantees a future for industries or sections of industries
which would otherwise have been overwhelmed by new technology.

Reflecting the structure of the defence industries, which are not very different from any other, the permanent arms race is characterized by a built-in
tendency for expansion involving a permanent process of technical change. But,
in a very important sense, this technical change is conservative. It is socially circumscribed by the relations of force, themselves the reflection of
the industrial structure. The characteristic of the relations of force is the
way they appear to be built around a particular technique of force, the weapon
system, the product of a particular industrial era. The weapons system com-
prises the weapons platform — the ship, aircraft, tank, etc. — the weapon, and
the means of communication. Whereas formerly, the weapon was the instrument

of the soldier, the soldier now appears to be the instrument of the weapons
system. The resulting organization is hierarchical, atomistic and dehumanizing.
It reflects the importance accorded to industrial products, particularly machines, in society as a whole. Furthermore, the weapons systems are themselves
ranked and subdivided into an hierarchical military organization, minimizing
the possibilities for individual or small group action. At the apex of the
American or British navy is the aircraft carrier, justifying aircraft to operate from its deck, destroyers, frigates and submarines to defend it, and supply
ships to replenish it. The bomber and battle tank have similar functions in
the air force and army. The liberal ideal of the fighter pilot as the modern
hero of individual combat is a convenient myth. In reality, 50 men are required
to operate each combat aircraft, together with the men required to operate sup-
porting aircraft so that the special importance accorded to the pilot is merely
symbolic.

The development of the armed forces has proceeded alongside the development of
the arms industry. Each weapons system was the product of a particular company
and the centre of a military unit. The manufacturing capabilities of a company
were at one and the same time the performance characteristics of a weapons system and the strategic doctrine of a military unit. The relationship between
different military units exactly paralleled the structure of industry. Changes
in the structure of industry, as in Britain in the late 1950s and early 1960s,
were associated with changes in the relations of force. A more current example
is the trend towards multinational defence companies in Europe, which is accompanied by new doctrines about the need to standardize and integrate European
armed forces.

This weapons system-based force structure excludes the possibility of a revolutionary technology, involving perhaps less expenditure and displacing traditional industries. New developments in missile technology, based on the modern
electronics sector, could, for example, have implications that are as revolutionary as was the development of firearms. Already, missiles have rendered
all weapons platforms extremely vulnerable. (Until anti-submarine detection
is more developed, the submarine escapes this generalization.) This fact alone
has reduced the grandiose marvels of modern technology — the aircraft carrier,
bomber or battle tank — to expensive absurdities. Indeed, the obsolescence of
the capital ship, of which the aircraft carrier is the current example, was
demonstrated as long ago as World War I. Yet the concept is defended, in the
vague terms of modern strategy as "flexible response" (US) or a "balance of
forces" across the "whole spectrum of operations" (UK),[7] because the weapons
system-based force structure is intimately connected to the structure of the
dominant industries in those countries that are believed to possess the most
military power.

If the aerospace, shipbuilding and vehicle industries, in their advanced oligo-
polistic phase, are characterized as a mode of production,[8] then it could be
said that this mode of production is reproduced in the permanent arms race.
This raises a number of interesting issues about the impact of exporting arms
to societies where this mode of production does not exist. Clearly, the permanent arms race is only one form of force to be found in the modern world. We
need to discover what determines the relations of force in Third World countries
and to what extent they are influenced by the imported techniques of force.

It is useful to start by making a broad distinction between two model forms of
force in underdeveloped countries. Obviously, much more refined distinctions
can be made, corresponding to complex class structures. The first model is the

pre-industrial army — the Bedouin levies of the Middle East, the retinue armies of pre-colonial Africa, the nineteenth-century militia and caudillos of Latin America.[9] Typically these are infantry or cavalry based; the weapon being still the instrument of the soldier. The method of recruitment and the organization reflects the relationships prevalent in society. Thus the Bedouin levies owe military service to their leaders, the sheikhs and kings of Arabia, in much the same way as feudal serfs owed military service to their lords in the Middle Ages. The weapons, however, are largely imported although the choice of weapons is delineated by the relation of force. In some cases, quite sophisticated weapons prove appropriate; the White Guard of Saudi Arabia has, since 1963, made use of Vigilant man-portable anti-tank missiles. In others, arms are designed in the metropolis especially for their use, viz. the ornate bayonets still manufactured by Churchill's gunmakers in London (owned, incidentally, by the American firm, Interarmco) for the use of Persian Gulf sheikhs. But these armies cannot make use of the major weapons which might whittle down their conservatism. This is why, for example, African armies have so long opposed the introduction of tanks.

This form of force does not necessarily involve capitalist relations of force, but it is dependent on capitalist techniques. In this it corresponds to the social formation in which it operates. This is generally characterized by the production of one or two basic commodities for export, sometimes by wage labour and sometimes on a slave or feudal-based mode of production. The revenue from these exports is spent on necessities (where not produced alongside the export commodity) and on prestige goods and arms for the ruling class. The arms are used directly for repression, to preserve the position of the ruling class.[10] Thus the social formation may not be capitalist, in the sense of employing capitalist techniques and utilizing a free market for labour, but it is dependent upon and essential to a capitalist world system.

The second model form of force is the industrial army. This is based on the weapons system concept which strictly limits the room for variation in the relations of force. With some qualification, the form of force thus becomes a reflection of the form of force prevailing in the metropolis. The rise of such armies is associated with the beginning of industrialization, and the need to create or preserve a social structure in which the industrialization process can take place. The pre-industrial armies used their guns directly for repression. The industrial armies, like their progenitors in the metropolis, are rarely used directly, except in external war against a competing ruling class with a similar form of force. When direct repression is necessary, they revert to the methods of the pre-industrial armies, or to the use of simple "intermediate technology" weapons, designed in the metropolis especially for the purpose. As in the metropolis, the true significance of the weapons system concept is political; it creates a commitment to industrialization and, more particularly, to a model of industrialization that is decadent by the standard of the most advanced industrial societies. The primary function of the industrial army is not so much combat as political intervention. It is through the military coup that the army preserves the system. The major weapons may have prestige significance and they may be used in external war and, on occasion, domestically. (Tanks and aircraft have proved effective as instruments of terror.) But, first and foremost, they orientate the soldier toward a particular political tendency.

If this analysis is correct and if the industrial army, in imitation of the permanent arms race, is the most common form of force to be found in the Third World, then some of the contradictory arguments of the development theorists could be reconciled. This political tendency would explain the positive findings of the "modernizers" measured in terms of attitudes towards growth and modern industry and, at the same time, it would explain the negative findings of those who emphasize the wasteful nature of militaristic industrialization and the importance of non-growth goals. But precisely because it is an explanation that is specific to one or more social formations, it does not preclude the exceptions. Indeed, revolutionary soldiers, citizens' armies, guerilla forces, etc. would be important to study in establishing the more general thesis about the political nature of organized force.

The military in the allocation of resources

The importance of the military in the allocation of resources has only been recognized relatively recently. Marx talked about the absorption of surplus population and the expenditure of food and liquor   Rosa Luxembourg pointed out the importance of arms expenditure as a method of realizing surplus value. But it is only with the rise of the permanent arms race that the allocative function of the military assumed such predominance, and it is primarily since World War II that Marxist arms economy theses, purporting to explain the survival of capitalism, have spread.

Surprisingly, very little has been written about the allocative function of the military on a world scale. The main work has been that undertaken by the Hamburg group. They argue that the military has a primary function in channelling resources from the periphery to the metropolis, quite apart from its function as organized force in creating the conditions in which this exploitation can take place. Because the surplus product extracted from the countryside is spent by the ruling class on arms, the peasantry in the Third World end up by paying for the continued existence of the defence industry in the metropolis. We have mentioned crudely how this operates in pre-industrial society where one or two commodities are produced for export, under highly inequitable conditions. With the beginnings of industrialization, the process becomes more complex. As well as arms and necessities not produced domestically, the revenue from commodity exports is now spent on imported capital goods which are used to produce manufactured goods for consumption mostly by the urban elite and by landowners. Whereas military expenditure previously consisted largely of expenditure of foreign exchange and could be seen as a method of channelling resources from the periphery to the metropolis, now the urban elite can claim a larger share of the surplus product and military expenditure can also be seen as a method of channelling resources from the countryside to the town. Military expenditure is paid for largely out of surplus product generated in the countryside and occasionally out of resources plundered in war but it is spent in the metropolis and in the towns. Apart from the soldiers' subsistence, local military expenditure requires repair and maintenance facilities, infrastructure such as roads and telephones, the manufacture of uniforms, etc. In some advanced cases, India or Brazil, the weapons are manufactured domestically from imported parts. (Often the cost of the parts is greater than the cost of the total system.) Of course, the country may be receiving foreign military assistance; but then it is also necessary to take into account the repayment of debt as well as the repatriation of profits from foreign-owned industries. The military assistance may eventually have to be paid for with agricultural earnings.

The Hamburg group emphasize the close connections between the military and the industrialization process. In Indonesia, for example, the military own various commercial and industrial enterprises and finance their own expenditure out of the profits. The Turkish Army have a military pension fund based on the most

modern and dynamic industries, often involved in joint ventures with multinational corporations. In this way, they argue, the interests of the military
and of foreign economic enterprise are fused. Indeed, it could be contended
that the military interest in industrialization is not so much ideological,
arising from the weapons system based force structure, as self-interested,
arising from a desire for self-sufficiency.[11]

This allocative function is not peculiar to the military. It could be carried
out by other state institutions. What makes the military especially suitable
is their role as organized force. This would include the suppression of rural
discontent, the acquisition of foreign resources through external war, and the
military coup to endorse an industrial strategy, where democratic endorsement
is absent. The analysis of the industrial army also indicates another aspect
to the debate about resources. Because of the nature of the permanent arms
race, the military would tend to imitate those industries which are on the
decline in the metropolis, thus condemning the periphery to continued backward-
ness and, through markets or profit repatriation, simultaneously helping to
prop up declining military powers.

EMPIRICAL EVIDENCE

Most of the analyses, described above, are necessarily speculative. Very
little empirical work has been undertaken in this field. And, presumably because of the complexity and variety of military institutions, there are few
conclusive results.

The empirical research that has been done can be grouped into three categories.
First, there are a number of statistical analyses of which the most important
are Benoit (1973) and Schmitter (1971).[12] These attempt to test various hypotheses about the nature of military institutions in the Third World and their
impact on economic and social change with such statistical indicators as military spending, degrees of military intervention, GNP, public spending, price
indices, tax burden, productivity, degrees of industrialization, etc. Secondly, there are a large number of case studies of the military in Third World
countries but very few address the issue of development. Most are concerned
with political or technical questions (about the military effectiveness of
Third World armies or the impact of arms on conflict). It is possible, however, to find a few relevant anecdotes and even, in some cases, some useful
empirical analysis. Thirdly, there are several compilations of relevant information which could provide invaluable source material for students interested
in making their own empirical studies. Every year, the US Arms Control and
Disarmament Agency (ACDA) publishes comparative data on military expenditure,
armed forces, GNP and population of 136 countries (US ACDA 1973, 1974). Since
1974, the Agency has also included statistics on the arms trade but has excluded data on public health and education spending, to be found in previous editions. The latter has been taken over by the Institute for World Order, which
now publishes "World Military and Social Expenditures" compiled by Ruth Sivard
(1974).[13]

An equally important source is the Stockholm International Peace Research
Institute's (SIPRI) annual publication entitled the "Yearbook on Armaments
and Disarmament". This includes fairly comprehensive data on military expenditure, the trade in major weapons, and military production in Third World
countries. In addition to the Yearbook, very detailed information about the
trade in major weapons is available in the 1971 report "The Arms Trade with

the Third World", and in the more recent publication, "Arms Trade Registers".

Of the two, the ACDA reports are probably the most immediately useful because of the comprehensiveness and comparability of the data. There are some short-comings, however. Unlike the SIPRI data, there is no detailed explanation of the sources and methods so that it is difficult to judge the accuracy of the information. Although the arms trade figures have the advantage of being all-inclusive, covering small arms as well as major weapons, they do appear to be incorrect in some instances. For example, the UK figures only cover sales from government factories; these account for only a third of total UK arms exports. Equally, the Chinese figures appear to be much too high; it is pos-sible that second-hand equipment has been valued at original acquisition cost. In contrast, any errors in the SIPRI figures can be established because the sources and methods of estimation are publicly available. Although the arms trade figures exclude small arms, they have the not inconsiderable advantage of being expressed both in monetary terms and in terms of individual transac-tions. With the SIPRI information, it is possible to track down the exact size, nature and source of individual major weapons imports to each Third World country; something which is extremely useful for detailed empirical work.

In addition to the publications of ACDA and SIPRI, there are many lesser sour-ces. The annual Military Balance, published by the International Institute for Strategic Studies provides patchy information about the size and armament of armed forces in selected Third World countries, as well as selective data about the arms trade. Statistical data about the arms trade was included in a series of studies undertaken at the Massachusetts Institute of Technology in the late 1960s (Leiss et al. 1970). Irma Adelman and Cynthia Morris include indicators for the political strength of the military in their statistical surveys of Third World Countries (Adelman and Morris, 1967; 1973). Finally, there are the traditional sources of information about the military, like "Jane's Fighting Ships" or "Brassey's Annual". These sources can be found in a Research Guide to Arms and Armed Forces, shortly to be published by the Inter-national Peace Research Association.

The weakness of statistical analyses derives primarily from the assumption that military institutions can be classified into one general category. If we take the contrary assumption that military institutions are a replica of the socie-ties in which they function, then we would not expect to come up with any use-ful general propositions that could be subjected to statistical tests except in so far as it is possible to generalize about different societies. In fact, although the results of statistical analyses are meagre, one or two interesting conclusions have emerged. But it could well be argued that these conclusions reflect less the characteristics of the military *per se* and more the fact that most military institutions in the Third World are the product of advanced in-dustrial society rather than indigenous society and that such conclusions tell us something about the industrial army.

One such result is Benoit's finding, discussed above, of a positive correlation between military burden and rate of growth of civilian output.[14] However, even this result cannot be considered definite. Benoit's data covers two periods, 1950-65 and 1960-65. Over the longer period, it could well be argued that the result is spurious since the high growth rates could also be explained by high bilateral aid. Although the regression analysis for the shorter period "points to (the military burden) as not only a significant determinant, but the stron-gest determinant", it might be objected that five years is too short a period

on which to base a finding of this kind. Schmitter finds, in his survey of
Latin American countries for the period 1950 to 1967, that militarism, which
he measures in terms of the frequency of military intervention, tends to be
associated with high rates of growth, control of inflation and public spending
but that these phenomena are much better explained by foreign dependence. "We
have shown, rather convincingly, that, in some penetrated societies as those of
Latin America, exogenous variables — especially the level of commercial and
financial dependence on the United States — do explain a wide range of outcomes,
including the rate of GNP increase" (Schmitter, 1971).

Whatever the direction of causation, neither Schmitter nor Benoit satisfactorily
explain the association between high military burdens or militaristic regimes,
high growth rates, and heavy external dependence. As we have seen, Benoit
suggests that, in addition to attracting foreign resources and stimulating
demand, military spending induces modernizing skills and attitudes. Quite
apart from the difficulty of testing this hypothesis, it excludes the alternative explanation that high industrial growth rates are the consequence of
increased exploitation established by force, and provide the mechanism for
channelling resources from countryside to town and from periphery to metropolis.
Interestingly, Schmitter provides some support for this view in his finding
that military rule tends to be associated with more inequitable tax structures,
with lower direct taxes and higher indirect taxes, particularly on exports and
imports.

Benoit's own example of India might be instructive in this respect. Benoit
argues that the 1962 war with China led to increased bilateral aid and increased
military spending, which led to higher industrial growth rates as a result of
demand stimulation and various modernizing inducements. This was made possible
by the import of American wheat which kept agricultural prices low. However,
and this takes the story beyond Benoit's period which ended in 1965, the advantages of this growth were swamped by the rise in food prices, when the supply
of American wheat dried up, and in oil prices and by the debt repayments on
those foreign loans, which Benoit sees as the beneficial effect of the Sino-
Indian war. The enormous growth in the armed forces has undoubtedly been important in overcoming dissension, both directly through repression and, indirectly, through ideology. For example, the railway strike of April 1974, which
threatened to burst India open over the impossibly high cost of living, was
settled indirectly by the appeal to "nation-building" sentiment, occasioned
by India's first atomic explosion.

A crude examination of the ACDA data might support the direction of some of
these conclusions. Table 5.1 shows the rates of growth of military spending,
arms imports and GNP per capita for selected developing countries. It is possible to pick out groups of countries, representing extreme situations. One
group, which includes Brazil, Taiwan, Iran, Israel, South Korea, Libya, Saudi
Arabia and Thailand, is characterized by high growth rates, high rates of
growth of military spending and military burdens that are above their regional
averages.[15]   These countries are also heavily dependent on the US or rich in
oil resources. A second group is characterized by high rates of growth of
military spending, low rates of growth of GNP and military burdens that are
above the regional averages. These are the war, or near war economies; they
include Cambodia, Chad, Egypt, Jordan, Somalia, North and South Vietnam, and,
curiously, Zambia. Finally, there are the low growth of GNP and the low growth
of military spending countries, which include Cuba, Equatorial Guinea, India
and Yemen (Aden). Of these only Cuba and Equatorial Guinea have military burdens that are above their regional averages. Cuba cannot be compared with

other countries because it has a people's militia, rather than an industrial army.

Table 5.2 presents some of Ruth Sivard's social indicators. It can be seen that the high growth countries and the war economies spend more on the military than on health and social services, while the low growth countries spend less. The exceptions are Brazil, Libya and Zambia. (Information on Yemen (Aden) is not available.) The figures for Brazil are, in any case, questionable since most social services are undertaken by the military and the budgets are not, therefore, readily distinguishable.

If we are considering these results in terms of the thesis that Benoit's findings are only applicable to industrial type armies, it is interesting to note that, with the exception of Cuba, the countries with a low rate of GNP growth and low growth of military spending have imported few major weapons. Further, most of the major weapons have come from the Soviet Union or China and, reportedly, have not been assimilated effectively into the armed forces. Cuba has, of course, made a conscious attempt to reshape the structure of its armed forces.

To explore the nature of these relationships in any further detail, statistics must give way to history. Unfortunately, the historical examples that have been written up are not altogether helpful. The "modernizers" have produced a number of case studies but none of these have provided much more than incident (Berger, 1960; Bienen, 1968; Lerner and Robinson, 1971; Lissak, 1964).[16] It has not proved difficult for critics, like Hurewitz (1969; 1975) to cite counter incident. Further, most of the "modernizing" case studies are the obvious ones, like Turkey and Egypt.

An important criticism of "modernizing" arguments is contained in Stepan's (1971) case study of Brazil. Stepan points out that "Brazil provided a particularly appropriate test case of the potentialities of military government because so many observers ... were initially (in 1964) very optimistic about the chances that the Brazilian military government would use its power to contribute rationally to economic and political development". These observers included the US government which "made a major financial and political commitment to the Brazilian military regime". Stepan criticizes the view that the military display more "cohesion", "stability" or "continuity of policy" than civilian politicians and analyzes the organizational cleavages within the military institution, how they relate to divisions in society as a whole and to divergent policies adopted by the military government. He does not evaluate the outcome of these policies but he does suggest that, despite the high economic rates of growth, the demobilization of "all mass change-orientated movements", the inequitable fiscal stabilization policy, and the widespread use of torture has deeply inhibited social development.

An interesting theme in Stepan's case study is his rejection of class-based analyses of the military institution. He finds that the social origins of officers is less important in explaining the behaviour of the military institution than its internal organization and the way this is affected by external change. For example, the change in the military's role from moderating intervention in politics to direct military rule is explained by the impact of economic and political crisis on military organization. The import of new military technology for counter insurgency enhanced the role of the sergeants. Because their increased military importance was not associated with any increase in social and political power, this led to the politicization of the sergeants,

TABLE 5.1
Rates of growth of military spending, arms imports and GNP *per capita*
for selected Third World countries, 1963-1973[a],
and military burden in 1972

	Rate of growth of military spending %	Rate of growth of arms imports %	Military burden[b] (1972) %	Rate of growth of GNP *per capita* %	Group of countries[d]
Algeria	- 0.1	- 6.1	1.7	3.8	
Chad	30.4	0	5.1	0.6	W
Equatorial Guinea	- 4.6	0	5.1	- 5.9	
Ethiopia	6.5	0	2.6	1.8	
Gabon	10.9	0	1.5	8.8	
Ghana	0.6	0	1.6	- 0.1	L
Libya	18.5	18.6	2.6	10.2	H
Nigeria	31.8	0	5.4	3.7	
Somalia	9.4	0	6.4	0.6	W
Sudan	15.1	0.3	5.2	- 0.9	W
Tanzania	31.2	2.1	2.4	3.0	
Uganda	33.8	0	4.6	2.0	
Zambia	18.2	0	5.8	0.1	W
AFRICA	6.5	13.6	2.8	2.9	
Argentina	1.0	5.3	1.5	3.3	
Brazil	9.8	6.7	2.5	4.7	H
Chile	2.0	1.3	1.7	1.9	
Cuba	1.7	- 5.7	5.1	0	L
Peru	6.2	7.0	3.3	1.3	
Venezuela	4.6	5.8	1.9	1.8	
LATIN AMERICA	3.9	25.8	1.8	2.8	
Burma	- 2.8	- 1.2	5.7	0.5	
Cambodia	17.5	7.6	16.1	- 2.5	W
China	8.0	0	9.0	3.5	
Taiwan	7.5	17.4	9.6	7.6	H
Indonesia	7.3	-23.8	3.4	3.0	
Korea, South	11.6	21.5	4.7	7.9	H
Laos	3.8	8.2	12.4	3.1	
Thailand	13.9	0.4	3.6	4.5	H
Vietnam, North	- 3.2	6.9	25.0	- 5.7	W
Vietnam, South	5.0	103.5	18.0	0.2	W
EAST ASIA	7.5	158.4	4.0	5.9	
Egypt	10.3	34.9	14.6	0.9	W
Iran	22.7	42.4	10.6	7.6	H
Iraq	9.0	7.4	12.8	2.5	
Israel	25.7	87.8	21.6	5.0	H
Jordan	7.1	5.4	17.4	- 1.1	W
Kuwait	13.2	0	2.6	- 0.7[c]	
Saudi Arabia	12.8	4.0	14.7	6.5	H
Syria	11.8	37.6	12.3	2.9	
Yemen (Aden)	1.2	3.2	17.4	- 0.7	L
Yemen (Sana'a)	3.1	0	3.8	- 8.8	
NEAR EAST	14.7	223.1	11.9	3.5	
India	2.2	- 5.2	3.6	0.9	L
SOUTH ASIA	2.9	- 3.1	3.8	1.1	

TABLE 5.2
Military and social indicators *per capita*, 1972
(millions US$)

	GNP (1)	Military spending (2)	Education spending (3)	Health spending (4)	Military/ Social spending (2)/(3+4)
Brazil	514	13	16	2	0.7
Burma	70	4	2	-	2.0
Cambodia	120	14	7	1	1.8
Chad	82	4	2	1	1.3
Taiwan	476	84	18	3	4.0
Cuba	628	33	31	17	0.7
Egypt	223	38	11	4	2.2
Equatorial Guinea	264	3	3	3	0.5
Gabon	916	10	5	3	1.3
Ghana	265	4	10	3	0.3
India	104	4	3	1	1.0
Iran	504	54	14	6	2.7
Israel	2344	484	133	25	3.1
Jordan	286	50	9	2	4.5
Korea, South	300	14	12	1	1.1
Libya	1982	48	101	53	0.3
Pakistan	109	9	2	1	3.0
Saudi Arabia	583	86	46	9	1.6
Somalia	71	4	1	1	2.0
Sudan	125	7	6	2	0.9
Vietnam, North	82	14	2	1	4.7
Vietnam, South	178	32	2	1	10.7
Yemen (Aden)	82	3	-	-	-
Zambia	359	17	21	12	0.5

Source: Ruth L. Sivard, World Military and Social Expenditures 1974
(New York: Institute for World Order, 1975).

Table 5.1: Notes

a All rates of growth are based on constant 1972 dollars.
b Military burden means the share of GNP devoted to defence.
c Explained by rapid increase in net immigration.
d Countries are grouped into three categories as follows:
    H = high rates of growth of GNP, high rates of growth of military spending,
          relatively high military burdens.
    L = low rates of growth of GNP, low rates of growth of military spending,
          relatively low, in general, military burdens.
    W = war economies characterized by low rates of growth of GNP, high rates
          of growth of military spending, relatively high military burdens.

Source: US Arms Control and Disarmament Agency, World Military Expenditures
and Arms Trade 1963-73 (Washington DC, 1974).

their association with the trade unions, and their support for Goulart, whom
their senior officers opposed. This, combined with Goulart's excessive (in
the opinion of the officers) use of political promotions and the fear that a
revolutionary government would disband the armed forces and create a militia
(as in Cuba) led officers to redefine their political role and their attitude
towards government.

In rejecting class-based analyses, however, Stepan appears to reject the
attempt to relate his organizational analysis to the class structure of society
as a whole. Because his analysis is, for the most part, ahistorical, he does
not seem to be able to explain the origins of the Brazilian type of military
organization and, hence, the lessons for other military institutions. He can
explain, for example, how the post-1964 Brazilian military government differs
from the post-1968 Peruvian government but not why (Einaudi, 1973).

There have been a few case studies from a Marxist perspective. One of the most
interesting is Anour Abdel Malek's study of Egypt which explores, in a very
detailed way, the development strategy followed by the army officers who seized
power in 1952 (Malek, 1968). Throughout the period under scrutiny, 1952-67,
the soldiers accorded primary importance to industrial investment but their
associated policy went through a series of different stages. The initial period, 1952-56, was characterized by an alliance with the peasantry, abolition
of the monarchy and political parties, and agrarian reform aimed at weakening
agrarian capital. After Suez came the Egyptianization or nationalization of
foreign economic interests and an attempted coalition with the Egyptian bourgeoisie. Finally, after 1961, the military inaugurated a full scale programme
of nationalization and created the Arab Socialist Union: the net result of
this process, according to Malek, was a society based on economic planning,
subject to the laws of the world market, moulded by the interests of a new
managerial class, based on an American and German influenced bureaucracy, and
a new land-owning class which emerged after the agrarian reform of the 1950s.
Thus the military achieved industrial growth, at the expense of the poorest
classes in society, based on the consumption pattern of the elite.

Malek does not consider the internal characteristics of the Egyptian Army which
led the Free Officers in the first place to challenge the status quo. This
issue is touched upon by Hamsa Alavi (1971 and forthcoming) in his study of
Pakistan, where he treats the army as a colonial creation, and by Ansari and
Kaldor (to be published) in their study of the role of imported military technology in the Bangladesh crisis. Ansari and Kaldor argue that military rule
in Pakistan was the consequence of the break-up of an alliance between the
Bangladesh peasantry and the Punjabi land-owning and urban classes, in opposition to Hindu rule. They show how the military government pursued a policy of
industrial growth, located in Karachi and the Punjab, at the expense of the
Bengali peasant, through a complicated system of controls on investment and
foreign exchange. Military spending contributed to this process because it
was concentrated in West Pakistan and financed by foreign aid or savings generated in East Bengal. They also emphasize the function of imported weapons
systems; both for society, in emphasizing the ideological role of the armed
forces in upholding the struggle against the Hindu, much as Bonaparte's army
recalled the French revolution, and, for the internal characteristics of the
military, in creating "an aspiration to the American model of development".
The failure to win the 1965 war was critical in undermining these functions,
especially because of the devastating effects of the American decision to halt
aid to Pakistan.[17]

None of these studies, however, except perhaps Malek's, can be said to establish their theses conclusively. This is largely because they lack detail.
Much more needs to be known about such issues as the economic and social lin-
kages between the military and society, and the nature of the internal organization, the degree of hierarchy, the type of training, etc. The problem is
that such detail would require field work of a very difficult kind and this may
be the primary reason for the inadequacy of empirical studies of armed forces.

CONCLUSIONS

What seems to emerge most clearly from this survey is the need for research
based on the inter-connections between an institutional analysis of the armed
forces and a class analysis of the society in which they operate. Development
theorists have tended to emphasize the institutional analysis, both in political
and economic terms. They have explained the military's political tendencies
by reference to inherent institutional characteristics sometimes making confusing use of the term "class", and they have explained the military's economic
impact in terms of direct absorption or mobilization of resources. In contrast,
some Marxists have tended to emphasize the class analysis of society in general.
They have treated the military as a more or less neutral instrument of the ruling class and looked at the economic impact of the military in terms of its
role in preserving a social system characterized by a particular allocation of
resources. Both approaches tell us something about the subject but both fail
to explain the differences in the behaviour of military institutions in Third
World countries.

Despite this *a priori* failure, it has proved possible to make some empirical
generalizations about the military in the Third World. In particular, there
appears to be a strong association between high military spending, high rates
of industrial growth, and foreign dependence. The mode of industrial growth,
whether based on free enterprise or on planning, seems to vary. I have tried
to suggest that this association can be explained in terms of imported military
technology, which imposes a common pattern on Third World military institutions,
a pattern which reflects the social structure of metropolitan countries as much
as indigenous society. The arms are used to extract resources to finance industrial growth, either directly through war or repression, or indirectly as
an ideological symbol of nationhood or whatever. The operation of the armed
forces, particularly the repair and maintenance of arms, at the same time provides a direct stimulus to industry. Finally, the political willingness to
carry out this role, whether in or out of government, stems from certain organizational characteristics imposed by certain kinds of imported military technology, namely, the weapons system. This pattern is repeated on a world scale.
Expenditure on arms and dependence resulting from the, perhaps implicit, use
of force or from the ideology of modern arms provides the mechanism for channelling resources from the periphery to the metropolis.

This suggests a wide range of research that could be undertaken in the future.
As organized force, we need to study the impact of military institutions in
war and in politics. The economic and social consequences of war, in the
Third World, is a much neglected topic. There are a number of basic facts to
be discovered: the destruction of human and physical resources, the acquisition of new resources when victorious, the reallocation of resources in consequence of social changes induced by war. The political tendencies of military
institutions must be analyzed with reference to organizational structure.
There is enormous scope for analysis of the origins, nature and determination

of different military organizations, ranging from Saudi Arabia's Bedouin levies
to China's People's Liberation Army, and consideration of the extent to which
this organization is moulded indigenously by its domestic functions in a given
social system, and the extent to which external factors, such as war or imported military technology, come into play. We also need to establish the way in
which ideology grows out of military organization and whether it is ideology or
self-interest (fear of disbandment, dependence on industry) which determines
military behaviour in politics.

This lays the basis for research into the second aspect of military institutions,
namely, their role in the allocation of resources. In a sense, this topic might
well be the most important and the most amenable to empirical research. It has
to go beyond the statistical assessment of resource absorption on which this
kind of research has hitherto been based. It must enumerate the direct links
of the military with the economy — its source of finance; its absorption of
foreign exchange, manpower, raw materials, etc; its expenditure and effects
on specific sectors (textiles, iron and steel, aerospace, vehicles, etc.);
its contribution to infrastructure — within the framework of a social allocation of resources supported by military activities. The work could be pursued
by topic as well as by locality; for example, the recent arms for oil deals,
the recent spread of multinational arms production, the social impact of new
military technologies, or the much neglected trade in small arms would provide
fascinating subjects for research.

In addition to the impact of domestic military forces on development, another
area of research, on which there is a good deal of evidence but almost no analysis, is the impact of foreign military forces on local development. The presence of US troops in Thailand or the US base in Eritrea, for example, clearly
have significant political and economic consequences, which ought to be studied.

Indeed, the possibilities for future research are so wide that there is little
point, at this stage, in making detailed specific suggestions. It is clear
that military activities are enormously important and some, such as war or the
coup, can invalidate development strategies based on research which may have
painstakingly examined the economy but neglected the armed forces. It is also
clear that existing research, while representing a beginning, is quite inadequate. Partly, this is because the military has been treated as a side issue,
not central to the problem of development. This perspective needs to be changed;
the military play an integral role in the process of economic and social change
and it may well be that development can only be achieved if this role is understood and altered.

NOTES

1. The Stockholm International Peace Research Institute (SIPRI), the US Arms
    Control and Disarmament Agency (ACDA), the International Institute for
    Strategic Studies (IISS), and the Center for International Studies (CIS)
    at the Massachusetts Institute for Technology.

2. Huntington says: "In the world of oligarchy, the soldier is a radical;
    in the middle class world he is a participant and arbiter; as mass soc-
    iety looms on the horizon he becomes the conservative guardian of the
    existing order" (Huntington, 1968).

3. It would be interesting to discover whether he would have obtained differ-

ent results had he based his calculations on budgetary shares rather than on output shares since defence represents a claim on governmental resources.

4. For a description of these programmes, see Barber and Ronning (1960).

5. Of course, it could be argued that the Vietnamese victory was not due to organization but to the limits of technology. Liebknecht argues that under capitalism, the last class-divided society, technology will reach an ultimate limit: "We can suppose that the time will come — even if it is far into the future — when technique and the easy domination by man of the most powerful forces of nature will reach a stage which makes the application of the technique of murder quite impossible, since it would mean the self-destruction of the human race. The exploitation of technical progress will then take on a new character; from a basic plutocratic activity it will to a certain extent become a democratic general possibility".

6. This analysis parallels Marx's distinction between forces and relations of production which, together, define the mode of production (see Kaldor, 1975).

7. Interestingly enough, political justifications for arms acquisition first made their appearance in the Anglo-German naval arms race. The Tirpitz plan for naval procurement was not conceived in military terms but in terms of the political need to challenge British hegemony.

8. Generally, the term "mode of production" refers to the more abstract prevailing social formation, i.e. slavery, feudalism, or capitalism. In the "Eighteenth Brumaire of Louis Bonaparte", Marx uses the term to describe the small-holding peasantry. This is the sense in which it is used here. An equivalent modern example might be housework.

9. These last might better be described as absence of form, reflecting perhaps profound social and economic disorder. The irregular guerilla bands and bandits of modern Bangladesh and Burma might be placed in a similar category.

10. This model has much in common with Terray's description of Gyaman in precolonial Africa. Here, long distance trade, including arms, led to the introduction of slavery, alongside a kin-based mode of subsistence production. The slaves were used to produce gold for export and the revenue was spent on prestige goods and guns to capture and maintain more slaves.

11. This might be likened to the French soldiers' partiality for champagne and cigars, paid for by finance capital.

12. Others include Nordlinger (1970) and Putnam (1967).

13. Ruth Sivard inaugurated ACDA's work on military expenditures and arms trade, when she was Chief Economist at the Agency.

14. According to Benoit, the correlation does not work the other way round, i.e. as countries grow, they spend a larger share of GNP on defence. He shows that military burdens are not related to absolute levels of income nor to tax revenues.

15. Thailand has a military burden that is below the East Asian average.

16. An example is Lerner and Robinson's Turkish case study and their descrip-
     tion of the large scale education programme introduced by the Turkish
     Army, with the help of American specialists. A journalist reported, in
     April 1959, on the way in which draftees were taught the relationships
     between effort and reward: "Visitors to a classroom were welcomed by
     this rehearsed teacher-pupil exchange in Turkish: 'What will you be if
     you do not learn to read and write?' asked the teacher. 'Privates'
     chorused the class. 'And what will you become if you study hard and
     learn your lessons?' asked the teacher. 'Corporals and Sergeants' the
     class answered enthusiastically."

17. This, incidentally, contradicts the argument that high military spending
     leads to foreign aid. Pakistan increased military spending after 1965.

The full references to the literature cited in the preceding
article and notes will be found in the annotated bibliography
at the end of this volume. The survey article and most of
the annotated bibliography originally appeared in World
Development, Vol. 4, No. 6, June 1976, pp. 459-482.

World Military and Social Expenditures: Some Comparisons

Ruth Leger Sivard

PRIORITIES ?

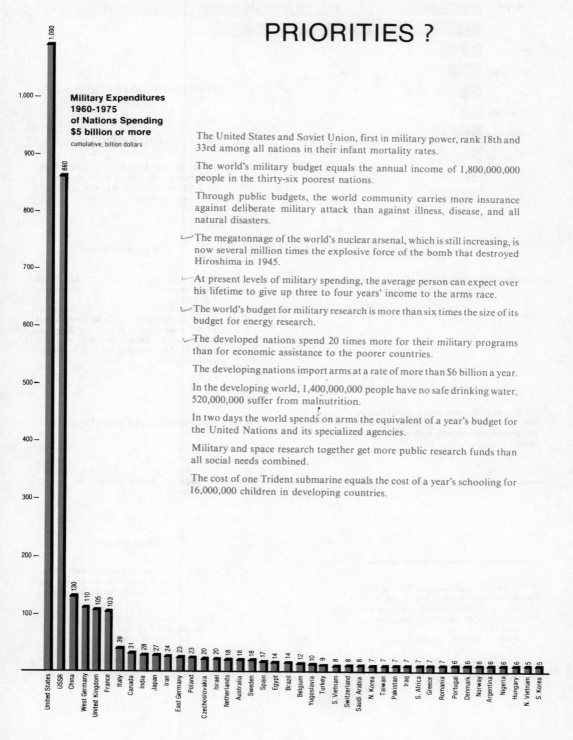

**Military Expenditures
1960-1975
of Nations Spending
$5 billion or more**
cumulative, billion dollars

The United States and Soviet Union, first in military power, rank 18th and 33rd among all nations in their infant mortality rates.

The world's military budget equals the annual income of 1,800,000,000 people in the thirty-six poorest nations.

Through public budgets, the world community carries more insurance against deliberate military attack than against illness, disease, and all natural disasters.

The megatonnage of the world's nuclear arsenal, which is still increasing, is now several million times the explosive force of the bomb that destroyed Hiroshima in 1945.

At present levels of military spending, the average person can expect over his lifetime to give up three to four years' income to the arms race.

The world's budget for military research is more than six times the size of its budget for energy research.

The developed nations spend 20 times more for their military programs than for economic assistance to the poorer countries.

The developing nations import arms at a rate of more than $6 billion a year.

In the developing world, 1,400,000,000 people have no safe drinking water, 520,000,000 suffer from malnutrition.

In two days the world spends on arms the equivalent of a year's budget for the United Nations and its specialized agencies.

Military and space research together get more public research funds than all social needs combined.

The cost of one Trident submarine equals the cost of a year's schooling for 16,000,000 children in developing countries.

Chart values (left to right): United States 1,090; USSR 860; China 130; West Germany 110; United Kingdom 105; France 103; Italy 39; Canada 31; India 28; Japan 27; Iran 24; East Germany 23; Poland 23; Czechoslovakia 20; Israel 20; Netherlands 18; Australia 18; Sweden 18; Spain 17; Egypt 14; Brazil 14; Belgium 12; Yugoslavia 10; Turkey 9; S. Vietnam 8; Switzerland 8; Saudi Arabia 8; N. Korea 7; Taiwan 7; Pakistan 7; Iraq 7; S. Africa 7; Greece 7; Romania 7; Portugal 6; Denmark 6; Norway 6; Argentina 6; Nigeria 6; Hungary 6; N. Vietnam 5; S. Korea 5

Major Arms Exporters
billion dollars, cumulative 1961-1975

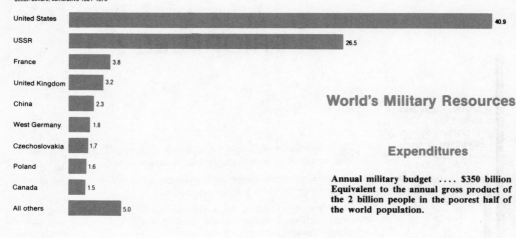

United States	40.9
USSR	26.5
France	3.8
United Kingdom	3.2
China	2.3
West Germany	1.8
Czechoslovakia	1.7
Poland	1.6
Canada	1.5
All others	5.0

"Military expenditures are a bottomless pit."
Nikita Krushchev, USSR, 1971

"What makes the arms race a global folly is that all countries are now buying greater and greater insecurity at higher and higher costs."
Alva Myrdal, Sweden, 1976

"The unrestrained competition among nations to build more arms, to sell more weapons, to deploy more forces is senseless, wasteful, but, above all, dangerous to our security."
Walter Mondale, United States, 1976

World's Military Resources

Expenditures

Annual military budget .... $350 billion
Equivalent to the annual gross product of the 2 billion people in the poorest half of the world population.

Personnel

Regular forces .... 22 million
Paramilitary .... 10 million
Civilians in military-
related jobs .... 25-30 million
Active military and civilian personnel equal to the population of France and Belgium. Additional 24 million in ready reserves, equal to the population of four Scandinavian countries.

Research and development

Annual R & D budget ..... $25 billion
Dominates public R & D effort, taking over 40% of total R&D budget; six times as large as public budget for energy research.

Weapons

Annual procurement budget .. $80 billion
Twice the size of the combined budgets for education and health in all developing countries.

Weapons inventory includes:
  124,000 tanks
  12,400 combat ships
  35,000 combat aircraft
  nuclear weapons representing
    50 billion tons TNT equivalent

World's Social Deficit

Income

Two and one-half billion people in the world's poorer countries share a total annual product averaging below $250 per capita.

For the very poorest, the economic advance since 1960 has meant a gain of $1-$2 a year in per capita income.

Education

One adult in four in the world is unable to read and write.

In developing nations, more than half the children of school age are not in schools.

Health

The rate of infant deaths to births in the poorest countries is 20 times higher than in countries with well-developed health programs.

95 per cent of the children born in the developing world are not immunized against common contagious diseases.

In rural areas of the developing world, the majority of people never see a doctor.

Life expectancy at birth is 25 years less in Africa than in Europe.

Food and water

Hunger is chronic among 520 million people in developing nations.

In Latin America, Asia and Africa, 1.4 billion people do not have access to safe drinking water.

"All governments should accept the goal that within a decade no child will go to bed hungry, that no family will fear for the next day's bread, and that no human being's future and capacity will be stunted by malnutrition."
World Food Conference, Italy, 1974

"The moral challenge of our day is nothing less than the ability of our civilization to use the technology of abundance to recreate, not destroy, the face of the earth."
Barbara Ward, United Kingdom, 1968

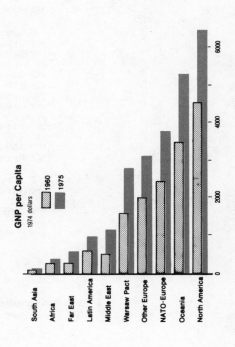

GNP per Capita
1974 dollars

1960
1975

South Asia
Africa
Far East
Latin America
Middle East
Warsaw Pact
Other Europe
NATO-Europe
Oceania
North America

OVERKILL AND

The blockbuster bomb of World War II had a power of *10* tons of TNT. The nuclear bomb that blew apart Hiroshima had *13.000* tons of TNT. Today a single nuclear warhead may have an explosive force of up to *25,000,000* tons of TNT.

"The belief that it is possible to achieve security through armaments on a national scale is, in the present state of military technology, a disastrous illusion".
Albert Einstein US 1950

It is now possible to deliver a bomb of 1 megaton (an explosive force of 1,000,000 tons of TNT) anywhere in the globe. Missiles can travel up to 9,000 miles and fall within a few hundred feet of the target.

A few soldiers pressing buttons can now deliver as much destruction to another continent as all the bombers of World War II.

War-oriented and people-oriented research

Government funding of research and development is also heavily weighted to military programs. Detailed data are available at present only for the United States and European Community *(Chart 7)*. The R & D patterns of these two areas differ, but it is the U.S. pattern that dominates since the USSR is believed by Western specialists to conform closely to it. These two nations spend three-fourths of the estimated $60 billion in public funds invested annually in all R & D. Their dominance puts weapons research at the center of the world's R & D effort, most of which occurs in the developed countries. Space research, also dominated by the superpowers, is the next most important R & D activity. The drive for preeminence in military and space results in some surprising contrasts in priorities, for example:

□ Military and space research together get more public R & D funds than all social needs combined.

□ More money goes into research on space than into research for the protection and improvement of human health.

□ Despite the shortage of petroleum, known dangers in the spread of nuclear power, too little knowledge of alternative energy sources, the R & D effort on energy still gets only one-sixth as much funding as weapons research.

Approximately 20 nations now have or will soon have nuclear power reactors. Within the decade, it is estimated, the by-product nuclear material they produce could make several thousand bombs a year.

UNDER-DEVELOPMENT

□ Usually the largest non-military program, government education expenditures are primarily for the school-age population (5-19) which now numbers 1.3 billion children, one-third of the world population. Total expenditures are 7 per cent less than military expenditures. For each school-age child they average $230 a year, as compared with military expenditures averaging $14,800 for each soldier.

□ For all public health, national health insurance, and health care under workmen's compensation, governments spend a little more than half as much as they do for military programs. The average is $44 per person, against military expenditures of $81 per person.

□ Official foreign economic assistance has a budget somewhat less than 6 per cent of the military expenditures of the donor countries. It provides the poorer nations with development aid amounting to $6 per capita, about two-thirds gift, one-third loan.

□ Expenditures for the United Nations and the operations of its world-wide programs in health, food, education, environment, labor, meteorology, etc., add up to less than $2 billion annually, the equivalent of two days of military expenditures.

□ A year's expenditures on international peacekeeping, another UN-supported activity, are equal to 3 hours of the world's expenditures on national military forces.

□ Arms imports in developing countries have expanded twice as fast as the gain in development aid and as the advance in their living standards represented by average per capita GNP.

□ Of the 83 developing nations which imported arms in 1975, more than one-fifth were among the very poorest nations in the world (average income under $200). These are the countries whose basic problem is insuring an adequate food supply for their rapidly growing populations.

□ In the last three years, while they invested $13 billion in foreign arms, the developing countries that are not oil exporters had a sharply rising external debt, their current account deficit increasing by $30 billion.

As a result of military coups, military officers now hold the key positions of power in over 40 percent of all developing nations.

"The vastly unequal relationship between the rich and the poor nations is fast becoming the central issue of our time."
Mahbub ul Haq, Pakistan, 1976

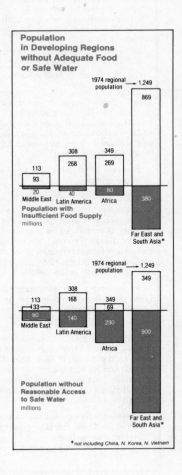

Population in Developing Regions without Adequate Food or Safe Water

1974 regional population → 1,249

Population with Insufficient Food Supply
millions

113 / 93	Middle East
308 / 268 / 40	Latin America
349 / 269 / 80	Africa
869 / 380	Far East and South Asia*
20	Middle East

1974 regional population → 1,249

113 / 33 / 80	Middle East
308 / 168 / 140	Latin America
349 / 69 / 280	Africa
349 / 900	Far East and South Asia*

Population without Reasonable Access to Safe Water
millions

* not including China, N. Korea, N. Vietnam

ALTERNATIVES

"Think what we could do if we were—all of us— to channel these vast sums of money [for arms] into other fields! We could eliminate pockets of poverty. We could improve health and education. If this is true for the United States how much more must it apply to the developing countries."

Eleanor Roosevelt, United States, 1963

Below are some of the purposes which could be furthered by redirecting a mere 5 per cent of the year's global military budget toward cooperative international endeavors.

The emphasis here is on the developing nations because this is where the most acute needs are concentrated and where four out of five of the world's children live.

What could **$17.5 billion**, a minor share of the world's military budget, do to begin to correct the world's social deficit?

This set of alternatives is put forward in a spirit of challenge—and hope. It is not intended as a blueprint for a disarmament dividend, nor a judgement among social priorities. It selects rather arbitrarily from a vast backlog of unmet needs, and holds these needs up against a very small fraction of the world's military budget in order to put the question again: How wisely are we using the world's limited resources?

Five million children in developing areas are killed every year by six contagious diseases preventable by immunization: diphtheria, whooping cough, infantile paralysis, measles, tetanus, and the childhood forms of tuberculosis. 95 per cent of the children born annually are not vaccinated.

A vaccination program to give protection against infectious diseases to all infants.

$600 million

Illiteracy and mass poverty are linked. One in four adults—700 million in all—are unable to read and write; their numbers have been increasing. They are cut off from knowledge which could improve their health, help them make more effective use of available resources, and permit them to participate more fully in the work and benefits of development.

Program to extend literacy to all adults by the end of the century.

$1.2 billion

In rural areas of the Third World a majority of the people have no access to professional health assistance, and the majority of births take place in homes without the assistance of trained personnel. Health auxiliaries, who can be trained in 3-6 months compared with 6 years for a medical graduate, have proved to be capable of handling 85 per cent of a village's health needs.

A preventive and community-oriented training program for a sharp increase in the numbers of medical auxiliaries.

$250 million

The number of people suffering from chronic malnutrition has increased further despite an improvement in the world food situation in 1976. More than 500 million eat less than the calories needed to maintain ordinary physical activity. External aid for investment in food and agricultural production has lagged behind goals agreed at the World Food Conference.

Increased development aid to improve the capacity of the Third World to grow its own food, and prevent malnutrition.

$3.0 billion

Up to two-thirds of the urban households in the lowest-income countries cannot afford the cheapest housing available. An estimated 300 million live in slum areas and shanty towns.

An expanded minimum-shelter program, incorporating self-help construction, for the urban poor.

$750 million

In Asia, Africa, and Latin America, 200 million pre-school children are chronically hungry. Malnutrition threatens their mental and physical growth and may prevent them from leading normal lives.

Supplementary feeding to ensure full development for 200 million malnourished children.

$4 billion

Infant mortality rates average five times higher in developing countries than in developed. High infant mortality, resulting from premature and underweight babies, is related to under-nourishment and anemia in women of child-bearing ages.

Supplementary feeding for 60 million malnourished pregnant and lactating women to protect their health and reduce infant mortality.

$1.5 billion

In the next ten years the entire increase in the world's school-age population will center in the Third World, where only half the children of school age are now attending school. Just to maintain the present enrollment, these countries will need 250 million new school places before 1985.

Major increase in the number of primary schools, with the addition of 100 million new places.

$3.2 billion

Over 1,000 million people in rural areas and 200 million in the cities are without reasonable access to safe water supplies. Water-borne diseases kill an estimated 25,000 people every day. Diarrheal diseases, associated with contaminated water, are the most common cause of death in children under five.

Hygienic water supply systems, toward the goal of clean water for all humanity by 1990.

$3.0 billion

"Adapted by kind permission from World Military and Social Expenditures, 1977, by Ruth Leger Sivard.

PART II

Disarmament and Development: What Can Be Done?

The Game of Disarmament

Alva Myrdal

My book is an attempt to study the policy question of disarmament from an international point of view.* It has grown out of *a gradually increasing feeling
of near despair after twelve years* of participating in multilateral disarmament
negotiations. There the superpowers have indulged in subterfuges and half-
truths, with their closest and usually most dependent allies following suit or
keeping silent. On balance, there has been no real advance towards limitation
of armaments. The competitive race between the two superpowers has steadily
escalated, and the militarization of the economy and national life of almost
all countries has intensified ....

The guiding principle in my criticism is rationality. The building up of the
giant military establishments has gone, and is going, right against what would
be rational from the point of view of the interests of every nation. This
applies as well to *the superpowers' policy of increasing armaments. It is
beyond all reason.* The book was intended to be an appeal to reason, but it
has also become an appeal to morality. How can we let the nationalistic security needs as defined and exaggerated by military and other vested interests
misguide our societies? How can we allow secretiveness and falsifications of
reality to motivate the continued arms race, with all the dangers and burdens
thereof? The common man should demand honest accountability of the policy-
makers. He has the right to question their ethics.

I address myself to the decision-makers — the governments and their advisers —
but my ambition is to be heard also by independent experts and concerned citizens in all countries. In the last instance, it is only by intensified public
debate that disarmament issues can be pressed forward. Something is fundamentally amiss when, even in democratic countries, disarmament can be such a dead
issue.

Greater security?

Every government defends its participation in the arms race as necessary to
guard its national security. But this is an illusion. What makes the arms
race a global folly is that all countries are now buying greater and greater
insecurity at higher and higher costs. The non-stop character of the arms
race also poses ever steeper obstacles to disarmament negotiations. While the
disarmers talk, the armouries that were to be dismantled are being built
higher and higher. Disarmament negotiations have, so far, been a sorrowful
Sisyphus game and a long series of missed opportunities.

Although statesmen and their military advisers do not want to listen and learn,
preferring to continue to use the woolly term, national security, in order to

*Extracted, with minor alterations, from The Game of Disarmament: How the United
States and Russia Run the Arms Race, by Alva Myrdal. Copyright c 1976 by Alva
Myrdal. Reprinted by permission of Pantheon Books, a Division of Random House,
Inc.

boost the defence budgets, the knowledge is now becoming commonplace among independent experts and writers that the stupendous increase in the quantity,
quality and cost of armaments has not resulted in any commensurable increase
in aggregate national security for the world. *A considerable body of evidence
indicates that a mutual stepping up of armaments leads to a decrease in national security, that is, safety against attacks.*

That the arms race is rapidly decreasing the security of all the lesser powers
is obvious. Also, the dynamics of the arms race increases the incidental
risks for third parties. If they line up with one of the superpowers in formal or non-formal alliances under the illusion that this guarantees their
security, they are then drawn even more tightly into that superpower game
which goes on above their heads.

Not even the two superpowers can gain greater security through the arms race.
Their nuclear-weapons strength long ago exceeded what might be needed even for
a "terror balance", that is, for a deterrent that forbids both, knowing that
retaliation lies in store at the already existing level of overkill, to use
force against the other. Temporary gains on one or the other side cannot make
it more tempting to use nuclear weapons for an attack. In addition, competition, inherent in the arms race, tends to make relative superiority unstable.

This element of instability in the arms race is a pending world danger. The
dangers of a collision are accentuated by technological development itself, as
warning times steadily decrease, thus *making it more and more probable that
war might occur through technical accidents and errors.* This is illustrated
by the fact that the time required for inter-hemispheric delivery of nuclear
bombs by missiles has shrunk to about ten minutes. The missile has also dras-
tically shortened the warning time and heightened the surprise element possible
between neighbouring nations on a continental land mass. The mechanical complexity and increasingly automated functioning between signal received and attack released make national security more and more threatened by technical
hazards.

"Limited war" over Europe

Where is the thoroughgoing responsible analysis of all aspects of the deployment of tactical nuclear weapons in Europe? Where is the political debate
about the effects of their use in a war and, generally, about their usefulness?

Discussion of the questions raised in expert circles about the wisdom of withdrawing all or certain types of them, the more vulnerable or more offensive,
has not reached the peoples of Europe. There is definitely no interest in public discussion of a realistic analysis (a) of the implications of drawing nuclear fire on to the European countries, nor (b) of the extent to which these
countries and peoples would be devastated ....

The European partners in NATO have preferred to have little public attention
directed towards the possible consequences of their NATO allegiance. Perhaps
they felt that they could not handle a twofold argument — continuing to appeal
to the USA for military commitment while informing the people at home about
the insecurity involved. The remarkable thing is that the public has acquies-
ced. Even in the non-aligned western countries there has been astonishingly
little discussion of these awkward issues or studies examining the consequences
of various scenarios, for example, those involving the use of the thousands of

tactical nuclear weapons deployed in the midst of Europe. These non-aligned neighbours to NATO countries have demonstrated a kind, but ultimately not very helpful, discretion in questions which concern the destiny of the continent as a whole.

There has as usual been more open discussion in the USA. There is has often been understood that the political consequences of presently relevant scenarios and damage estimates are ominous. As former ambassador to NATO Harlan Cleveland has pointed out:

> It is natural for Americans to press for effective, which
> is to say large-scale, use of nuclear weapons on the battle-
> field — enough to "stop the enemy in his tracks". But this
> conjures up for Europeans the picture of a Europe devastated
> while the United States and the Soviet Union remain intact.

This matter was not brought up at the European Security Conference, where it ought to have headed an urgent agenda. Nowhere so far are views heard from the citizens of Europe who will, after all, be the victims if there is a super-power war in Europe.

They should, if they were enlightened participants in a dialogue about the defence of Europe, join with the independent experts and state it clearly: *these tactical nuclear weapons are not needed in Europe, either for deterrence or for defence.*

In fact, and that should be the overriding concern, the USA does not need to have these weapons in Europe. If it maintains its strategy of using its nuclear strength to defend Western Europe, it need only detach some of its submarines, equipped with nuclear warheads on ballistic missiles, targeted and ready to fire in case of an attack against Western Europe. That should be sufficient to deter any such attack.

Scissions in the alliances

Even if their peoples have been kept uninformed, it must be assumed that the West European governments and their expert advisers are fully aware of the wholesale destruction of their countries and the killing and maiming of a very large portion of their peoples that would occur in case of even a limited nuclear war in Europe ....

Towards a strategy for new attempts

Against the background of the long history of defeat, it sometimes looks as if the task to reach effective agreements on important disarmament measures were impossible, that mankind is doomed to continue an ever intensified arms race and a relentless militarization of the world. If this is to be our fate, it would be equally impossible to trust that the political balance between the superpowers will secure peace. This balance is being undermined by technological advances which keep open the possibilities of surprising breakthroughs in new weapons systems, decreasing warning time and weakening the barriers against all kinds of mistakes and misinterpretations. Security is further eroded by the probable future spread of nuclear weaponry to more countries. The danger of a major cataclysm is real. Bertrand Russell towards the end of his life

reckoned the possibility of human survival on earth till the next century to
be only 50 per cent.

I decline to accept a defeatist view. To be realistic it is necessary to recognize the facts. The arms race is irrational, and we are not permitted to
let unreason stand unchallenged. Hope of reversing the trend must be built by
untiring efforts to educate peoples and governments to recognize their true
interests. This means effectively attacking the forces within the countries
that are propelling the arms race within the arms race. There are mistaken
but widely spread ideas about the importance of production and modernization
of armaments for industrialization and employment. There is ambition in the
military sector to dispose of bigger defence budgets and competition between
the armed services for a share in new investments. The technological imperative to improve the performance characteristics of all military devices is
kept alive by scientists and the technical cadres. Additionally, the very
idea of balancing and the thoughtless acceptance of the thesis that every advance in military strength by "the other side" is reason for "matching" it is
irrational.

Many of the above factors are expressions of the competitive spirit prevailing
in our societies. All converge in what Dwight D. Eisenhower in his last pres-
idential message to the United States nation called *the military-industrial
complex, to which must now be added academic*. These forces are represented in
legislative assemblies. They are particularly strong and visible in the USA,
but they operate in all countries, including the Soviet Union.

We must oppose the arms race not only on the grounds of its irrationality but
also on grounds of morality. Each new generation of arms becomes more inhumane.
Every new war tends to become more cruel. For centuries rules about how warfare is to be conducted have been accepted as international law, but these
rules are now disregarded in the most flagrant way. They must be expanded,
modernized and respected. They must guide our efforts to restrain the use and
production of and trade in cruel weapons ....

In attempting to formulate *a rational and ethical strategy for disarmament*, I
conclude from experience that we have regrettably to give up the holistic
approach of General and Complete Disarmament by means of an orderly series of
steps for implementation and a pre-set timetable. That approach has a long
history in both the League of Nations and the United Nations. It has always
ended in failure.

The sober conclusion of those who stand for the ideal of disarmament is that
in the present world situation what we must aim at is *a strategy for limitation
and reduction of specific arms* and other preparations for war as part of a comprehensive programme. Attempts hitherto made to agree on specified arms limitation measures, however, have been far too piecemeal. No treaties to abstain
from production and use of weapons have been concluded, only marginal steps
have been taken, and even these are not effective. On the prime issues, such
as the nuclear arms race between the superpowers, the negotiations up to now
have been futile.

A strategy that is both realistic and courageous must be found to limit and
reduce arms and eliminate some of them immediately. *A new comprehensive grasp
of the disarmament problems is necessary*. While abandoning the attempt to get
a general agreement in one stroke, we must seek a solution that combines specific measures into an integrated whole. These may take the form of international

legislation, multi- or bilateral agreements, or of unilateral moves forward on the road to the acknowledged goal.

A gross miscalculation

The despondency over mankind's present drift towards disaster is exacerbated by senseless overkill capacity, more arms having already been produced and deployed than could ever be used. This is particularly true of nuclear weapons, especially strategic ones in the arsenals of the superpowers; tactical weapons, intended for battlefield use, deserve special attention from a political point of view with a focus on specific regions.

For this evil the superpowers are almost entirely responsible. Each has accumulated and is continuing to accumulate stockpiles of atomic weapons which have long since been much more than enough to destroy the other power and the whole world many times over. By the end of the ten-year term of SALT, each will be capable of destroying the other, not 50 times over as at present, but 100 times over. Why?

Realistically, *the problem is how much weaponry is needed for a strategy of deterrence. This is the only relevant question.* Continuing to match each other's destructive capacity is irrelevant. ... In reality the situation between the two superpowers is this: neither the United States nor the Soviet Union can possibly want to use nuclear bombs deliberately against each other, knowing that they would immediately draw the holocaust on to themselves. This is the assumed purpose of the terror balance. When we and they know that a fraction of their nuclear fire strength is enough to deter the other side from ever courting such a fate, the intrinsic irrationality of the superpowers' holding and augmenting their giant nuclear armouries is immediately evident.

Militarily, the size of nuclear forces needed for deterrence is spoken of as second-strike capabilities. In simpler words, what counts is how much is needed for retaliation. The superpowers must calculate how much they would have left after having suffered a nuclear attack, and how much they estimate they would need for retaliating with unacceptable damage on the adversary.

It should be quite clear that the size of the second-strike capability cannot be measured in the number of warheads and delivery vehicles they have now, but must refer to the chances of having enough operable which could be fired from an invulnerable position. Thus the salient military concern must be to harden the silos for land-based missiles, or to make them mobile or, as the most effective means so far available to preserve invulnerability, to give preference to submarine-based ballistic missiles. Without entering here into a discussion of how much might be left for a second strike, it is enough to know that *both superpowers are confident of having such securely retained capabilities far beyond what is enough for retaliating* with an insupportable blow. As the threat of such a blow is most effective when directed against centres with civilian populations, the second-strike force is usually described as a counter-city force. And the force available for that deterrent is surely much more than sufficient on both sides. But the relevant answer as to how much capacity retained is enough for deterrence cannot be and need not be given in quantitative terms. The calculation becomes psychological-political more than military. Is it or is it not enough deterrence for each of the superpowers already to run the risk of being hit by one megaton nuclear bomb? Or do they see any war aims for an offensive that could justify several of their own big cities

being sacrificed when the retaliatory blow comes? Even their entire nation
devastated?

A succinct answer, indicating that the low figure of one bomb is probably enough for a credible deterrent, was given in a statement by former Special
Assistant to the President for National Security Affairs, McGeorge Bundy, made
shortly after leaving his post:

> In the real world of real political leaders — whether here
> or in the Soviet Union — a decision that would bring even
> one hydrogen bomb on one city of one's own country would
> be recognized in advance as a catastrophic blunder; ten
> bombs on ten cities would be a disaster beyond history;
> and a hundred bombs on a hundred cities are unthinkable.

The above statement was quoted by Herbert York, who, among other prominent
posts, has held the job of Director of Defense Research and Engineering in the
Department of Defense under Presidents Eisenhower and Kennedy. He added:

> My personal view is that Bundy is right: that from one to
> ten are enough whenever the course of the events is being
> rationally determined.

The reservation about a decision made on rational grounds is important. Of
course, there can be no calculus for lunatic decisions. ...

How can it be explained that the numerical limits in the Vladivostok agreement
allow each of the two superpowers to increase its arsenal by multiplying nuclear warheads into the tens of thousands, altogether representing more than a
million Hiroshimas?

There are but two possible explanations, both indicating basic flaws of thinking. One is that the military planners have not concentrated on (the strategy of) deterrence, by which they should only be occupied with retaliatory
capacity, but are more or less wittingly ensnarled by matching or balance. Or
that they do not sincerely aim at deterrence but allow themselves, under that
label, to proceed right into some wild war-fighting scenarios.

A further sign is the small degree of attention that the military planners pay
to problems of defence, in the narrow sense of how much and what is needed to
defend their territories against possible attacks. All scenarios and all weapons development work is concentrated on offensive categories. The ulterior
aim of winning a world war is seemingly always present in the minds of the
superpowers. The quantitative level, set in SALT, and the freedom left for
endless qualitative improvements and innovations indicate that both sides are,
in fact, attempting to proceed to first-strike capabilities, that is, to anni-
hilate or at least totally disarm the adversary. The thinking of the planners
is obviously concerned more with war-fighting than deterrence, even first use
of nuclear weapons. The crucial question can hardly be which of these governments will be the victor after both have fought to the last bomb and quite
possibly the last major population centres. ...

Some conclusions

Part Two of my book outlines an Active Disarmament Agenda. The agenda must give priority to the most decisive aspects of arms regulation, even if only in a preliminary way by laying down guidelines. The following examples are not meant to indicate a time sequence, but rather to suggest an order of priority.

1. *Quantitative disarmament of nuclear weapons and their delivery vehicles* by sharp curtailment of both strategic and tactical arsenals. Aim: agreement on de-escalating towards a minimum deterrent.

2. *Qualitative disarmament of nuclear weapons* by total cessation of further development of such weapons, both strategic and tactical, as well as of further development of their delivery vehicles. Immediate action: a comprehensive test ban to fasten the padlock on the ongoing proliferation of nuclear weapon types and on the spread of nuclear weapons to additional countries. Agreeing on a time-limited moratorium might be a first step.

3. *Similar quantitative as well as qualitative disarmament of conventional weapons* by mutually balanced reductions of arms production and by regulating and restricting trade in arms.

4. *Prohibition of production, stockpiling, trading, and deployment of chemical weapons.*

5. *Prohibition of the use as well as the production of cruel antipersonnel weapons*, i.e., weapons characterized as causing "unnecessary suffering".

6. *Prohibition of indiscriminate warfare befalling civilian populations, as well as prohibition of environmental warfare.*

7. *Agreements on demilitarization of ocean space*, not only prohibiting installations of certain weapon categories, but also regulating the deployment of tracking, refuelling, and other devices for military purposes.

8. *Agreements on eliminating foreign bases*, withdrawal of tactical nuclear weapons from foreign territories, and prohibiting passage through foreign territorial seas.

If lack of progress threatens to stultify these disarmament negotiations, other steps must be resorted to. Much more important measures than hitherto can be taken and much stronger pressures exerted on substantive issues by independent action of the great majority of non-aligned states. I wish to exemplify the avenues that lie open by listing four points which refer back to several proposals made in previous chapters. The order does not necessarily reflect priorities, but rather a possible time sequence, dependent on how speedily the suggestions can be made feasible for being carried out within the UN framework.

1. *Some actual arms limitation agreements* can be reached independently of the superpowers. The best example is one practically ready for implementation; the Treaty against the production, stockpiling, and testing of chemical weapons. It neither requires global coverage nor instrinsically stands in need of the concurrence of the nuclear-weapons states. A great number of countries are ready to forswear not just the use but also the procurement of chemical means of warfare. It is in the interest of the underdeveloped countries to do so, as chemical warfare so patently risks "downhill wars". They should remonstrate against the immorality of recourse to these horror weapons. If the superpowers and their most obedient allies turn out to be the only ones standing aside from such a treaty, so much worse for the judgement of them in the eyes of the

world. Thus a treaty committing its parties not to produce chemical means of
warfare or allow any deployment of such weapons on their territory would be
quite important in itself, even if originally adhered to only by a core of
dedicated nations. By means of clauses on regular review conferences and a
majority rule for accepting amendments, it would hold itself open for improvements and adjustments in the light of accumulated experience.

2. *The decision to establish an International Verification Agency* can likewise
be made in the United Nations by majority vote. It can at least be set up on
an interim basis, e.g. in respect to chemical weapons and seismological detection from a distance of nuclear explosions. There is absolutely no reason to
wait for compliance by the nuclear-weapons powers.

3. *A number of exploratory and preparatory studies* can readily be instituted
by a majority in the United Nations. Usually this would continue to take the
form of authorizing the Secretary General to call on a group of experts, the
experts sometimes being seconded by interested member states but sometimes
being independent. This is a proven technique for moving matters forward, even
if one of the superpowers boycotts the study (as in the very important report
on napalm). There are qualified experts available, not least because the scientific communities are taking a more and more active role in studies in the
arms field. The technique can be applied in a much more systematic way in
order to accelerate progress and build up pressure in one area after another.
Not least should the purpose be to educate the people and the politicians by
laying bare the facts about the unreasonable course of the arms race in such
a way that the knowledge compels change.

Note

This summary of the Game of Disarmament is reprinted from Development Dialogue,
1977:1, pp. 10-16.

Ways and Means to Generate the Political Will

Inga Thorsson

Aggression may be inherent in mankind but war, which engages masses of people in battle against each other, is a learned behaviour, developed in historical times, and, as such, can be unlearned, and ultimately eliminated entirely.

The thwarted intelligence of man has led technological development into greater and greater destructive capacity, and the experiences of warfare have penetrated into the lives of more and more men, women and children.

Fortunately, the constructive, rational side of the human intelligence has gained strength to react. The ideal of peace, of a life in co-existence, understanding and co-operation, has always been the follower of the destructive forces of war. As armaments and warfare in the 20th century involved more and more human and financial resources, so the movement for peace has grown stronger and more forceful. The insane cruelty of the First World War opened the eyes of men and women all over the harassed European continent. Also, national leaders were concerned about the rapid and massive increase in military spending. As Dave Noble has pointed out in his War and Peace Book, the Washington Naval Conference in 1921 and the ensuing naval limitation pacts of the 1920s and 1930s resulted from a desire to divert money from a naval arms race, in order to cope with the economic strains that the industrialized world was then experiencing.

Disarmament between the World Wars was a movement engaging all, from private men and women to leading statesmen. One of the most prominent forces of this drive was Philip Noel-Baker. He tells us himself of his experiences in his great work on the Arms Race: "Before the World Disarmament Conference met in February 1932", he says, "almost every question concerning manpower, the reduction and limitation of armaments and weapons, and the limitation of military expenditure had been meticulously debated, and in many matters a practical solution had been found."

The work of the League of Nations was particularly thorough and complete in the matter of budgetary limitation of armaments. As Noel-Baker underlines, discussions were conducted at a high level of government responsibility, they were assiduously pursued and they led to wide agreement on possible technical solutions. But still they failed to lead to successful political action.

Disarmament efforts have continued through the 1960s and 1970s, this time through the UN. In the late 1950s, at the same time as the gradual defeat of colonialism and the emergence of the new nations of the Third World, a new idea came into the discussion — this was the concept of peaceful development, which was diametrically opposed to the waste of resources on destructive purposes.

Already in the late 1950s, proposals were made for the utilization of resources released by disarmament for development purposes. In the following decade discussions continued. The economic and social consequences of the arms race

93

were analyzed. The issue of development again came into focus in 1972 with
the report on Disarmament and Development whose conclusions are still valid,
and will, I hope, soon be taken up for renewed consideration and follow-up
efforts.

The New Approach to Peace

A more dynamic, more constructive outlook on peace has emerged. We have now
reached the stage where disarmament alone, although an absolute necessity, is
not enough. The stockpiles of arms are in themselves a mortal threat to mankind but there are also other threats to our existence. Disarmament for peace
is not sufficient: it must be supported by development for peace.

The situation of the world around us can be painted in a picture of the darkest
possible colours. On one hand, the arms race absorbs for deadly purposes 40
million dollars every 24 hours. On the other hand, immeasurable poverty affects
the lives of three-quarters of the men, women and children in the world around
us. The efforts for disarmament must therefore be an inextricable part of the
efforts to solve the common problems of our time, problems which ultimately
involve our very survival, the possibility to continue the human experiment.

There are four billion people on this planet. Of these, roughly one quarter
lives in the industrialized world which, with all its drawbacks and problems,
at least offers for most of its population food, shelter, education, and on
average a certain prosperity. Moreover, three quarters of the income of the
world this year accrued to persons in the industrialized countries, increasing
further their consumption capacity.

At the same time, there are one billion people, the poorest quarter, who suffer
for want of the most elementary basic necessities of human life: food, clean
water for themselves and their cattle, shelter, clothes. They have the barest
of incomes, little or no opportunities of being productively employed with a
reasonable return, no chance of ever improving their own situation, in spite
of their individual efforts. Half of them are children, under the age of 15,
who not only suffer for the present, but, even more tragically, if they survive
to become adults, will have little chance of developing normal health and intelligence. This billion people, a quarter of the humans of the globe, will
receive at most $2\frac{1}{2}$ per cent of the world income this year for improving their
levels of living.

In the words of Sean MacBride: "Grossly unfair economic conditions, which still
condemn most human beings to starvation, disease and poverty, constitute in
themselves aggression against their victims".

The Basis for Action: Disarmament with Development

Experts in the economic aspects of security policy do not doubt that the economic imbalance and the tensions between North and South may lead to outright
war. We must intercept such a future war by another, where North and South
are on the same side, fighting against the common enemies of injustice and inequality.

The absurdity of the situation today is that incredible sums are wasted away
on weapons which are unusable in the war against poverty. These weapons are,

on the contrary, by their mere existence, a threat to the whole of humanity in
two respects. Firstly, they are extremely dangerous in themselves, and secondly, they divert resources from the struggle against starvation and need.

According to World Bank estimates, the basic investments required to overcome
the fundamental obstacles to development would be somewhere in the region of
12½ billion dollars a year over the next decade. An allocation of this size,
if supported by proper social structures, would meet the basic necessities of
human welfare — food and shelter, water supply and transportation, education,
health care. In The Home of Man, Barbara Ward sets these requirements in contrast to the actual level of military expenditures. She concludes: "If we take
the World Bank's estimate of basic needs, we reach the remarkable conclusion
that the entire proposed spending of work for peace for an entire decade would
amount to no more than half the world's annual bill for weapons".

In other words, barely 5% of what is now directed to military purposes would
be sufficient for an initial victory over the aggression of poverty on one
billion people.

However, we must not let our effort to reach economic and social justice wait
for an eventual slow-down and halt in the arms race. The fight must be carried
out on two fronts simultaneously. The war against inequity must be waged by
its own inherent necessity; development efforts must continue in far more intensified fashion independently of progress in disarmament, so long waited for
in vain. At the same time, we must never slacken in our efforts to demonstrate
to those engaged in the arms race, that they are, in fact, racing against their
own interests. They have reached, and now surpassed, the level where a further
increase in military power will not enhance their security. Rather, their way
to security lies through increasing their efforts to conquer world poverty, and
lay the foundation for economic and social equality.

The arms race has been explained to us in all its terrifying detail. Military
spending, military research and development continues at a rate previously
unknown. In the words of Professor Bernard Feld at the MIT: "The world is
entering upon perilous times, perhaps the most dangerous period in its entire
history. It is my judgment that the odds are around 1 in 3 that a nuclear weapon will be used in a conflict situation before the year 1984, and that the
chances are greater than 50/50 for nuclear war to occur in the years remaining in this century" (Bulletin of the Atomic Scientists).

The two superpowers together account for 60 per cent of the world's military
expenditures, a proportion which is larger than their share of the world's output, estimated at 45 per cent. As Mrs. Ruth Leger Sivard has shown in World
Military and Social Expenditures, the combined annual military expenditures of
these two countries alone substantially exceed the value of the annual GNP of
the continent of Africa In conventional as well as nuclear weaponry, the two
superpowers control more military force than all the other nations combined.

These facts are frightening enough in themselves. But there is another aspect
of this military dominance which is even more disturbing: that is, the US and
the USSR together account for 75 per cent of the world's arms trade. Through
competitive marketing activities they drive up the sales of the most modern
weapons; through favourable licensing arrangements they encourage the spread
of more and more sophisticated technology and productive facilities. Furthermore, military aid several times exceeds foreign aid given for development purposes. As Frank Barnaby's paper shows, weapons proliferated by the major mili-

tary powers to the conflict-stricken areas of the world are of the most sophisticated kind, incredibly accurate and extremely efficient.

Far from abating conflicts and promoting world security, weapons sales and
military aid in fact escalate fears and aggression. They never aim at coming
to grips with the underlying causes of a conflict.

Disarmament

Disarmament efforts continue to involve thousands of people all over the world
Here, again, the superpowers have been active. Some results have been reached
in SALT, and other bilateral negotiations which are welcomed. However, our
optimism in this respect should, for two reasons, be guarded.

1. Development in the armaments field tend to bypass disarmament agreements,
    making them ineffective. I would tend to agree with Barnaby and Neild that
    these bilateral disarmament negotiations seem to have led, on the whole
    and paradoxically, to a continuing armaments race.

2. There is also a risk that a bilateralization of disarmament negotiations
    will neglect the interests of other countries concerned. Disarmament is a
    concern to every single man, woman and child in every single country. The
    issue at stake is the survival of the human race. The outcome of SALT and
    other bilateral talks will have direct bearing on that issue. With this
    in mind, Sweden and many other non-aligned countries have pressed the
    superpowers for results in their negotiations.

At the same time we are continuing to work for a strengthening of multilateral
disarmament efforts. Activities of the Conference of the Committee on Disarmament (the CCD) in Geneva have been intensified. For this reason I am inclined
to disagree with those who advocate its break-up. Rather, it is of vital importance that the small and non-aligned countries members of the CCD join forces and play as active a role as possible, e.g. in submitting their own proposals for disarmament agreements, such as texts for a CTB agreement.

As for the United Nations, a General Assembly Ad Hoc Committee met last year
in three sessions to discuss the role of the UN in the disarmament field. The
proposals of this committee aimed at activating the organization as well as its
member states, giving the UN new responsibilities and strengthening its secretariat unit. These proposals have largely been accepted by the General Assembly and are now being implemented.

In the discussions of the Ad Hoc Committee the role of the Non-Government
Organizations was stressed in more than one context. Even if the rules of the
house, in accordance with the Charter, prevent the NGOs from taking part in
the actual debates, they have a very important task, both in raising public
opinion at the national level (by exerting pressure on politicians responsible
for disarmament negotiations) and in lobbying in the corridors of the UN.
Disarmament negotiators, multilateral and bilateral, have often enough been
severely criticized, even ridiculed, for the lack of results in their work.
They are rightly criticized, but less correctly ridiculed. The lack of momentum in the negotiations is deplorable enough, but it is still important that
negotiations are at least carried on. It is for enlightened, concerned and
involved citizens to impress upon politicians and decision-makers the need to
speed up activities and present concrete results.

Disarmament and Development

At the same time, it is important that we do not content ourselves only with the actual disarmament efforts. World disarmament is needed for world development — but equally, world development is a prerequisite for world disarmament. Not until we have arrived at a situation of reasonable equity and economic balance in the world, will it be possible to develop conditions for a lasting disarmament.

In spite of the many problems afflicting the highly developed countries in the present crisis of capitalism and free market forces, a number of countries of the industrialized world today have still proved it to be possible to reach a situation of general social stability, where internal conflicts are, generally, solved by negotiations according to agreed rules. On a national level we work at eliminating the causes of conflicts — social injustices, economic inequalities, regional differences. This has been accepted by all democratic political parties for a long time as necessary for the functioning of our modern societies. Why are these lessons not applied also to the international society?

This will require fresh thinking and new approaches; it must not be bounded by stereotypes already known not to work.

In recent years, in one context after another, fresh thinking *has* been applied, concrete proposals have been put forward on norms, methods, and tactics, for constructive work with these problems. Important examples are the global UN conferences during the 70s, the 6th and 7th special sessions of the General Assembly on the international order, the Hammarskjold Foundation report What Now?, studies such as that by the Leontief group for the UN on the future of the world economy.

Studies, research and debates are going on in numerous national and international groups, in industrialized as well as developing countries. The RIO group, working on Reshaping the International Order under the eminent leadership of Professor Jan Tinbergen, scanned the situation of the world, sector by sector, including, for the first time in the context of global problems, the armaments race. We confirmed the shortcomings, the wants and scarcities with regard to the most elementary of human needs. In addition, we worked out integrated strategies for initiating and negotiating a multi-dimensional change, which would, as we expressed it in our report, lead to "a life of dignity and well-being for all".

Like the World Bank, we found that a yearly instalment of around 15 billion dollars for 10 years should be sufficient for meeting the basic necessities. Out of these, the developing countries already set aside some 3-4 billion for social development, leaving some 10-12 billion dollars to be contributed by the industrialized countries, indeed only 4 per cent of the yearly cost of weapons.

The RIO report proposes the negotiation of comprehensive packages of proposals, implying a process of give and take, an element of collective bargaining. A precondition for successful negotiations is, of course, the substantial strengthening of the negotiating position of the most disadvantaged countries. This implies fundamental changes in the power structure of the world since true interdependence can only be established between equals.

For the negotiations, we put forward three distinct packages of proposals:

1. proposals aimed at removing the gross inequities in the distribution of
    world income and economic opportunities;

2. proposals to ensure a more harmonious growth of the global economic system,
    and

3. proposals to provide the beginnings of a global planning system.

We stress emphatically that the highest priority should be afforded to working
out a "global compact on poverty", designed to attack the worst forms of poverty all over the globe over the course of the next decade. "Such an effort",
we say in the report, "would, effectively administered, serve not only the
cause of equity and justice but should improve political stability and advance
the date when population stability would be achieved and concessional aid
would no longer be required".

Once there is a truly serious decision taken for constructive co-operation towards new social and economic goals, in a spirit of equality rather than of
competition in power, or military might, the financial costs for the rich
countries and the political costs for the poorest countries are both within
manageable limits.

Mrs. Sivard, whom I have quoted already, admirably illustrates the effects of
such a redistribution of resources by saying: "What could 5 per cent of the
total military expenditures — 15 billion dollars — do to reduce the world's
vast social deficit?" And she presents the following possibilities* for
international co-operative programmes for peaceful purposes — together, as
she says, representing "a start on a formidable fund for peace".

For 200 million malnourished children, supplementary protein feeding to ensure full brain development	$4 billion
For poor countries on the edge of famine, increased agricultural investment to enlarge food production	$3 billion
Expansion of primary schools, with the addition of 100 million new places for children not now attending school	$3 billion
Emergency aid and a permanent international relief force to assist disaster-stricken countries	$2 billion
World-wide programme for prevention of dental decay by fluoridation	$1.5 billion
Basic education for 25 million adults now illiterate	$1 billion
World-wide campaign to eradicate malaria	$450 million
Iron supplement to protect 300 million children and women of childbearing ages against anaemia	$45 million
Vitamin supplement to protect 100 million children 1-5 years against blindness caused by Vitamin A deficiency	$5 million
Total	$15 billion

---

*op. cit. 1976. Further details and slight variations of these proposals
will be found in the centre section, taken from the 1977 version of World
Military and Social Expenditures.

Political Action

This is where we have to start from. These are the alternatives which should
be pressed on politicians, to generate the will for constructive action.

The task seems to be obvious to any rational being. Unfortunately, the truth
is that politics is seldom a rational business. The responsibility now rests
with orindary people to wake up the world, to start a mass movement for peace
and development.

The problems *are* indeed tremendous. When pointed out to people in terms of
doom-saying, they can quite easily be made to seem so overwhelming, that many
will find the prospects for the future unbearably dismal. This might well be
counter-productive to our purpose, as it easily creates feelings of hopeless-
ness and despair, paralysing the will of action.

Recalling something said in one of C.P. Snow's Eliot-books: "When men believe
that events are too big for them, there is no hope". I agree with those who
emphasize, instead, that the necessary and far-reaching changes in attitudes
and actions cannot be motivated by fear-creating doom-sayers. On the contrary,
the active and positive support of these changes can be enlisted through presenting a positive image of a future *that is possible*, once the will to constructive action is mobilized.

To me, working since my early youth within the labour movement, that would
seem to be from all points of view a very appropriate illustration to the mass
movement needed. Looking at the formidable effects of workers' action, we wit-
ness an irresistible tide of change surging over Europe, over the world. From
the late 19th century, after the turn of the century, and during the following
decades, thousands, millions of people were engaged by the ideals of solidarity,
of justice and equality — winning political power in one country after another.
This year, a century later, we are about to start the same movement, this time
on an international scale: for solidarity, justice, and equality over the
world.

It is my firm belief that this new action, the movement of "humanistic socialism", will prove as strong and irresistible a force as the labour movement —
creating a world in which opportunities and the means to use those opportunities are more equitably distributed.

We must counteract the stupefying forces of the present world system, which
hypnotize people in the industrialized world into a false security and happi-
ness, based on the acquisition of more and more sophisticated material goods,
at the same time closing their eyes to the real dangers, looming higher and
higher around them.

We must start by alerting every single man and woman and, in particular, young
people (on whom the hypnosis may not yet have had full effect) to a sense of
real participation in a true life, instead of merely consuming one manufactured
by industrial technology. We must inspire them to take the responsibility for
themselves, for their people — for the world. To create a sense that we ourselves, each and every one of us, truly matter, that each has a power of really accomplishing something. Without faith in our own life we will not care
about the lives of others.

But this is clearly not enough.

D.W.D.—H

The Basis for a New Effort

Politicians and concerned citizens must also reach an understanding on both
the programme and methods of change.

First, we have to accept that we still do not know enough about how the transformation from societies competing in a deadly armaments race, to societies
joining forces for a constructive change to justice, equity and well-being for
all, will take place. Modern societies are immensely complex, with very fixed
structures. How do we move such societies into a completely new direction,
based on new values and attitudes regarding international solidarity? This is
the great political challenge facing us.

Secondly, how are we to achieve it? Again, from the common experience of all
those who have worked in the labour movement, we have learnt that it pays to
organize enormous pressure from below, on the existing political structures.
In order to obtain the necessary strength to achieve this, we have to find the
ways and means by which to reach beyond those already converted, to reach those
who do not yet know enough and/or who do not yet have the necessary will to act
in a co-operative effort in their own interest.

Fundamental to all our efforts is information, education. We must repeat the
illustrative facts and figures of the arms race and the economic inequities.
We must throw new light on them, set them into a new perspective. We must un-
tiringly bombard people, that these are issues that matter in a concrete way,
to each one of us, to the development not only of societies far away, but to
that of our own society, and consequently, to our own jobs, our own ways of
living and to generations coming after us. We must keep hammering into people
that each and every one is responsible, each and every one can do something
about it.

We know that the military systems of the world exert a very hard pressure on
responsible politicians and decision-makers. This is due to a number of reasons — the inherent dynamics of technological development, supported by the
excessive budgetary secrecy, as well as heavy industrial interests, aside from
hard-core arguments of security policy.

To be able to exert counter-pressure, we must start by scrutinizing all those
arguments, put forward in support of a continuing strong arms industry and
trade, from the point of view of rational utilization of national and global
resources.

What about the half million scientists and the millions of workers, engaged in
military research and military industrial production all over the world? In
times of serious unemployment, the persistent argument is that we must not
make matters worse by making also these people unemployed. This argument is
made to look more and more relevant, the more directly you are involved in
local politics. Yet it is an invalid argument. The services of the half-mil-
lion scientists are more demanded in fields of constructive development — in
medical services, improvement of the human environment, development of alternative sources of energy, nutrition, education. There are dozens and dozens
of objectives with vast development possibilities. Similarly, the work of the
millions of industrial employees will be demanded in industries, producing
capital and other goods for the enormous potential markets of the three quarters of the world that are still called "developing".

Since military expenditures are, largely, unproductive, a redirection of military industry might be directly beneficial to the productivity of a country. These are matters which should be further investigated.

What tax-payer would not wish his money to be economically productive? What politician would stand up to defend a waste of tax-payers' money on unproductive purposes, moreover purposes that are not only unproductive, but directly fatal?

Military expenditure also has a directly inflationary impact on our economies. What politican would stand up to defend the maintenance of an industry causing inflation?

Mrs. Alva Myrdal has proposed that governments should be requested to work out plans for a redirection of their military industries, and to give in regular reports on these plans, and their continuous updating, to the UN. Plans should also be drawn up for a diversification of military production, to prevent it from monopolizing either a specific industry, or a specific community.

There is still the security argument: "After all, we must be prepared to pay for our security". National security is a recognized objective of the efforts of a society. But, in the nuclear age, is our security really promoted by unlimited armaments?

In 1958, this question was answered by Philip Noel-Baker, in his pertinent way. "The romanticists", he says, "are those who still believe that modern armaments can make a nation safe. There is no military defence today for any nation, except in drastic measures of disarmament, embodied in a multilateral treaty to which all governments subscribe".

Since 1958, armaments have escalated unto a level where there are 15 tons of explosives in store for every single man, woman and child all over the world. This is beyond the level where it is at all possible to keep any nation in any way secure.

Diffusing economic and social tensions

At the same time, as we have seen, other than purely military factors are growing in importance in the relations between states. The grave economic imbalances affect all countries negatively. Lasting security will only be obtained through an equitable economic and social development, a development leading to cultural freedom, and a deepfelt respect for human rights. Politicians and decision-makers of the industrialized countries must realize that it is in their own interests — and in the interests of their own societies — that the economic and political imbalances of the world are corrected.

People of the industrialized countries must co-operate with people of the developing countries in exerting pressure on politicians at home and abroad on the inevitability of a reshaping of the world system at all levels. Reforms are necessary on a national level in the developing and developed countries alike, as well as on a regional level, and on a global level. The eyes of politicians on both sides must be opened for development options of a long-term nature, and for the long-term consequences of alternative world orders.

It is in this work, in the analysis of the global situation, that disarmament

becomes particularly relevant. Options must be clearly presented: arms or
development? How much arms? What kind of development?

Real negotiations on the future world order must get started. An attempt at
one form of negotiation has been made in the North-South dialogue in Paris,
which, as was to be expected, has demonstrated the vast difficulties of such
efforts. We will be able to learn a lot from the experiences of the Paris
negotiators. Even if the results may seem discouraging, we must continue —
although not necessarily in the same form. It is only in co-operation between
industrialized and developing countries in a state of self-reliance that we
may eventually find a mode of survival.

The term "global rationality" has been coined to characterize the necessary
atmosphere for this development to take place. I believe that we would be able
to create such an atmosphere by establishing and winning recognition of four
main principles:

first   —by achieving universal recognition of the equality, in theory and
            practice, between nations and people;

second —by reaching a universal recognition of the global and interrelated
            issues of our time, leading to growing interdependencies between
            nations;

third   —by reconciling this fact and the need of earlier suppressed and still
            underprivileged states for national self-assertion and self-reliance;

fourth —by working for constructive steps towards real disarmament for the
            achievement of rational and responsible management of resources, for
            true economic and social development, for a life in peace, dignity
            and well-being for all.

The implementation of measures inspired by such an atmosphere requires a continuing process of change. It is sometimes said that development is a historical process, which by necessity takes time. Through the convergence of several forces at work, we seem, however, to have arrived at a moment of historic
discontinuity, which, if the opportunity it offers is properly used, could
result in fundamental and constructive changes in the present world order.

Postscript

The above contribution represents the main contents of a statement given at
the UNA Conference for Disarmament and Development in early January 1977.
Since then, disarmament efforts have taken up a new momentum of considerable
strength. The reason seems to be the decision by the General Assembly in late
1976 to convene the Special Session of the Assembly devoted to disarmament in
May/June 1978. This decision has already shown its importance in at least
three ways:

First: The Special Session is being prepared by an ad hoc committee, the
            fourth meeting of which is being held in January-February 1978. Its
            work so far has proved to be both constructive and productive. Even
            more — it has been carried out in a positive spirit and with the
            active participation of the leading powers in the two military blocks.
            At the General Assembly regular session in autumn 1977 there was even

some expectation in the air that already before the Special Session, and to a great extent because of its being convened, some results in disarmament may be forthcoming. The Session itself will not solve, through negotiation, any disarmament problem. But it will have to be seen as an important first step in a new phase of disarmament efforts. A forceful and well planned follow-up, through implementation of the programme of action that is generally supposed to be adopted by the session, is therefore of imperative importance to the world in the next few years.

Second: Based on a proposal by the Nordic countries, the Special Session is supposed to initiate a UN study on the impact of the arms race on economic and social development. The study will have to examine the ways in which material and human resources are utilized, as well as the effects of armaments on international and national economies. It will have to lead up to providing the world with the necessary mechanisms to meet the requirements of a redeployment of national resources from military purposes to constructive and peaceful ends. This would include mechanisms for re-allocating resources to development efforts in the developing countries. This could dramatically alter the prospects for economic and social development, nationally as well as internationally, and promote the ultimate realization of the goals of a new international economic order.

Third: All through the year of 1977, non-governmental organizations have stepped up their activities to arouse public opinion and establish effective pressure on governments finally to do something for disarmament. Well planned conferences have been held, meetings between government representatives and concerned citizens have been organized, efforts are being made to reach mass media — these activities represent a forceful expression of the will of people to demand effective action towards disarmament and peace — indeed, the strongest expression since the end of the second world war.

Objectives and Means for Linking
Disarmament to Development

Richard Jolly

If measures of disarmament are to be combined effectively with measures for poverty-eradicating development at least four steps must be taken:

1. There must be a shift in the world pattern of production away from armaments production, particularly in the main armaments producing developed countries but also within many, if not most, of the developing countries.

2. There must be a corresponding shift towards a more peaceful, development-oriented pattern of production and consumption, focussed particularly on the needs of the poorest groups and poorest countries.

3. Internationally the flows of foreign exchange and resources sustaining present expenditures on the purchase and production of armaments and other military requirements need to be reduced and replaced by flows to meet the requirements of this different development pattern.

4. The coalitions of interest, political and economic, commercial and technical, public and private, national and international, which sustain the present flows of armaments and military expenditures will need to be consciously weakened or shifted in ways which reduce the momentum of the arms race and gradually build up "vested interests" for implementing and sustaining the other three changes.

Merely to identify these four steps is to indicate something of the problems which their implementation on a sustained basis will involve. Financial estimates of what might be saved by measures of disarmament and what might be available for spending on measures of development are striking but altogether too simple. It would be fortuitous if the structural shifts out of armaments production were exactly to match the new requirements for basic needs production in terms of either employment, investment, exports or imports, public revenue or expenditure — let alone all of these together with the political repercussions which they would set in train.

Yet at the same time, it is clearly incorrect to argue that such changes are a together out of the question. On certain historical occasions, decisive changes of this sort have taken place. Moreover, the measures now required are clearly long term and over the long term changes of structure, large and small, planned or unplanned, are continuously taking place and will continue to do so. The issues involved in deliberately planning for a measure of *conscious* structural change in the future relate therefore to the extent to which objectives can be clarified in advance, the specific steps to achieve them identified and the means to pursue them effectively agreed by those with power to support or obstruct their achievement.

What therefore might be appropriate development objectives for a programme combining development with disarmament?

Strategies for Poverty-focussed Development

The critical economic priority in the Third World is for many more developing countries to redirect their economies towards strategies focussed on the elimination of poverty and the provision of basic needs for all their population. This priority has been increasingly recognised in the last few years, though inevitably action lags far behind rhetoric and resolutions in national and international meetings. For the purposes of such strategies, basic needs have been defined to cover:

(a) basic consumption needs — essentially food to meet minimum consumption and nutrition standards, clothing and housing;

(b) basic essential services — access to clean water, sanitation, basic education, health facilities and public transport;

(c) productive employment, defined as the opportunity to earn sufficient income in cash or kind to enable individuals and their families to meet their basic needs;

(d) participation — the opportunity for all groups to influence the decisions which affect themselves and their local communities.

In its major document for the World Employment Conference, Employment Growth and Basic Needs: A One-World Problem,[1] the ILO estimated that in 1972 there were some 1,200 million persons in developing market economies living in poverty, of whom some 700 million were so poor as to be "destitute". This document and the international conference at which it was discussed in 1976 identified some of the main elements of national economic strategy to provide for these basic needs. It noted that in many, if not most, developing countries, a continuation of development on the pattern of the 1950s and 1960s would still leave hundreds of millions of persons in poverty at the end of the century. To avoid this a major change of strategy would be required, not minor alterations of direction, let alone marginal improvements to past performance. In many developing countries, the whole thrust of strategy, rural and urban, would need to be changed, to give much greater priority to meeting basic needs in all regions, all sectors and all areas of government policy. For the majority of the poorer nations, the strategy would not mean a neglect of economic growth but the need for a combination of growth *with* redistribution. Neither growth nor redistribution on their own would be sufficient to provide basic needs for all before the turn of the century.

These domestic changes of strategy will need to be supplemented and supported internationally to enable countries to provide the additional resources which they, particularly the poorer nations, would require to implement a basic needs strategy within a reasonable time horizon. But changes in international relationships and practices will also be required if developing countries are to achieve a greater degree of "self-reliance", the fuller control over their own economies and resources required to effect these basic changes of economic direction and strategy. These international changes over a wide field of economic and social issues are increasingly seen as part of a more general need for a New International Economic Order, which has received strong emphasis from Third World countries over the last few years.

These core ideas have attracted growing support to the point where they probably now represent a consensus among the development community of the main priorities for current development strategy, national and international. They would therefore seem appropriate priorities to embody in an integrated prog-ramme for combining measures of world disarmament with world development.

Possible Links with Disarmament — the resources involved

The links between these development priorities and disarmament have until recently received relatively little attention. Of course, certain individual groups and specialist committees — and far-seeing individuals — have never lost sight of the connection between world development and world disarmament. The United Nations has produced over the years since the Second World War a steady stream of reports on these themes. But largely the two major challenges of development and disarmament have remained separate.

In part this separation may be because there is no logically necessary link between the two issues. Indeed there is a strategic argument for not linking them directly, lest difficulties in achieving one are used as an argument for postponing action on the other. The 1972 UN groups of experts on the economic and social consequences of disarmament, for instance, stated in their report:

> "Disarmament and development are of the greatest importance
> to the world community. But fundamentally they stand separ-
> ately from one another. The United Nations has agreed to
> seek each one vigorously in its own right, regardless of
> the pace of progress in approaching the other. Specifically,
> nations have agreed that national and international efforts
> to promote development should be neither postponed nor
> allowed to lag merely because progress in disarmament is
> slow."

> "However, disarmament and development can be linked to each
> other because the enormous amount of resources wasted in
> the arms race might be utilized to facilitate development
> and progress. Furthermore, the blatant contrast between
> this waste of resources and the unfilled needs of develop-
> ment can be used to help rouse public opinion in favour
> of effective disarmament, and in favour of the achievement
> of further progress in development particularly of the
> developing countries."

In the last two or three years, however, the blatant contrast between the scale of world expenditure on armaments and the severe limits on expenditure set by recession and measures to combat inflation has made the link between disarmament and development almost inescapable. The volume of resources con-sumed, the bias in the technologies created and the whole direction of develop-ment encouraged by this massive concentration on armaments have long passed the point when either the *level* or the *pattern* of armaments expenditure can be ignored or treated as a problem separate from that of eradicating world poverty.

The costs of this diversion of resources into armaments and military activities is indicated by the staggering size of the financial expenditure incurred each year. As a world total and as a share of national budgets in many countries, both rich and poor, such expenditure equals or exceeds the large sums spent on the resources directed towards all forms of health or education, let alone the much smaller sums spent on most of the basic needs of the poorer sections of the population. The World Bank has estimated that the provision of basic needs

for the poorest quarter of the world's population, roughly between 800 and
1,200 million persons, would cost $125 billion in capital expenditures over
the next 10 years. The stark contrast between the nobility of this objective
attainable with an expenditure of merely *one-twentieth* of that projected for
world armaments over the same period underlines the disastrous and inhuman
diversion to armaments which might otherwise be turned to peace and humane
progress.

Structural Changes

Inevitably, such global, financial estimates of the waste and diversion of
resources into armaments which might otherwise be turned to basic development
are vastly over-simplified. Their very simplicity has an obvious attraction
in terms of headlines to hit the media: they contain no doubt a rough and
ready truth in the recognition that the estimated *financial* costs of providing
for many of the world's basic needs within a decade are less than half one
year's expenditure on armaments. But clearly the figures are no more than the
roughest orders of magnitude since, as explained already, very much more is
involved than a shift in public expenditure. Indeed, such financial estimates
can be seriously misleading because they tend to divert attention from the political and social dimensions of the changes involved — and even to disguise the
changes in the economic *structures* which would be required in both developed and
developing countries and in the nature of economic relationships between them.[2]

Within the industrialized countries, these changes would be far from marginal:
movement would be required out of the armaments-related industries into those
involved with the production of peaceful goods and parallel changes in research
and development, transportation, government and private finance, possibly even
regional policy would be needed. These would not be easy to accomplish, nor
would they be once for all changes. Moreover, the dynamics of the industrialized economies would be significantly altered, with the thrust of technological
development moving significantly out of the armaments, defence, air and space
related industries into others more directly focussed on the needs and welfare
of ordinary people.

This is not to suggest that the resources freed by disarmament would not be
immensely useful in improving living standards and life-styles in developed
countries as well as in support of a programme directed towards the eradication
of poverty. Nor is it to doubt the conclusion of the UN Working Party on
Disarmament and Development that

> "most of the resources released by disarmament, total or
> partial, will be readily transferable to other uses — for
> example, manpower, food, clothing, transport, fuel and
> products of the metal and engineering industries ...
> according to [our] analysis, the number of industries
> suffering negative impact would be smaller when the replace-
> ment for military expenditure is assistance to developing
> countries than when the replacement is domestic personal
> consumption". (*op. cit.* para 37)

Moreover, there may be positive effects on growth or potential growth: an MIT
study estimated these to be a gain of 1 per cent in growth rate for each 1 per
cent reduction of GNP devoted to military uses. And finally, there will be
beneficial effects in moderating the rate of inflation due to the reduction of
such large expenditures on essentially unproductive uses of resources.

There is no doubt that in the long run these changes could offer wide and very large benefits within industrial countries and in making it possible to meet other objectives, directed in particular to meeting basic needs in less developed countries. The extent to which all this could follow from any specific measures of disarmament is technically almost beyond present calculation, if large non-marginal changes are involved. All one can say is that the freeing of resources could be very large indeed, incomparably larger than anything we have seen so far within programmes of international aid.

These resources could be of enormous benefit to the Third World, but major changes of domestic policy would, in many cases, also be required if they are to contribute effectively to the meeting of basic needs. Indeed, the critical needs are not primarily matters of increases in expenditure or even of major transfers of resources from the industrialized countries. They are, as explained above, more fundamentally a matter of a total change in the direction of development in the Third World — in ways which strengthen the production of goods and services which meet basic needs. The institutions and patterns of production, land ownership and government administration may also need restructuring to ensure that all persons, but particularly the rural poor, have sufficient incomes and the opportunities and position to enjoy them. The diversity of situations within Third World countries is too great to generalize in more detail over the specific changes that would be required. In countries which are predominantly rural, with existing structures heavily weighted to the advantage of a small urban elite, the whole balance of development between the rural and urban sectors and within the rural sector would need to be altered. In countries where the external economic relationships have dominated the whole pattern of internal development a move to a greater degree of self-reliance will be essential.

It would be wrong to underestimate the fundamental nature of these changes. Roughly half the Third World countries are ruled by military regimes and a shift from military expenditure to peaceful, poverty-focussed development may obviously represent a fundamental change in the very base of power which sustains the regime. One can scarcely expect this change to be willingly accepted, let alone actively welcomed. At the same time, it would again be wrong to dismiss out of hand the possibility of such changes taking place. In the first place, there is a diversity of situations within the Third World. In some, including some military regimes, recent years have seen a move against the trend of increasing military expenditure and a strengthening of broad-based development-focussed activities. Second, it may sometimes be in the interests of a regime precisely to support and seek such changes — to widen their base of popular support, even to implement the ideals of a reforming government. Third, internationally there can be pressures on Third World regimes to lower military expenditure and to give greater emphasis to meeting the basic needs of their populations.

For the purposes of assessing the possibilities, one can identify three groups of Third World countries. In the first group are those countries, probably fairly few, already clearly committed to a development strategy which gives high priority to raising the living standards of the mass of the population and to the eradication of poverty. Almost any additional resources provided from abroad to these countries will further these objectives but at the same time their objectives are being and will be pursued regardless of outside support. At the other end of the spectrum is the third group of countries, usually in the power of a narrow elite, whose concern with mass welfare or poverty eradication is paper thin, if expressed at all. Without fundamental

changes in the direction of their development strategies, there is little that
the international community can do to improve the lot of the poor within these
countries: even a large inflow of additional resources from abroad will readily
be diverted into the pockets of the rich and powerful.

Often preoccupation with these two groups of countries or situations leads
people to argue that there is nothing which the international community can or
need do to relieve Third World poverty. But this is to ignore a third group
of countries, in the middle of the spectrum, in which the balance of interests
and power offers some freedom of manoeuvre. Development strategies or policies
in these countries are by no means directed primarily to mass welfare or poverty
eradication — but they do give some place to these objectives and with additional resources and outside support could give more. It follows that programmes linking measures of disarmament to development in these countries should
have a special place in a world programme of disarmament and development.

The Starting Points for Change

To see the problem as one of changing structures of production and international
economic relations is to identify a different strategy or at least emphasis for
a programme of disarmament focussed on development. The arena of decision and
negotiations is in part shifted away from the international world of disarmament and diplomacy and towards a multiplicity of national centres and groups
involved in decision-making about national structures of production and consumption, public expenditure and trade. The starting point, particularly within
rich countries, are those groups in government, industry and unions which have
a stake in the present patterns of production and a voice in determining how
they will change in the future. The focus must be on the industrial-military
complex and, one must now add, its technological research complexes, long ago
identified by Eisenhower as critically sustaining the present military concentration. These groups, in different ways in different countries, are involved
in the coalitions of interest which have led to the present situation. They
will be involved in the changes which move away from it. This will only be
possible if these changes are planned in ways which provide employment and incomes to replace those which a reduction in armaments and military activity
will imply.

The changes are obviously formidable, perhaps so formidable and fundamental
that many may doubt whether they could ever be possible. It would be a dangerous mistake to underestimate the nature of the changes required. But at the
same time for three reasons it is difficult to argue that the situation is
completely unalterable. First, one has seen changes of greater relative magnitude before — at the end of the Second World War for a number of countries and
at the end of the First World War (and on other occasions) for a more limited
group. When the political and economic conditions are right, substantial disarmament, with attendant changes of economic structure, can take place, as it
has already. Second, the structural changes involved in a shift away from the
armaments production and military activities, though enormous, are no larger
than certain shifts in the structure of economic production which have taken
place in recent years within many individual countries and in the nature of
trading relations between them — the run down of coal, textile, electronics
production within many industrialized countries, with the rise of production
in these sectors in parts of the Third World, notably in Mexico, Brazil, Korea
and some of the smaller successful Third World exporting nations. Shifts in
the structure of production do take place — if only the dynamic of change is

right. Third, as explained above, the changes would not merely be possible
but could have major beneficial effects on employment and the pattern of development in the developed countries themselves. Indeed in terms of taxation,
inflation, technological advances and the freeing of resources for other uses,
there is a strong case for arguing that these changes would significantly
raise the living standards of the majority of people in the industrialized countries themselves — an important factor when assessing likely political support.

From Disarmament to Development

If disarmament for development will require this broad-ranging set of changes,
one can at least summarize the critical arenas for action and some potential
alliances which may make it possible. There are perhaps four. First, within
the industrialized countries, the adjustments away from the production and export of armaments must be linked to a more fundamental questioning of the whole
pattern of development. The broad issue is how to achieve an alternative development pattern, altering gradually but steadily and fundamentally many of the
trends of recent decades in order to move to a more human-centred style of
economic and social life. Second, within developing countries, the same fundamental changes of structure and development patterns must also be considered —
though inevitably with more emphasis on basic needs, at least in the foresee-
able future. Third, internationally critical relationships between countries,
particularly those related to the international division of labour, need to be
brought under some measure of international co-ordination and control. This
will mean a much closer integration of changes in national production and international trade. Clearly, with national planning so often discredited and in
disarray, we are far from a position where comprehensive international plans
of production are either feasible or even desirable. But this is no reason for
defending the international anarchy which currently prevails, economically and
legally with respect to most shifts of production and flows of resources. This
underlines the fact that serious measures to lower the level of armaments activity are only part of the broader measures to achieve a re-structuring of national and international economic activity. Fourthly, these measures must provide for a continuing concern with security and political control. Here, there
is probably a need for more attention to regional arrangements in which the
simple polarizations of the post Second World War would give place to a more
complex set of political and even military relationships, to ensure minimum
needs for security but to avoid, as far as possible, escalations beyond them.

Equally, if not more, important for security will be measures to diminish
"structural violence" — the extremes of inequality and exploitation which are
found too often within the world economy and which current political and economic institutions too readily permit. The enormity of current expenditures on
armaments and military measures designed to tackle situations of "direct violence" (but often ironically contributing directly to them) contrast startlingly
with the paucity of expenditure and effort explicitly designed to diminish
"structural violence". Of course, measures to tackle both "direct" and "structural" violence involve risks and uncertainties, but this is no justification
for such an enormity of overspending in one direction and such disproportionate
underspending in the other. This ultimately is the reason for arguing that
security and defence could be enhanced if measures of disarmament were combined
with measures of development.

NOTES

1. See also the report and resolution of the conference, also published by
    the ILO (Geneva), Meeting Basic Needs: strategies for eradicating mass
    poverty and unemployment, 1977.

2. There are also more technical economic reasons why purely financial measures
    of resource use based on existing market prices are inappropriate when non-
    marginal changes are being considered and when base period prices are often
    "administered" or determined in markets heavily influenced by government or
    a few large companies. For all these reasons a variety of disaggregated
    measures of the resources used in military activities and how they distort
    development patterns are almost certainly a better guide to the real costs
    of military and armaments activities than a single financial statistic.

Approaches to Disarmament

Robert Neild

Arms trade and disarmament — the different approaches

It may be useful to outline the alternative approaches to disarmament and ask what can we expect from each. The first is the traditional global approach in which it is proposed that all nations should agree in a treaty for General and Complete Disarmament simultaneously to disarm according to an agreed timetable. It is an approach devised from the inter-war years when disarmament essentially concerned the major European nations plus the US and Japan — a small, largely contiguous group for whom simultaneity of action was important if no one was to gain a transnational advantage. This approach is often backed by a global statistical drama — produced by estimating how much a cut in military expenditure would release for various virtuous purposes. One example of this is the supposed link between a world cut in armaments expenditure and an increase in international aid devoted to meeting basic needs. This approach has been pursued on a number of occasions since the Second World War.

In parallel have gone the negotiations of partial disarmament measures (or "arms control" measures). The partial test ban (which reduced pollution), the ocean bed treaty, SALT and MBFR negotiations are examples which have led essentially to cosmetic measures — proposals which the military do not object to, and which give the appearance of progress, but which essentially are agreements about not doing things that nobody wants to do, or negotiations which purport to make progress but produce nothing. Both general disarmament, and the production by the UN of global reports expounding statistical dramas, have been looked upon fairly cynically, in my view, by the superpowers and their followers, including Britain.

There is everything to be said for keeping up the pressure for general disarmament but we must recognize the difficulty of the approach. One is asking for agreements from governments which are dominated by the military and by intellectual strategists. It is very unlikely that the governments of the Superpowers, with their present political bases and interests, will agree to anything like a major measure of disarmament. We must therefore be very hardheaded and critical in keeping up pressure for progress and yet refrain from implicitly endorsing partial measures and phoney negotiations which are little more than a charade.

The second main approach is to decompose the problem and explore measures to reduce military expenditures and armaments trade within limited geographical areas. One obvious proposal is to stop the arms trade and in that way to isolate the arms race in some degree within an area of the advanced countries. The difficulty with this approach is that a flat embargo on exports primarily affects those countries that cannot produce arms themselves whilst leaving those which can in a much stronger position. For example, if arms are cut off from the countries surrounding South Africa, South Africa itself will continue to produce arms on her own and black neighbours will have been relatively weakened. An alternative is to explore the possibility of regional agreements

for disarmament. These might involve, for example, some limitation on the
level of armaments in each country of a region. These would need to be supported by agreements from supplying nations, to the effect that they will not
try to break the agreement by forcing arms in and they would need to be backed
up by their acceptance of some central monitoring system run by the recipient
countries themselves. The purpose of such a system would be to see that arms
are not pushed into the region in ways that break agreed limits. The merit of
measures of this kind is that instead of being actions imposed by the supplying nations on weaker nations, which imply an element of dictatorship and dis-
crimination, one is suggesting, where possible, that regions should voluntar-
ily make their own arrangements. The supplying nations should be committed to
support any agreement only if requested by the parties to the agreement. Obviously such co-operation will not be easy. It will depend on finding suitable
areas, both with limited arms levels and with sufficient political harmony between one nation and another. Secondly within the nations involved, the governments and rival factions must not be tempted to seek the sort of militarist
route to maintaining their position within their society which needs outside
support. In other words, one is assuming that one has a set of countries
which are either in a state of innocence or somehow have escaped from the kind
of militarized societies which presently exist. Clearly this will not be easy,
but possibly, by starting small, one might be able to find areas of the world
where this kind of approach might be feasible.

Restraint by individual arms suppliers is a third desirable and feasible policy.
Besides political and military difficulties, however, this involves economic
difficulties particularly with respect to sophisticated arms. These arise because the technological race to develop weapons has resulted in huge research
and development costs before any armaments are actually produced. This means
the burden of producing weapons-systems becomes extremely great, particularly
for smaller producing countries, unless one exports to help cover the enormous
overhead costs.

Conversely, to stop exporting may imply that one has to stop producing sophisticated weapons which in turn may lead either to dependence on other suppliers
(thereby compromising one's freedom of action) or neutrality or the adoption
of an alternative strategy such as civilian resistance.

Having described the difficulties of national restraint in arms exports, we
can examine its advantages by studying Sweden as a test case. Sweden has a
remarkably sound policy involving virtually no exporting of arms. The arms
that Sweden exports are on a very limited scale and directed to countries who
are very unlikely to use them.

The benefits are, first, that to the extent that the number of countries supplying arms is reduced, the degree of competition may be diminished which in
turn can improve the possibilities of restraint by agreement or collusion
amongst the remaining suppliers. In this context, however, one should note
that difficulties have occurred at those odd moments when the Russians and the
Americans have agreed not to supply arms, or to limit the supply of arms (to
the Middle East for instance). In these cases, lesser powers have eagerly
filled the arms vacuum, thereby nullifying the initial agreement. Nevertheless
the possibilities of collusive restraint are probably greater the fewer the
number of suppliers. On the other hand, the purchaser is left in a more polar-
ized position having to choose from a more limited number of suppliers. The
second benefit of restraint relates to the basic anti-militaristic posture
which the Swedes have taken. This posture is in part a cause of supply res-

traint and in part a consequence of it: once a country has adopted a policy
of restraint in supplying arms, then the anti-militaristic philosophies and
policies of arms restraint interact, thereby reducing the power of the vested
interests of the military establishment.

At the moment the difficulties of achieving restraint in arms export from the
UK would be great because of the recession following the rise in the price of
oil. This has given the oil countries substantial foreign exchange which they
happily spend on arms. In addition, there are powerful economic forces inducing the industrialized nations to compete in selling arms to the Middle East.
I believe this to be a short-sighted policy even in military terms, as it
appears unlikely that the Middle East market for weapons will stabilize at anywhere near its present level. But it is important to stress that the basic
difficulty of getting a policy of abstinence adopted in a country like Britain
involves the commitment to an anti-military posture and attitude to the
nation's security problems and interests. This virtually requires the effective withdrawal from the Arms Race and the Cold War, as well as from the arms
export business.

Canada is a country which has effected this withdrawal. It was involved
through the commitment of troops in Europe but has quietly withdrawn from it
and spends very little on defence as a result. It now has a rather positive
policy on disarmament. Canada provides a good example of the kind of approach
that George Kennan referred to in his article when he advocated unilateral
action. The relevant question is: can and should we get the United Kingdom
to withdraw its troops from Germany, rid itself of nuclear weapons, stop exporting weapons and generally adopt a far nearer approximation to a disarmed posture?

Whether a country can do this seems to depend essentially on its assessment of
whether the Soviet Union is now an aggressive power. It also depends on how
a country rates its own contribution to NATO and, hence, if it thinks on balance that the removal of its contribution would add significantly to the risks
of military invasion.

I take the view that essentially the Soviet Union is a country with an over-
extended empire which it has great difficulty in holding down. It has lost
Yugoslavia and Albania. It has had major revolts in all the remaining colonies, except Bulgaria, which have been put down by the colonial forces or by
Soviet invasion. This is the major reason why the Soviet Union has strong
military forces in Eastern Europe and why it continues to play up the threat
to NATO, in order to justify its presence holding down its colonies. Thus
there is no united menacing block confronting NATO in Europe. It is for these
reasons that I believe Britain could also adopt a policy of unilaterally win-
ding down its military position and basically challenging a fundamental assumption of the Cold War, namely that the Warsaw Pact is monolithic and has aggressive intent in Western Europe.

Achieving Popular Support and Understanding

If these are the policies I believe we should follow, the next question is:
what methods can we use to encourage people to put these things across? Now
one method is to calculate the benefits of redeployment; for example, the
amount of tax reduction resulting from disarmament. However, I feel that this
is essentially static and narrow. The real benefits from disarmament would

come from a higher rate and quite different pattern of growth of the UK economy over a long period.

There is rather strong evidence that military expenditure has become increasingly incompatible with development, or even growth, as conventionally defined
by GNP. There are interesting examples of rapid growth, in the 19th century,
of countries which pursued development on a fairly militaristic basis. The
two best examples are Germany and Japan. Like other countries, they were
essentially seeking to catch up with Britain which, through accidents of history, was the first nation to have an agricultural and industrial revolution.
Britain was thereby able to industrialize and achieve a supreme competitive
position and consequently the ability to acquire an empire on the cheap with
extraordinarily little military expenditure. Both Germany and Japan were seeking to achieve economic strength and gain empires at the same time, but the
fact that they were pursuing militaristic and imperial ends did not prevent
their growing extremely fast. The main reason is that until the end of the 19th
century armaments were fairly similar to machines in the type of inputs and
skills they required for their production. They were also relatively cheap.
The basic policy which such countries followed was to develop basic industries
such as steel, shipyards, engineering and railways (for the purpose of moving
their forces and other things). As a result, they invested in heavy industry
and infrastructure of a kind necessary for civil development but with a par-
tially military intent. The actual arms themselves were relatively small items
of expenditure superimposed on this main effort directed at industrialization.

What has happened progressively since that period is that arms have become
increasingly specialized and exotic, particularly since the Second World War.
The advent of the nuclear weapon was of supreme importance in giving the scientists a kind of dictatorship in military policy which they never had before.
With the advent of the nuclear weapon, the scientists had succeeded in producing an artefact of such astonishing power that they were virtually given free
reign in the nuclear countries to spend what they liked on research and development in the military field in pursuit of these weapons, counter-weapons,
delivery systems and anything else they could think of. The result was an
horrifying expansion of scientific and technological effort into research and
development which fairly swiftly divorced the production of advanced weapons
from that of most ordinary civilian products. It is this fact of the rising
price of weapons and their ever increasing sophistication, which explains the
growing divergence between civil and military products, and between the allocation of resources required for growth and that required for production. This
helps to explain why in recent periods, those countries which have opted for
heavy military spending such as the United States and the United Kingdom (and
even the Soviet Union) have rather poor rates of growth whereas those with
fairly low rates of military spending, such as Germany and Japan, have achieved
relatively high rates of growth. In this way, the conflict between arms and
growth in its traditional sense has become more acute than ever before.

One hears frequent reference to the Lucas aero-space workers and the possibilities and interests of people in the armaments industry in contributing to
development by producing products which would be valuable in the less developed
world. Although this is valuable, I have some reservations because the main
motive for disarmament should not originate in a paternalistic attitude towards
the less developed countries. Instead of thinking about how we can directly
contribute to development, we need to think more about how we can reorganize
and develop our own society to ensure it is viable in the long run in a more
disarmed state and without the levels and patterns of consumption which may be
not sustainable in the long run.

We should start to experiment and explore new patterns of living. We must put our own house in order before we consider assisting with the direction of other countries. I take the total world view that disarmament requires development in the sense of reshaping our own society into one which really fulfills our ideals and which is economically sustainable without pollution or the exhaustion of the environment. The fatuity of the limitless pursuit of growth without concern for the environment has already begun to take root and cannot fail to gain further support. The nature of events will be such that the contradictions of the present system will become more apparent and people will react against it more forcefully. We ought to conduct genuine experiments in which chunks of territory are isolated and cordoned off. Within such areas people should be asked to experiment in organizing themselves in different ways in order to discover their own living conditions. This would produce experimental communities which achieve quite different patterns of living with quite different uses of exhaustible resources. In sum, the important thing for the rich countries is to look for alternative patterns of life. In order to move this way peripheral countries, such as Britain, should contract out of the superpower blocs and all they stand for.

Disarmament and Development

United Nations 1972

An extract from the 1972 report of the Group of Experts
on the Economic and Social Consequences of Disarmament.

THE INTERRELATIONSHIP BETWEEN DISARMAMENT AND DEVELOPMENT

Disarmament would contribute to economic and social development through the
promotion of peace and relaxation of international tensions as well as through
the release of resources for peaceful uses.

In the Report of the Secretary-General entitled Economic and Social Consequences
of the Arms Race and of Military Expenditures,[1] it is observed that:

> "International suspicions and fears ... damage the economic
> and social well being of the world by impeding exchanges
> between peoples whether these be of trade and flow of cap-
> ital, or of knowledge and technological 'know-how'. If
> there were no arms race, trade and other exchanges would
> almost certainly be easier."[2]

The same report observed:

> "... One major effect of the arms race and military expen-
> diture has been to reduce the priority given to aid in the
> policies of donor countries."[3]

> "It would take only a 5 per cent shift of current expen-
> ditures on arms to development to make it possible to
> approach the official targets for aid."[4]

The unanimous conclusion, presented in the same report, contains the following
statement:

> "... A halt in the arms race and a significant reduction
> in military expenditures would help the social and economic
> development of all countries and would increase the possi-
> bilities of providing additional aid to developing countries."[5]

The Link With Respect to Resources in General

The transfer to peaceful uses of resources used in each country for military
purposes will bring about greater satisfaction of civilian needs of the country. The resources thus released, sometimes referred to as the "disarmament
dividend", can be redirected to raise standards of living and to promote faster
growth, in particular through higher expenditures in fixed investment and in
education and training of manpower.

In the developing world as a whole, the share of gross product claimed by military expenditure is a little more than 4 per cent;[6] in 17 developing countries, mostly in the regions at war in the Far East and the Middle East, the

average share climbs to around 13 per cent. On the other hand, in 46 countries, mainly in Africa and Latin America, the average share is only 1.5 per cent of their gross product. In some instances the armed forces are engaged in civil activities which would need to be continued and financed from civil budgets. Therefore, there will be considerable variation among developing countries in respect to the magnitude of their own "disarmament dividend".

In case of general and complete disarmament — and also, to a lesser extent, when the cuts in military expenditure are significant, but less than total — economic assistance granted by developed to developing countries could and should be greatly increased and would merit high priority in the allocation of released resources.

The higher the level of *per capita* income of a developed country, the stronger is the case for it to contribute to the promotion of growth in developing countries, not only through increased economic aid but also through increased international trade. Special care should be taken to facilitate imports from the developing countries and to assure for them fair terms of trade.

In order to take full advantage of the possibilities for development offered by the "disarmament dividend", organized actions will have to be taken by Governments as well as by the international community.

Many developing countries import their arms from abroad. Although many of these arms are provided as aid or on easy terms, disarmament would still release significant foreign exchange resources which could be used for the import of investment goods necessary for economic growth.

As disarmament is accomplished, the amount of military aid granted by the developed countries should, instead of being merely suppressed, by used for the expansion of economic aid to developing countries.

While it would bestow great economic benefits on developing and developed countries, if the necessary policy measures were introduced, it could make an important contribution towards closing the increasing economic "gap" between them. This would also apply to situations where the cuts in military expenditures are smaller, yet significant. Since military expenditures now absorb a larger proportion of the combined GNP of the developed than of the developing countries, a general (proportional) reduction in military expenditures will increase the non-military part of the GNP of the first group of countries proportionally more than that of the second group. However, a simultaneous increase in the fraction of GNP in the advanced donor countries allocated to international development assistance could not only prevent a widening of the "gap", but contribute greatly to its closing.

Such a rise in the fraction of their combined GNP allocated by developed countries to development assistance would have to be larger the greater the difference between the military expenditures — expressed in percentages of their respective GNPs — of the two groups of countries.[7] When applied to the configuration of GNP, military expenditure and development assistance estimated for 1970, a rough calculation shows that a 20 per cent general reduction in military expenditures, for example, would contribute not only to the satisfaction of urgent economic needs of both developed and developing countries, but also to the reduction of the economic gap between the two groups if such developmental assistance were raised globally in the same proportion or slightly more.

Recognizing that each donor country will want to determine its own policies
for expanded economic assistance, the Group hopes that these decisions will
secure an adequate increase in assistance for development.

The Group suggests that consideration should be given to progress in disarmament in the periodic reviews and appraisals of progress towards achieving the
goals and objectives of the International Development Strategy for the Second
United Nations Development Decade.

The Link with Respect to Specific Resources

Most of the resources released by disarmament, total or partial, would be
readily transferable to other uses — for example, manpower, food, clothing,
transport, fuel and products of the metal and engineering industries. Budgetary action to raise civil demand will be enough to induce redeployment of
released resources either to investment or to consumption, public or private.

Some other resources, for example, nuclear weapon plants and military aircraft
and missile plants may not be readily transferable. Some alternative civil
uses may be found: for example, satellites and other techniques developed by
the military could be used more than they are now in the search for natural
resources and in international meteorological work. But only a part of the
specialized resources could probably be absorbed in ways of this kind. For
the rest, other industries will have to be brought into the areas where the
specialized military production has been concentrated and retraining programmes
will be needed for those whose skills become redundant.

Regional development policies and retraining policies of the required types
exist in many advanced countries. But even in some of the countries where
these policies exist, for example some of the countries of Western Europe,
there is often the threat of serious unemployment in particular areas when
work on, for instance, a military aircraft project, is completed or cancelled.
The industry is often reluctant to change, and sometimes the Government places
new military orders to sustain employment, thus perpetuating the arms race.
To prevent this happening, the Group suggests that Governments, when placing
orders for specialized military production or creating specialized plants
likely to give rise to these difficulties in the event of diarmament, should
make advance plans to deal with the redeployment to peaceful work of the manpower and plant (in so far as the latter is reusable).

Apart from catering for these areas of special difficulty, all countries might
be urged to consider what would be the most valuable ways of redeploying resources from military to civil use and to consider, in particular: (a) which
resources now used by the military might make a particularly valuable contribution to development in any area; and (b) in the light of such an assessment,
which specialized resources would be suitable as aid or technical assistance
from developed to developing countries. Planning of this kind would benefit
from international co-operation.

The Group believes that the feasibility of making such plans should be explored
now. Changes in the composition of military programmes, with no decline in
total military expenditures, have already made numerous scientists and engineers redundant in some countries. Some of this unemployment could have been
avoided by advance planning of links with development. The ingenuity and resourcefulness displayed in the Second World War in converting facilities to

serve military purposes was impressive. To fail to devote equal ingenuity and
resourcefulness to converting military facilities to serve peaceful ends, including the development needs of developing countries, would be inexcusable.

Research and development needs special consideration. The world's expenditure
on research and development has grown tremendously since the Second World War,
but a very large part of the effort has been military. It is estimated by the
Secretariat that world expenditure on research and development now amounts to
$60 billion, or about 2 per cent of world gross product, of which about $25
billion is for military purposes. An overwhelming part of these expenditures
are made in the advanced countries.

These research and development resources, when diverted to peaceful uses, might
have a great impact on development. A large and imaginative increase in peaceful research and development budgets will be required if all, or even a large
part, of the research and development manpower employed on military work is to
find peaceful research and development work. It is not possible for us — or
probably for anyone — to say what would be the fruits of an expansion in peaceful research and development of the magnitude which disarmament would permit.
All we can say with certainty is that there is a vast range of problems in the
developing countries and that there are huge sophisticated resources absorbed
by military research and development in the developed countries. The range of
possibilities for transfer appears to be extremely wide. Our conclusion is
that it would be useful constantly to consider what disarmament steps are in
the offing, how far these may release resources and how these may best be used
to promote development either at home or in the developing countries. Secondly,
more concrete study may be needed of the question of how the very large research and development resources that would be freed by general and complete
disarmament might be redeployed.

We considered what specific resources would be released for development by the
four partial measures we adopted as hypotheses. We came to the following conclusions:

(a) A comprehensive test ban. It seems uncertain whether peaceful nuclear
explosions will prove to be attractive economically very soon. If they do
prove to be attractive economically, it is important that they should be made
available to the non-nuclear weapons countries, under appropriate international
arrangements. There appears to be great continuing scope for the development
and application of nuclear energy; resources released by a comprehensive test
ban might directly or indirectly permit an expansion of effort here. The resources involved would not, of course, be nearly as great as those resulting
from complete nuclear disarmament. It is estimated that complete nuclear disarmament would offer promise of additional benefits. More than 20,000 nuclear
scientists and engineers would become available, some of whom could be assigned
to assist the peaceful nuclear programmes of developing countries if plans for
this purpose were made. If 2,000 tons of fissile material were released for
peaceful purposes it would be enough to provide the initial and replacement
fuel over their useful life for an installed capacity of about 100,000 electrical megawatts of thermal reactors or an installed capacity of about 500,000
electrical megawatts of fast breeder reactors. For comparison with these figures, the current estimates of the total installed capacity of nuclear power
plants are 300,000 electrical megawatts in 1980 and 1,000,000 electrical megawatts in 1990.[8]

(b) Chemical disarmament. Biological disarmament has already released resour-

ces that are valuable for research into disease, animal and human. Chemical
disarmament would add resources useful for ecologically acceptable pest control
and toxicological research. If the laboratories used for chemical (or biological) warfare work were converted to civil uses and opened up, they would not
only offer first-class technical facilities but might also help to engender
confidence that disarmament was being observed, the more so if international
exchanges were encouraged.

(c) Demilitarization of the sea-bed and deep-sea environment. Sea-related
activities of benefit to developing countries could, with appropriate planning,
be stimulated by complete demilitarization of the sea-bed and deep-sea environment and by naval and other disarmament. In general, developing countries
could share in the benefits resulting from better utilization and management
of the ocean space, and from accelerated development of marine resources, for
example under international arrangements. These benefits would be made possible by expanded programmes of research and exploration using water-borne
devices and remote sensing from satellites and aircraft. Mineral exploitation
of the sea-bed could be facilitated, enabling the world community to better
utilize this common heritage of mankind.

(d) The elimination of all foreign bases and withdrawal of foreign troops.
This measure would influence the balances of payments between the countries
with troops or installations abroad and the countries where those troops or
installations are sited. The nations withdrawing troops and facilities would
enjoy a gain to their balances of payments and probably a reduction in their
total military expenditures — though some of the troops and facilities withdrawn from abroad may be maintained at home. In the areas from which the with-
drawals took place, there might be a reduction in foreign exchange earnings.
This would be outweighed by the change in political conditions, the possible
reductions in local military expenditures and the other developments with
which this measure would surely be associated. Nevertheless, there should be
an increase in non-military aid where necessary, to facilitate transfer to more
normal activities.

The Group suggests that as large as possible a proportion of development assistance should be channelled in ways which would contribute to international co-
operation in joint projects of rapidly growing importance for the world community. Apart from multilateral assistance programmes, which have advantages over
bilateral programmes owing to greater acceptability in some circumstances,
emphasis needs to be placed on new international undertakings, such as the
establishment of an international regime for the sea-bed, projects to change
regional climates and the regional internationalization of certain civil avia-
tion services (e.g. for natural resources surveys and assistance in disasters).

MOBILIZING PUBLIC OPINION IN FAVOUR OF PROMOTING DISARMAMENT AND DEVELOPMENT

The goals of international disarmament must constantly be kept alive in the
minds of the people of the world, with the hope they raise to avert war, to
strengthen peace and security between nations and to foster a climate of co-operation for progress. The Group considers that at the present stage public
opinion should be mobilized mainly with a view to following up the results
already achieved in the field of disarmament by new steps towards general and
complete disarmament. In the continuing multilateral negotiations for disarmament, there are formal commitments to follow up some of the partial agreements already made with further agreements in the same field, for example, a

comprehensive test ban in place of a partial test ban, a ban on the possession
and production of chemical as well as biological weapons, and also the general
demilitarization of the ocean. The Group calls upon public opinion to work for
the achievement of agreements on disarmament at all levels — bilateral, regional and international. The idea of the Disarmament Decade could be utilized
in such publicity endeavours, not least in order to keep public opinion concerned with obtaining real achievements before the Decade is up. If agreement
is reached on holding a world disarmament conference, and if the conference is
held, this would facilitate the mobilization of public opinion; and the Group
hopes that such a conference would enable all countries, on an equal footing,
to compare ideas concerning every aspect of disarmament.

Likewise, the goals of promoting economic development in order to secure social
development for all people in all nations, must receive a greater share in the
building of public opinion everywhere. The plans for the Second United Nations
Development Decade should help to keep progress in that direction under constant review.

The purpose of mobilizing public opinion for both these imperative goals —
disarmament and development — may be effectively served by constantly publici-
zing reminders of the blatant contrast between the waste of resources on armaments and the great unfilled needs of social and economic development.

In particular, the shocking discrepancy between world expenditures for armaments and for aid to the poorer nations should be regularly publicized.

In implementing such action schemes for public information, some of the more
specific statements and recommendations of this report should be utilized.
For example:

(a) In United Nations reports on disarmament and on development the comparison
between military and civilian expenditures should be brought to the foreground.

(b) Within the framework of the periodic reviews and appraisal of progress
towards achieving the goals and objectives of the International Development
Strategy for the Second United Nations Development Decade, progress in disarmament should be given consideration, and considerable publicity should be given
to the ensuing debate.

(c) The appeal voiced by a group of experts in 1971 in the report entitled
Economic and Social Consequences of the Arms Race and of Military Expenditures[9]
should be reiterated. The Group wants particularly to support the general
recommendation: "In order to draw the attention of the Governments and peoples
of the world to the direction the arms race is taking, the Secretary-General
should keep the facts under periodic review".[10] In particular, the Secretary-
General should endeavour to include, in his periodic reports to the Economic
and Social Council and the General Assembly on the economic and social consequences of disarmament and of the arms race, statistics for each country, as
far as they are available, showing in addition to military expenditures and
their impact on social and economic development, development aid given or
received. Military aid should also be recorded, both for donor and for recipient nations in relation to the statistics required above, in so far as they
are available.

(d) Public discussion in international forums and within Member States should
be encouraged in regard to the statement in the present report that unless

disarmament savings are accompanied by a sufficient increase in development aid, the income gap between developed and developing countries is apt to widen.

(e) The imagination of the public in all countries should be kindled by information on conversion possibilities as indicated above.

(f) Public opinion within Member States should be alerted to the planning for alternative, civilian uses of resources, facilities and manpower, which is recommended to be made as part of planning military production and purchases.

(g) In particular, all media should draw attention to the tremendous inherent potentialities of redirecting military research and development to development objectives. Comparisons of facts such as the contrast between military research and development costing $25 billion a year and health research costing only about $6 billion are telling examples which should be played up by mass media in order to appeal directly to human interest.

The objectives of disarmament and development could be effectively promoted if the public in each country were kept informed of hopeful moves in these directions made in other countries.

Appeal should be made to mass media in general as well as to the information services of the United Nations and organizations of the United Nations family to develop programmes of information on the subject of this report.

SUMMARY OF CONCLUSIONS AND RECOMMENDATIONS

Disarmament and development are of the greatest importance to the world community. But fundamentally they stand separately from one another. The United Nations has agreed to seek each one vigorously in its own right, regardless of the pace of progress in approaching the other. Specifically, nations have agreed that national and international efforts to promote development should be neither postponed nor allowed to lag merely because progress in disarmament is slow.

However, disarmament and development can be linked to each other because the enormous amount of resources wasted in the arms race might be utilized to facilitate development and progress. Furthermore, the blatant contrast between this waste of resources and the unfilled needs of development can be used to help rouse public opinion in favour of effective disarmament, and in favour of the achievement of further progress in development, particularly of the developing countries.

So far, in the field of disarmament, several important international agreements on certain types of arms have been reached; they have been "partial" or "collateral" measures mostly of a non-armament character. They may have forestalled increases in military spending but they have not reduced it.

World military expenditures in 1970 were roughly $200 billion, i.e. 6.5 per cent of the GNP of the countries of the world. Military expenditures of the countries which provide aid for development are estimated to be approximately 6.7 per cent of their GNP, or 25 times greater than the official development assistance they provide. The major part of the world's military expenditure is made by a very small number of countries; the six main military spenders are responsible for more than four-fifths of the total. The developing coun-

tries spend approximately 4.2 per cent of their GNP, or only about 7 per cent
of the world total, although for some of them the share of military expenditure
in their GNP is high.

An agreed programme for the Disarmament Decade does not exist. General and
complete disarmament under effective international control remains the main
objective. Its achievement would represent a momentous political change and
would release massive resources for peaceful uses. We agree with the authors
of earlier studies that there would be no insuperable technical difficulties
in ensuring the redeployment of the released resources to peaceful uses. Partial measures are a second best, but more of them may be introduced before
agreement is reached on general and complete disarmament.

The two principal aims of policies of world-wide economic and social development are the increase in the levels of living of all peoples and the reduction
in income disparities both within and between countries. On the basis of the
modest achievements of the First United Nations Development Decade, and even
if growth objectives of the Second United Nations Development Decade are
attained, the problem of reducing mass poverty and unemployment in the less
developed regions of the world still remains. More efforts therefore should
be made by the world community. While, in the opinion of the Group, developing countries bear responsibility for adopting adequate measures to mobilize
their own resources more effectively, and for reducing income disparities, the
solution of that problem would, in many developing countries, depend on the
contribution to their external resources made by expansion of their exports
and also, to a significant extent, on stepped-up foreign assistance.

Disarmament would contribute to economic and social development through the
promotion of peace and the relaxation of international tensions as well as
through the release of resources for peaceful uses. The transfer to peaceful
uses of resources used in each country for military purposes will bring about
greater satisfaction of civilian needs of the country. The resources thus
released, sometimes referred to as the "disarmament dividend", can be redirected to raise standards of living and to promote faster growth.

There will be considerable variation among developing countries respecting the
magnitude of their own "disarmament dividend". In case of general and complete
disarmament — and also, to a lesser extent when the cuts in military expenditure are significant but less than total — economic assistance granted by developed to developing countries could and should be greatly increased and should
be given higher priority in the allocation of released resources. Since military expenditures now absorb a larger proportion of the combined GNP of the
developed than of the developing countries, a general (proportional) reduction
in military expenditure will increase the non-military part of the GNP of the
first group of countries proportionally more than that of the second group.
However, a simultaneous increase in the fraction of GNP in the advanced donor
countries allocated to international development assistance could not only
prevent a widening of the "gap", but contribute greatly to its closing.

The Group suggests that consideration should be given to progress in disarmament in the periodic reviews and appraisals of progress towards achieving the
goals and objectives of the International Development Strategy for the Second
United Nations Development Decade.

Most of the resources released by disarmament, total or partial, would be
readily transferable to other uses — for example, manpower, food, clothing,

transport, fuel and products of the metal and engineering industries. Budgetary action to raise civil demand will be enough to induce redeployment of these resources either to investment or to consumption, public or private. But other resources — for example, nuclear weapon plants and military aircraft and missile plants — may not be readily transferable.

The Group suggests that Governments, when placing orders for specialized military production or creating specialized plants likely to give rise to transfer difficulties in the event of disarmament, should make advance plans to deal with the redeployment to peaceful work of the manpower and plant (in so far as the latter is reusable).

Apart from catering for these areas of special difficulty, all countries might be urged to consider what would be the most valuable ways of redeploying resources from military to civil use and to consider, in particular: (a) which specialized resources now used by the military might make a particularly valuable contribution to development in any area; and (b) in the light of such an assessment, which specialized resources would be suitable as aid or technical assistance from developed to developing countries. Planning of this kind would benefit from international co-operation.

Research and development needs special consideration. The world's expenditure on research and development has grown tremendously since the Second World War, but a very large part of the effort has been military. These research and development resources, when diverted to peaceful uses, might have a great impact on development. A large and imaginative increase in peaceful research and development budgets will be required if all, or even a large part, of the research and development manpower employed on military work is to find peaceful research and development work. There is a vast range of problems in the developing countries and there are huge sophisticated resources absorbed by military research and development in the developed countries. The range of possibilities of transfer appears to be extremely wide.

The goals of international disarmament must constantly be kept alive in the minds of the people of the world. The Group considers that at the present stage public opinion should be mobilized mainly with a view to following up the results already achieved in the field of disarmament by new steps towards general and complete disarmament. The Group calls upon public opinion to work for the achievement of agreements on disarmament at all levels — bilateral, regional and international.

Likewise, the goals of promoting economic development in order to secure social development for all people in all nations must receive a greater share in the building of public opinion everywhere. The shocking discrepancy between world expenditure for armaments and for aid to the poorer nations should be regularly publicized.

The appeal voiced by a group of experts in 1971 in the Report entitled Economic and Social Consequences of the Arms Race and of Military Expenditures[11] should be reiterated. The Group wants particularly to support the general recommendation: "In order to draw the attention of the Governments and peoples of the world to the direction the arms race is taking, the Secretary-General should keep the facts under periodic review".[12]

Public opinion within Member States should be alerted to the planning for alternative civilian uses of resources, facilities and manpower now used for military purposes.

Appeal should be made to mass media in general as well as to the information services of the United Nations and organizations of the United Nations family to develop programmes of information on the subjects of this report.

NOTES

1. Economic and Social Consequences of the Arms Race and of Military Expenditures (UN publications, sales no. E72.IX.16).

2. Ibid., para. 95.

3. Ibid., para. 104.

4. Ibid., para. 107.

5. Ibid., para. 120.

6. Ibid., Annex I, Table 2, p. 28.

7. A concise formulation of these relationships has been worked out by Wassily Leontief and some other members of the Group.

8. Estimates supplied by the International Atomic Energy Agency.

9. See Note 1 above.

10. Ibid., para. 120(4).

11. See Note 1 above.

12. Ibid., para. 120(4).

From Military Expenditure to Development Assistance: A Proposal

United Nations 1975

> Extracts from Report of the Secretary-General, UN:
> "Reduction of the military budgets of States permanent
> members of the Security Council by 10% and utilization of
> part of the funds thus saved to provide assistance to
> developing countries". UN, New York, 1975.

INTRODUCTION

The history of proposals to freeze or reduce military budgets goes back a long
way. As far back as 1899, at The Hague Peace Conference, the Soviet Union
proposed ceilings on army and navy expenditures with the aim of preventing an
arms race. In the years between the First and Second World Wars, there was a
great deal of discussion, for example at the Preparatory Commission of the Conference on Disarmament, about budgetary control and standardized military budgets. Since the Second World War, at various times and in various forums, a
large number of countries have made formal proposals for military budget reductions. This has been a special concern of the United Nations General Assembly.

None of these formal proposals has as yet resulted in action; the conditions
for success were not there. We would stress two such conditions. First, there
has to be a sufficient degree of trust between nations; this was clearly lack-
ing in the 1930s. Secondly, there has to be a sufficient supply of information
to maintain the participants' confidence that any agreements are being observed.
In both these respects the conditions now are, in our view, more propitious
than they were. We have had over a fairly long period a process of increasing
detente among the major Powers. Furthermore, the means available to nations
for collecting and evaluating information have also become sophisticated year
by year.

The origin of this particular study is to be found in an initiative of the
Union of Soviet Socialist Republics specifically linking disarmament and development. On 25 September 1973, the Union of Soviet Socialist Republics proposed
to the General Assembly, at its twenty-eighth session, that it should include
in its agenda, as an important and urgent question, an item entitled "Reduction
of the military budget of States permament members of the Security Council by
10 per cent and utilization of part of the funds thus saved to provide assistance to developing countries" and it included in the proposal a draft resolution.[1] In the course of the debate certain differences of opinion emerged
concerning the Soviet proposal. In order to preserve the impetus provided by
this proposal, the representative of Mexico proposed a second resolution of a
procedural nature. The General Assembly, at its 2194th plenary meeting, on 7
December 1973, adopted simultaneously resolutions 3093 A and B (XXVIII) initiated by the USSR and Mexico respectively and bearing the same title as the
item.

By resolution 3093 A (XXVIII), the General Assembly recommended that all States

permanent members of the Security Council should reduce their military budgets
by 10 per cent from the 1973 level during the next financial year; appealed
to those States to allot 10 per cent of the funds so released for the provision
of assistance to developing countries; expressed the desire that other States,
particularly those with a major economic and military potential, should act
similarly; and established the Special Committee on the Distribution of the
Funds Released as a Result of the Reduction of Military Budgets to distribute
the funds released, for the provision of assistance to developing countries. ...

REDUCTION OF MILITARY BUDGETS

Objectives: The Economic and Social Consequences of Military Budget Reductions

The objectives of a reduction in military budgets are clear. The first is
that, as a measure of arms control and disarmament, it should be a step along
the road to a more peaceful world. The second objective is to release resources for economic and social welfare; and these released resources should be
used both for the benefit of the State making the reduction and, through international assistance, for the benefit of developing countries — a view which
the Group emphatically endorses.

Few people would deny that international security could be maintained with far
lower general levels of world military expenditure than at the present; equally,
few would deny that, as a general rule, if the major Powers were to reduce their
arsenals and force levels substantially, this would decrease the likelihood of
military conflict between them.[2] We do not argue that the levels of military
force are the only factor determining peaceful relations between States; but
they are a major factor.

If military budgets were reduced, this would help to improve the general international climate. The arms limitation agreements so far reached are evidence
of this.[3] They have been important, not only in their own right, but also
because they have helped to strengthen international confidence. Reductions
of military budgets, as a further measure of partial disarmament, would lead
to greater mutual understanding between States and peoples. Each step taken
towards disarmament may help to make the next step easier.

The economic benefits which could be derived from military budget reductions
are equally indisputable. The burden which military expenditure imposes on
the economy was the subject of another report, and we do not propose to go over
the same ground again.[4] However, we would like to single out from that report
one point whose saliency has increased in the last three years. During these
years, there has been a marked increase in world-wide concern about the longer-
term adequacy of the world's natural resources; there is a greater recognition
that some resources are indeed finite, and less easy assurance that adequate
substitutes will be developed and produced in time.   There is less easy
assurance, for example, about solutions to the world food problem — a problem
which is not for the future, but is here now. We are not suggesting that there
is any generally agreed view about the quantification of the long-term adequacy
of resources, but simply that many more serious-minded people are concerned
about the matter than was the case three years ago. To take one example: it
is widely argued that by the end of this century, formidable new civil technological advances will be needed if the world is to provide a tolerable standard
of living for its inhabitants; in this light, the employment of nearly half a
million scientists and technologists on developing weapons of war seems even

more of a waste than it did before.

The alternative potential uses of the resources freed from military expenditure are myriad. Certainly there would be transition problems — and the larger the scale of reduction, the larger these problems would be. We also recognize that some countries may feel less confident than they did a decade ago of their ability to manage their economies precisely as they wish. None the less, we are still prepared generally to endorse the conclusions of the report on the economics of disarmament[5] that the problems of transition can be met.

Developed countries reducing military budgets would understandably employ a substantial part of the resources released for their own use — by raising investment or public or private consumption. There is indeed a danger in the present world climate of opinion that countries would pre-empt the whole of the released resources for their own use. If this were to happen, the consequence would be that the relative gap in the standard of living between the developed and developing world would widen even further. Hence the importance of the provision in the resolution which provides our mandate — that a portion of the funds and resources saved should be devoted to international assistance to developing countries.

The problems and possibilities of this transfer of resources were thoroughly examined in 1972.[6] We can perhaps usefully add an illustration quantification appropriate to our own report. If the major military Powers were to channel approximately 1 per cent of the resources currently devoted to military expenditure to development aid, the addition to the flow of aid would probably be of the order of $2 thousand million, at 1973 prices. This would increase that flow by no less than 20 per cent.

Reduction of Military Budgets in Accordance With General Assembly Resolution 3093 A (XXVIII)

It is against this background — recognizing the waste of resources in the current levels of world military expenditure and the urgent need for resources for development aid — that we turn to the examination of the specific proposal contained in resolution 3093 A (XXVIII). The terms of this resolution have already been set out in the introduction.

The proposal for reductions in military budgets was addressed in the first instance to the permanent members of the Security Council; it seemed reasonable that the first steps should be taken by those countries — all nuclear Powers whose military expenditure was highest. However, the resolution expressed the desire that other States — particularly those with a "major economic and military potential" — should also join in. This would have the advantage that cuts in the military budget of permanent members of the Security Council would not be offset by increases in the budgets of their allies in military blocs.

The proposed reduction in military budgets is a single-stage measure — a cut of 10 per cent in the published military budget for the 1973 financial year. The measure was envisaged by the sponsor as five concurrent unilateral reductions; in this way it was hoped to avoid the complex problems that would arise with a formal agreement. ...

The resolution also proposed a quantitative link between the reduction in the use of resources for military purposes and the increase in aid; that 10 per cent of the cut should be devoted to international assistance for developing countries.

Resolution 3093 (XXVIII) found widespread support in the General Assembly and was welcomed by a large majority of the developing countries. However, there were differences of opinion about the ease with which the resolution could be implemented. The Union of Soviet Socialist Republics (the sponsor of the resolution) has made it clear that, in its view, it is an indispensable condition that all permanent Security Council members should implement the reductions. We note that China declared its opposition to the measure and that France, the United Kingdom of Great Britain and Northern Ireland and the United States of America abstained on the vote in the Assembly. However, the idea of the general approach of military budgets reductions was a seed which fell on fertile soil. ...

Military Budget Reductions: Consideration of Alternative Options

The Soviet proposal is one way to reduce military budgets; it concerns the totals only, for a single year, and involves a reduction by a specific percentage. Here we also consider certain other options. (At this stage we are simply setting them out, without discussing implications, problems and difficulties.) Such options could, for example, cover some particular component of the total — such as research and development (R & D). Then again the form of the limitation proposed can be a percentage, as resolution 3093 A (XXVIII) suggests; it could also be a ceiling, or the reduction might be prescribed in absolute terms. The reductions proposed can obviously be large or small, and can be for a single year or for longer periods. One of the interesting variations examined is an expenditure cut which is linked with a limitation on some component of military force; it might be linked, for example, with some limit on the number of men under arms. The mode of agreement can vary — from mutual example to formal agreement. Resolution 3093 A (XXVIII) proposes as participants permanent members of the Security Council and other States with major economic and military potential. Other groups could be considered; for example, there could be agreements among groups of States in particular regions to reduce military budgets; such agreements would also be most constructive and a number have already been proposed.

All these different forms have different requirements, different possible effects on security and, indeed, different consequences for the release of resources for development aid. These questions are discussed below.

MEANING AND MEASUREMENT OF MILITARY EXPENDITURE

Scope and Content of Military Budgets

A prerequisite for negotiating the reduction of military budgets in two or more countries is agreement on what is and what is not to be included in military budgets. The problem of defining the scope and content of a complex aggregate is encountered in many international comparisons — e.g. of health or education — but it is critical where a State's decision on allocations to national security and international development assistance will depend directly on the measure of comparative military budget levels. Unfortunately, there is no accepted conceptual standard of the definition and coverage of the military sector. Moreover, the great variation in the range of activities included in military budgets prevents reliable quantitative comparisons without extensive adjustment of the basic data. To name but three examples of such divergences, some countries include the payment of military pensions in their military budget and others do not. Civil defence is sometimes included and sometimes excluded; indeed, in some countries private citizens are required to incur expenditure under this heading. In some countries, the cost of the development of atomic weapons has been borne by agencies other than the Ministry of Defence. Therefore, in the hope of providing a more precise yardstick with which military budgets can be compared, the following analysis focuses on States' expenditure for military purposes — in brief, military expenditure irrespective of either classification in State financial accounts or method of financing, within or without the government budget. The Group notes that there seems to be general agreement that military expenditure customarily includes outlays on the following: pay and allowance of military personnel; pay of civilian personnel; operations and maintenance; procurement of weapon systems; military research and development; military construction; military aspects of atomic energy and space; and stockpiles of military equipment and materials. There are also other expenditures which, under certain circumstances, could be treated as military expenditure — for example, outlays on civil defence, para-military forces and military aid. ...

Valuation of Resources in the Military Sector

Negotiators attempting to agree on equivalent reductions in military budgets will be concerned to ensure, as far as possible, that these cuts do represent equivalent reductions in military power. It cannot automatically be assumed that this will be so. First of all, the military power of a country does not, of course, depend on the military expenditure of just one year; it depends on the total stock of military "capital" (weapons, bases, accumulated technical knowledge, and so on). Military expenditure in any particular year just maintains and adds to the pre-existing stock. So negotiators will have to have confidence, first in the reliability of the estimates and, then, in the acceptability of the initial levels of military capital.

Another reason why it would be difficult to forecast the effect on military power of a given cut is the difficulty of developing a set of relative prices for military goods and services which reflects their comparative usefulness in producing military power as perceived by national decision-makers. This problem is exacerbated by the rapidity of technological change which makes it even more difficult to define the unit of military output. Even where the authorities are using military resources efficiently, there can only be a rough correspondence between changes in military expenditure and changes in military power.

Alternatively, expenditure in the military sector may be valued in terms of resource cost and the appropriate criterion of valuation would be "opportunity cost" — in this case the value of civil goods and services that could be obtained if resources were shifted from the military to the civil sector. This valuation concept is particularly relevant for measurements of the "burden of defence" and of the resources that might be released through a disarmament agreement. However, while prices in fact always diverge from opportunity costs within the civil sector in all economies — to an extent that in turn varies widely between countries — the gap between opportunity costs and prices used in military budgeting in many countries is even wider. The net effect of the divergence may well be an underestimate of opportunity cost in the military sector, to the extent that military authorities may be able to command resources at low or even zero cost. However, there also exist prominent examples of overvaluation of resources used in the military sector.

Especially for agreements extending beyond a single year, there is the problem that rates of price increase differ considerably from country to country — particularly in recent years. Allowance would have to be made for differential price change to avoid inequitable effects on an agreement to reduce military expenditures. The construction of price indices to "deflate" military expenditure encounters not only the standard "index-number problems"[7] but also the difficulties of defining the output whose price change is to be measured. Rapid technological change makes the problem of separating price and quality changes more formidable for military than for civil goods. For example, it is difficult to disentangle that part of the sharply increased cost of a fighter aircraft which is due to pure price change from that part which reflects an increase in performance. When opportunity cost is the appropriate criterion, this difficulty is eased by using price indices from pertinent civil sectors.

The comparisons of military expenditure among countries are analogous to comparisons within one country over time. For international comparisons, special rates for translating the military expenditure of different countries into a common currency — corresponding conceptually to the price indices used within one country — should be calculated and multiple answers are again unavoidable.[8] (United States Arms Control and Disarmament Agency estimates of post war trends in world military expenditure are shown in Figure 11.1. Note: The figures represented are preliminary Arms Control and Disarmament Agency figures, later to be revised.)

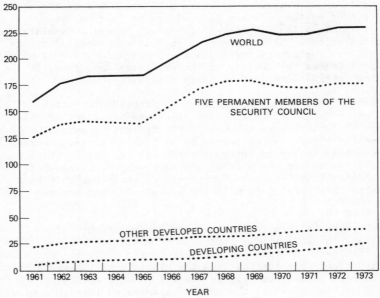

Fig. 11.1   Post-war trends in world military
             expenditure: United States Arms
             Control and Disarmament Agency (ACDA)
             estimates *(Absolute figures in con-
             stant 1970 dollars)*

NOTES

1. Official Records of the General Assembly, Twenty-eighth Session Annexes, agenda item 102, document A/9191.

2. This is not to say that all reductions of military expenditure of all kinds will increase national security; the problems of reallocations of expenditure which might lead to the opposite result are discussed elsewhere.

3. The Treaty Banning Nuclear Weapon Tests in the Atmosphere, in Outer Space and Under Water (United Nations, Treaty Series, vol. 480 (1963), No. 6964); the Treaty on Principles Governing the Activities of States in the Exploration and Use of Outer Space, including the Moon and Other Celestial Bodies (General Assembly Resolution 2222 (XXI), annex); the Treaty for the Prohibition of Nuclear Weapons in Latin America (Official Records of the General Assembly, Twenty-second Session, Annexes, agenda item 91, document A/C.1/ 946); the Treaty on the Non-Proliferation of Nuclear Weapons (General Assembly Resolution 2373 (XXII), annex); the Treaty on the Prohibition of the Emplacement of Nuclear Weapons and Other Weapons of Mass Destruction on the Sea-Bed and the Ocean Floor and in the Subsoil Thereof (General Assembly Resolution 2660 (XXV), annex); the Convention on the Prohibition of the Development, Production and Stockpiling of Bacteriological (Biological) and Toxin Weapons and on their Destruction (General Assembly Resolution 2826 (XXVI), annex); the Soviet-American agreements on the limitation of strategic arms, 1972 (United States, Department of State Bulletin, 26 June 1972) and 1974 (New Times, Moscow, 3 July 1974); the Treaty between the United States of America and the Union of Soviet Socialist Republics on the Limitation of Underground Nuclear Weapon Tests (A/9698); and others.

4. UN publication, Sales No. E72.IX.16.

5. UN publication, Sales No. 62.IX.1.

6. Disarmament and Development: Report of the Group Experts on the Economic and Social Consequences of Disarmament (UN publication, Sales No. E73.IX.1).

7. The "index number" problem refers to the awkward situation where the measurement of the average price change between two periods produces two possible answers depending on whether one uses quantities of the first or second period as weights in developing an aggregate average. Both solutions are equally valid.

8. For example, in comparing the output of two countries A and B, the procedure is to value all the items in each country first at A's prices — giving figures which, say, show A's total as 5 per cent higher than that of B. Then the whole operation should be done again, valuing each item at B's prices, to derive figures which might show A's total as 5 per cent lower than that of B. The procedure becomes very complicated for a number of countries, and it will be necessary to draw up multilateral agreements in such a way as to avoid the necessity for extensive international value comparisons.

Economic and Social Consequences
of the Arms Race

United Nations 1977

The following extract is from one of the latest reports
issued by the Secretary General of the United Nations.[1]
It was prepared by a group of 12 consultants drawn from
both East and West as well as from the Third World.

Introduction

The main features stressed in the first report on the Economic and Social
Consequences of the Arms Race and of Military Expenditures, submitted to the
General Assembly in 1971[2] retain their entire validity today. Indeed, arsenals
have been growing in size and sophistication and new types of weapons of even
greater destructive power have been developed or have become operational in the
meantime. The threat inherent in vast accumulations of weapons, and of nuclear
weapons in particular, continues to grow. The cost of the arms race for the
world as a whole and for the vast majority of countries has continued to rise,
while the problems of development and the urgency of social needs are as acute
as ever. The threat of war, the risk of final obliteration and the immense
human and material costs of the arms race are still the reasons which make
disarmament imperative.

But there are a number of features which have changed in the intervening period,
some of them radically new, some of them merely extrapolations of trends which
were already beginning to make themselves felt in the 1960s and which add to
the urgency of the need for disarmament. Predictably, as the major powers have
made no progress in actual reductions of their arsenals but have continued to
expand and refine them, the arms race has proven increasingly difficult to
confine geographically. New powers are emerging with a regional military pre-
eminence and the number of countries on all continents which are being drawn
into the overall arms build-up, acquiring ever more sophisticated weaponry, is
increasing.

Also on the cost side of the arms race, the situation has been changing for the
worse. In the 1970s many countries experienced deep recession and severe
inflation. Most others were affected indirectly by its impact on international
trade and by the disruption of the international system of payments. As a
result, government programmes in the social and economic fields have in many
cases had to be revised downwards. At the same time, though for partly different reasons, problems of environment preservation and resource conservation
have gained a new prominence and have been the cause of growing concern.
Against this background of a darkened economic outlook and a greater awareness
of the scarcity of resources and the fragility of the physical environment, the
continued mindless and uninhibited wastage of the arms race becomes ever more
incongruous and unacceptable.

In the field of international relations as well, profound changes have taken
place. New countries and groups of countries have risen to economic and poli-

tical prominence. Old patterns of alignment are in many cases felt as a fetter
on the social development of countries and a hindrance to the development of
international co-operation on the basis of sovereignty, equal participation of
all States and equal rights and duties. These trends have found their most
systematic and explicit expression in decisions to move towards the establishment of a new international economic order.

The 1970s have been proclaimed as the Disarmament Decade. Two-thirds through
it, it is already possible to begin to take stock. This period has been characterized by a consolidation of détente among the main protagonists in the
arms race, by the adoption of a number of partial agreements, bilateral and
multilateral, on the limitaticn of armaments. The Helsinki Conference on Security and Co-operation in Europe was of particular importance for the consolidation of détente. But these results have been far from sufficient to turn or
even to stem the tide of the arms race. It is already apparent that the
Disarmament Decade is not likely to produce the results hoped for, and that
in planning for the next the reasons for that failure will have to be carefully
considered. For there can be no relaxation of effort. Genuine and substantial
disarmament, particularly nuclear disarmament and particularly of those countries whose military arsenals and military budgets are the most massive, remains
a task of the greatest urgency. All countries and Governments share responsibility for taking effective action to halt and reverse the arms race so that
genuine security can be achieved and one of the main hindrances to social and
economic progress can be removed. ...

Current stocks of nuclear weapons are sufficient to destroy the world many
times over. These weapons and the missiles, aircraft and artillery to deliver
them are constantly being diversified and their performance characteristics
improved. The numbers of nuclear warheads in arsenals is not known, but the
number of carriers of different types is known with a fair degree of accuracy.
From these numbers it can be inferred that in 1974 so-called "strategic" nuclear
forces in the United States and the Soviet Union included 10-11,000 thermo-
nuclear warheads deliverable from missiles or bombers.[3] This number has been
rising very fast. Nuclear weapons arsenals are also increasing in other nuclear
weapons states. Figures given by SIPRI indicate that the number of missile-
deliverable warheads of the two major nuclear Powers increased from about
3,700 in 1970 to nearly 12,000 in 1976, a rise by more than a factor three.[4]
Their combined explosive power is believed to be equivalent to 1.3 million
Hiroshima-size bombs.[5] With regard to so-called "tactical" nuclear weapons the
situation is more uncertain. Their number is believed to be about four times
larger than the number of "strategic" nuclear warheads, but their combined
explosive power is but a fraction of the latter. According to one source it is
equivalent to about 700 million tons of TNT or to some 50,000 Hiroshima-type
bombs.[6]

Even though plausible estimates of numbers of major types of conventional
weapons such as aircraft, fighting vessels and tanks could be constructed for
most countries,[7] aggregate figures are not very meaningful for the reasons
just given. Only for fighting vessels are figures available which attempt to
measure the current value of stocks, taking account of the size, vintage and
armament of fighting ships and making allowance for technological improvements.[8]
Even these estimates are based on assumptions which are open to challenge, and
they can provide no more than a crude indication of trends. They indicate that
the total number of fighting ships in the world has changed little over the
years, although the value of the world stock (in constant dollars) doubled from
1960 to 1970 and rose by a further 30 per cent from 1970 to 1976. This pattern

appears to be valid for several other types of armaments as well: world stocks reckoned in numbers have remained fairly constant, but in terms of cost and performance world stocks are increasing very rapidly and, in the 1970s in par- ticular, current models have been spreading very fast to an increasing number of countries. This is true in particular of modern aircraft. Only 13 devel- oping countries had supersonic aircraft in 1965. A decade later that number had risen to 41. Over the past 30 years a few major arms-producing countries together developed and procured over 70 distinct types of interceptors, fighter and attack aircraft and twice as many variants of these types. To this may be added 30 to 40 types or variants cancelled before they went into production. Even after correcting for inflation, the unit price of fighter aircraft has been doubling every 4 to 5 years, rising from about \$0.25 million per aircraft (in 1975 prices) during the Second World War, to well over \$10 million today, reflecting improvements in performance and armament. All aspects of the cost of most modern weapons systems, development, manufacture, operation and main- tenance have risen very sharply.

Since the present report deals with the economic and social consequences of the arms race and military expenditure, the main stress in the following para- graphs will be on the enormous volume of men and resources devoted to military purposes and withheld from useful civilian production. But the distinguishing characteristic of the present arms race is the continuous qualitative change in the weapons and equipment being produced and deployed. It is primarily this feature that gives the arms race its momentum and it immeasurably compli- cates efforts to stop or control it.

The past decade has seen a continuous stream of new developments in the sphere of nuclear and conventional means of warfare. Because these technological and qualitative changes have not displayed the spectacular, eye-catching qualities which characterized some earlier developments, such as the advent of the atom bomb or of space technology, there is a danger that it may seem as though military technology was remaining relatively unchanged. Such complacency would be entirely unjustified. Recent developments have profoundly influenced mili- tary capabilities, world-wide destructive potentials and strategic conditions, possibilities and doctrines. In several respects, it will be seen later, these developments greatly reduce the perils of the nuclear arms race. In the key respect of technological development and its implications, the arms race is today as intense and danger-ridden as it has ever been. ...

The Arms Race in the Social and Economic Development Conditions of the 1970s

Under conditions of full utilization of the factors of production the delet- erious economic effects of the arms race on consumption, public or private, and on investment, are directly measured by the volume of resources absorbed for military purposes. When factors of production are idle, when, as in many countries today, there is deep recession and rampant inflation, the processes at work are different, though their effects are not less serious compared with those under conditions of full employment. In periods of recession when men and machines are idle, there is general waste of economic resources, and arma- ments production does not directly withdraw resources from civilian use, though it may do so (and frequently does) in some bottle-neck sectors. But growing expenditure on armaments is not an efficient way of combating recession. Expenditures on such items as education, health, housing and social welfare are more effective means for both economic and social reasons. First, the maintenance of high and rising armaments expenditures in the face of stagnating

or falling government revenues may lead countries to economize in such areas
as health, education, and welfare with all the negative social consequences
this entails. Second, since in recent times recession tends to go hand in
hand with high rates of inflation ("stagflation") and, in some cases, with
heavy balance-of-payments deficits, high arms expenditures have proved to be
a hindrance for economic policies leading out of recession. High government
expenditure on armaments increases demand without increasing the volume of
saleable or exportable goods. It thus intensifies the problems of inflation
and of the external balance. Military expenditures, therefore, reduce the
effectiveness of expansionary policies or even lead to restrictionary measures
in other fields which tend to prolong recession and unemployment. To the
direct waste contained in armaments production is added the indirect wastage
of unused resources. ...

One of the main economic problems of the first half of this decade was the
accelerating inflationary process in many countries of the world. Theory and
data are not at the point where the role of the military expenditure in stimulating inflation can be quantified, but consideration of the various ways in
which it can have an effect suggests that its contribution is not inconsequen-
tial. High military expenditures sustained over a long period of time are
likely to aggravate upward pressures on the price level in several ways.
First, military expenditures are inherently inflationary in that purchasing
power and effective demand is created without an offsetting increase in immediately consumable output or in productive capacity to meet future consumption
requirements. This excess demand creates an upward pressure on prices throughout the economy. This effect is stronger, the weaker and more narrow the
productive base. Where military expenditure contributes to the creation of
money for deficit financing of central government expenditure inflationary
pressures are generated by the resultant increase in the stock of money. Similarly, if military activities contribute to the emergence of deficits in the
balance of payments in reserve currency countries then the stock of money and
thus inflationary pressures grow in other countries. Second, there are reasons
to believe that the arms industry offers less resistance to increases in the
cost of labour and of the other factors of production than do most other industries[9] partly because of its highly capital and technology-intensive character,
and partly because cost increases in this sector can more readily be passed on
to the customer. These increases in the cost of the other factors of production then spread to other sectors of the economy, including sectors where the
rate of growth of productivity is lower, forcing up their prices as well.
Finally, and more generally, the diversion of substantial capital and R and D
resources away from the civilian sector impedes the long-term growth of productivity and thereby renders the economy more vulnerable to inflationary pressures. Inflationary trends, whatever their origin, tend to be exported, affecting other countries in the form of price increases, scarcities or in other
ways, depending on the circumstances. The inflationary impact of military
expenditure on the prices of exported military goods to developing countries
results in a deterioration of their terms of trade.

Altogether, it is clear that some of the major economic problems of recent
years, rapid inflation, trade imbalance and the disequilibria in international
payments, are aggravated by the maintenance of large military efforts, even if
the contribution of the arms race to these problems cannot be indicated in
quantitative terms. In particular there can be little doubt that the effects
of sustaining large military expenditures over a long period has contributed
to current inflation and its persistence in times of economic recession and
high unemployment. A significant reduction in world military expenditure

would help in bringing inflation under control. ...

This is not contradicted by the fact that in many countries a considerable
fraction of the work force is now either unemployed or underemployed. For
people are not unemployed because there are no more needs to satisfy. They
are unemployed or underemployed because of recessions or structural problems
in the economy, and these are themselves aggravated by high military expenditures. In most developed market economies the use of demand stimulus which
could deal effectively with unemployment has been inhibited by fears that it
would enhance inflationary tendencies and adversely affect the balance of payments. But, as already noted, inflation and, in some cases, balance-of-payments
deficits have probably been aggravated by high rates of military spending sustained over a long period. In any case, under appropriate conditions, funds
released from military budgets can be used to raise demand in the civilian
sector without stimulating inflation and, generally speaking, without affecting
the balance of trade either way. Indeed, to the extent that military procurement is more inflationary than most other forms of expenditure, a dollar for
dollar reallocation of monetary resources to civilian ends would in the longer
run ease inflationary pressures and leave greater scope for policies to curb
unemployment.

Despite these obvious facts there is a tenacious myth, dating back to German
rearmament prior to the Second World War, that high arms budgets protect against
unemployment or at least mitigate it. This belief has an air of self-evidence
and is reinforced when, as has often happened, Governments have given publicity
to the supposed employment benefits of arms procurement they were contemplating,
without adding that alternative uses of the same funds would create jobs as
well, normally many more. As a consequence it is still today a widespread
belief that disarmament or discontinuation of some specific weapons programme
would swell the ranks of the jobless, particularly when unemployment is already
high. It should be stressed that such conceptions are wrong. Military outlays
are not unique in their ability to generate employment. In fact, whereas military expenditures obviously create jobs in the industries supplying the armed
forces, the growing high-technology component in military expenditures has
eroded their direct and their overall job-creating potential. Today there is
rapidly accumulating evidence that high military budgets instead of alleviating
overall unemployment, contribute substantially to it. According to the United
States Government estimates (and only for this country do figures seem to be
available) a billion dollars of military expenditure creates 76,000 jobs.[10]
But if the same amount is spent for civilian programmes of the Federal Government it creates on average over 100,000 jobs, and many more than this if channelled into activities that are particularly labour-consuming. Calculations
indicate that if the same one billion dollars were released for private consumption by means of tax cuts it would create 112,000 new jobs.[11] In other
words, a 10 per cent cut in the military budget, that is to say, a cut of $8
to 9 billion and a corresponding tax reduction, could diminish unemployment by
0.3 million, and more than this if cuts and alternative programmes were selected with a view to maximizing the effect on employment.[12] Thus, the proposition
that military expenditure generates employment at least as, if not more, effectively than non-military expenditure is demonstrably false.

In the case of technological innovation, no less than in the case of manpower
and unemployment, the true impact of high military expenditures has mostly been
clouded in myth. The basic fact of an enormous diversion of resources has been
disguised by excessive claims about the importance of civilian spin-offs from
military research and development.[13] The drive for continuous improvement in

weaponry and military equipment, so the argument goes, has been an important
spur to technological progress and, so it continues, without the urgency of
military demands, funds on a sufficient scale would not have been forthcoming.
A limited number of examples, always the same, are cited to prove the case:
nuclear power, air transportation, radar, space technology and a few more.
Yet a sober assessment indicates that the claims are grossly exaggerated, and
even the standard examples are not all of them convincing.[14] In fact it is
remarkable how many inventions of the greatest civilian importance in production techniques, in materials, in power generation, engines and appliances, in
all fields of surface transportation and in communication owed absolutely
nothing of their origin and very little, if anything, of their subsequent development to military R and D, even if they were often adopted by the armed
forces and adapted to military requirements at a later stage. Military spin-
offs from civilian research have been incomparably larger than civilian spin-
offs from military research. The truly remarkable fact is how little, not how
much new has come to the civilian sector from military R and D efforts. Product
development in the sense of incremental improvements in materials, in miniatur-
ization, in performance, in reliability, etc., has in some cases been made under
military auspices, simply because this is where research and development funds
have been readily available. ...

The trade in arms has opposite effects on the economies of importing and exporting countries. What is involved is a highly unequal exchange, detrimental in
particular to efforts to bridge the gap between poor and rich countries. For
the importer of arms it is in economic terms a pure waste of surplus which
could have been used productively. Even when weapons are provided as gifts
there are maintenance, operation and infrastructure costs to be included on
the debit side. In contrast to the import of civilian goods these outlays
raise neither consumption nor production and generate no future output from
which to pay for them. Not so for the exporting country. That part of its
arms production which is destined for its own armed forces again figures to a
first approximation simply as an economic loss. But its production of weapons
for export is no different in economic terms from any other export production.
In some cases it may be in fact more advantageous than other kinds of export
because the advanced-technology component in arms exports is particularly high.
These exports therefore tend to stimulate important sectors of the economy of
the exporting country, such as mechanical engineering, electronics and the
industries supplying these sectors. Recent arms deals involving highly sophisticated equipment have enhanced these tendencies since the price of such equipment often includes a large component to pay for R and D costs. In addition
to orders for existing weapons, some recent contracts have even involved the
development of new or improved weapons systems specially for export to the
contractor. In this way importing countries are subsidizing military R and D
in the arms exporting countries. This also applies when instead of importing
weapons, countries produce them under licence. In most cases this subsidy is
of marginal importance for the exporting country but in a few cases the viabil-
ity of certain national arms industries or of particular companies is significantly affected. In a very real, although often marginal way, importing countries are thus helping to perpetuate the lead in military technology of the
main arms exporting countries and to sustain the rate of innovation and obsolescence in weaponry. ...

Conclusions and Recommendations

The main task of this report has been to analyze the social and economic

consequences of the arms race. What emerges with particular force is the
multiplicity of those consequences, not only in the field of security proper,
but in all aspects of civil life. The social, political, technological and
industrial options of countries are affected by their participation in the arms
race. International policies, not only in the military field, but also in the
fields of international trade and of co-operation and exchanges generally, are
influenced by the climate of confrontation and apprehension engendered by the
arms race. Many of the major problems faced by the world community, problems
of development, economic imbalance and inflation, pollution, energy and raw
materials, trade relations and technology, and so forth, are enhanced and
exacerbated by the arms race. Progress in other areas such as health, education, housing and many more is delayed owing to lack of resources.

This question of the relationship between armament and disarmament, on the one
hand, and other aspects of social, economic and political development, on the
other, has received all too little attention in the past. This report has
attempted to indicate these interrelations, but an adequate analysis would
require much deeper study. It is remarkable, for example, that recent studies
of the future of the world economy, analyses relating to the establishment of
a new international economic order and the United Nations conferences on a
variety of contemporary problems which have been held in recent years have in
most cases omitted consideration of the implications of the arms race altogether, despite its obvious and massive implications in each of these cases.
From every point of view it would be an advantage if in such studies and analyses and in the elaboration of programmes and recommendations the consequences
of and for the arms race were specifically considered. Both aspects of the
problem need to be taken into account: on the one hand, the volume of resources
consumed on the arms race and the socially constructive uses to which they
could be put; and on the other hand, the social, political, economic and
institutional processes, both domestic and international, whereby changes in
military policies affect the future course of development in other fields and
are themselves affected by it.

Discussion of the consequences of the arms race — social, economic and military-
political — presupposes some conceptual view of the phenomenon itself. Likewise, effective progress towards disarmament presupposes some understanding of
the forces and processes that drive the arms race along. There is a growing
body of literature on this question, but it is mainly confined to consideration
of one or a few countries and to exposition of the one or the other particular
model of the armaments process. The impact on disarmament efforts has therefore been virtually non-existent. What seems to be needed is not only an
elaboration or integration of these several approaches to obtain a clearer
understanding of the interplay of forces that sustain the arms race, but the
gathering together of these separate strands in a way that could inform and
guide action. What is even more needed is a clear outline of the views of
different countries and groups of countries as to what constitutes the fundamental mechanisms of the arms race. Effective action to reverse it would seem
to presuppose some agreement as to where the problem lies and what it consists
of. It is not the task of this group, whose terms of reference were to examine
the consequences of the arms race, to do more than call attention to the fact
that there is here an area where further study is called for.

It has been stressed throughout this report that the two most important goals
of the international community, disarmament, on the one hand, and development,
on the other, which the States Members of the United Nations are committed to
pursue vigorously, each in its own right, are in fact intimately linked.

Development at an acceptable rate would be hard if not impossible to reconcile with a continuation of the arms race. Research and development is one area where the misdirection of efforts is glaring. In this as in other respects, vast resources, badly needed for development, are being consumed as countries make ever greater sacrifices for military purposes.

Conversely, substantial progress in the field of development is increasingly understood to be essential for the preservation of world peace and security. These cannot in the long run be preserved in a world where large and growing economic gaps separate the countries of the world. Genuine security cannot be assured by the accumulation of armament but only through disarmament, co-operation and the growth of exchange and interdependence in a world of diminishing inequalities.

Substantial progress in the field of disarmament would represent a decisive turning point as regards development, imparting new momentum to efforts in this direction and greatly facilitating progress in this field. Progress towards disarmament would release internal material, financial and human resources both in developed and in developing countries and would permit their redeployment to purposes of development. In the case of many developing countries, these resources are relatively small in absolute terms, but in other cases they are very substantial, and in all cases the impact on development would be significant. The relaxation of the climate of fear, hostility and confrontation which progress towards disarmament would bring about, would remove some of the barriers now hampering international exchanges in general and the free circulation of raw materials and advanced technology in particular, and would greatly facilitate the free choice by each country of its particular path towards development. Last but not least, substantial progress towards disarmament would represent major savings in industrialized countries and would make possible substantial increases in development assistance. In fact, disarmament should be so designed that this close connection between disarmament and development gets full recognition. Provisions to ensure the transfer to development purposes of part of the resources released, provisions to ensure that measures of armaments limitation are so designed that they do not impede the transfer of technology for peaceful ends and other similar provisions must be an integral part of disarmament measures.

The 1970s were proclaimed Disarmament Decade, but through the first two thirds of that decade progress has been meagre and fell far short of what the vast majority of members of the international community would genuinely prefer. A number of agreements, several of them of great importance in their own right, have been reached, but progress has been much too slow to constrain the momentum of the arms race to any significant extent, let alone reverse it. If results in the future are to be less disappointing than in the past the reasons for this failure must be carefully examined. In this report a number of factors which may be important in this respect have been considered: the inertial forces which tend to develop in a qualitative arms race, the system of reciprocal compulsion it generates, and the fact that partial agreements on limitations are easily overtaken by developments in other areas of the arms race.

All of this points to one of the serious shortcomings of disarmament efforts for over a decade: the lack of a comprehensive scheme in which partial measures would find their place and, supplementing each other, would add up to a coherent strategy. General and complete disarmament under effective international control must remain the ultimate goal. Agreements to regulate and confine the arms race in the meantime are means and, in some cases, pre-condi-

tions for achieving that goal, but they cannot take its place. Effective
restraining measures in one field, even if they are adopted, can be circumven-
ted, and in the longer run new countries would be likely to enter the competition. In this context, it is imperative that negotiations on general and
complete disarmament should receive greater and more urgent attention than has
been the case in the past.

Effective progress towards disarmament presupposes the elaboration of an overall plan, persuasive in concept and workable in application, a "Strategy for
Disarmament" as it were. This must be based on a thorough assessment of the
problems involved, the forces propelling the arms race and the experience of
the past. It should involve specification of priorities, decision on targets
and adoption of programmes and, where appropriate, time-tables. This strategy
must be comprehensive enough to ensure a fair and equitable response to the
concerns of every country, and flexible enough to permit taking realistic and
concrete steps in the immediate future, in intermediate stages and in the final
stage. In short, a framework is needed within which endeavours can be co-ordinated and against which progress can be measured. This is no less essential in
the field of disarmament than it is in the field of development, or in any
other field where a multiplicity of efforts is to lead effectively to a common
goal.

It is not the task of this group to outline such a strategy, but some points
of particular importance emerge from our work. Measures of disarmament and
military disengagement affect the vital interests of all States, directly or
indirectly. All States must necessarily be engaged in the task of eliminating
the sources of conflict and tension, and of moving rapidly to the adoption and
implementation of disarmament measures under effective international control.
The determination of tasks and priorities must engage the participation of all
States, even though specific measures may often be negotiated more effectively
in regionally or otherwise limited fora.

Indeed, to impart a new momentum to disarmament efforts it seems necessary not
only to engage all countries in these endeavours on a basis of equality, but
also to involve the peoples of all countries more actively and in a more coherent and organized fashion than has been the case hitherto. A variety of movements and organizations — political, professional, religious and others — can
play an important role in this respect, and have in fact done so in the past.
The negative consequences of the arms race, in terms of endangering their
existence and in terms of social and economic sacrifices, affect all peoples
of the world. They have an obvious right to information about the military
policies and programmes of Governments and their implications. Much of the
secrecy in this field is not justified by military requirements. In some
cases, it results from mere tradition; in others, it serves such purposes as
shielding questionable or unnecessary armaments programmes from public scrutiny
and public criticism. Without endangering the security of any country much
greater openness of information could and should be applied in this field.

Given the character of the present arms race, effective disarmament will presuppose progress in two directions simultaneously: curtailment of the qualitative arms race, and reductions of military budgets. The first involves the
erection of boundaries against further developments in weaponry. The agreements on biological weapons and on anti-ballistic missile systems are steps in
this direction. Responsibility for continued and more rapid progress in this
respect overwhelmingly rests with the main military Powers and with the two
largest Powers in particular, which are alone in producing the full range of

modern weapons and where most innovations in military technology and all innovation in nuclear weapons and their means of delivery originate. It is particularly important that mutual limitations agreed upon by the largest Powers
should involve important qualitative limitations of nuclear-weapon systems and
should involve curtailment of military research and development.

The second major task of immediate urgency is to bring about substantial reductions in the military budgets of all countries and particularly of those whose
military budgets are the highest. All countries share responsibility for
taking prompt steps in this direction. In conjunction with this, steps must
be taken to facilitate the conversion of industries and installations to civilian ends. Not only would substantial budget reductions mean a turning point
in efforts to achieve disarmament and to diminish the risks of war, they would
also release internal resources for the social and economic development of
countries and greatly improve the prospects for the necessary expansion of aid
to developing countries. What is needed is the adoption of a specific time-
schedule for gradual but substantial co-ordinated reduction of budgets, first
of all of those of the largest and most heavily armed countries and of strategic rivals locked in confrontation, specifying criteria and proportions for
these reductions and ensuring that they are irreversible and that the means
saved are in fact allocated for peaceful purposes. If such cuts in military
expenditure are not accompanied by any further specifications, it is to be
expected that they would in many cases primarily affect the size of conventional
armouries and of standing forces. Indeed, countries able to do so might be
tempted to compensate a decline in numbers by improved performance, in other
words by a more vigorous pursuit of the qualitative arms race. This again
indicates the importance of co-ordinating partial measures adopted in different
fields.

Nuclear disarmament must be given the highest priority both because of the
intolerable threat posed by nuclear weapons, and because current and foresee-
able developments in their means of delivery and in the doctrines governing
their use, and the prospect of their proliferation to new States will enhance
this threat and could make disarmament vastly more difficult in the future.
As regards nuclear weapons proliferation, regional limitations and restraints,
such as the establishment of nuclear-free zones, would constitute important
steps. An important step would also be the conclusion of a comprehensive
nuclear test ban treaty. Progress in the direction of nuclear disarmament
would be greatly facilitated by agreement on certain targets and time-schedules
for phased reductions in the nuclear arsenals and for outlawing the use, development, production and possession of these weapons.

Finally, regional disarmament and disengagement designed to diminish the sources
of tension and conflict must be part of a comprehensive approach. There is
need, on the one hand, for general targets regarding military disengagement on
land and on the seas, dismantling of military blocks and withdrawal of troops
and bases from foreign territories, and, on the other hand, for immediate consideration of specific areas and regions, such as Central Europe, the Middle
East, the Indian Ocean and the Mediterranean, taking full account of the precise character of the security problems of the countries concerned. Progress
in these areas is again linked to or even conditional upon progress in the
limitation of the arms race of the main Powers and their regional disengagement.
It should be borne in mind that the bulk of the world's military expenditures
is being devoted to the accumulation of conventional arms. The build-up of
conventional arms in many parts of the world in recent years has generated
increasing concern. Without denying the overriding importance of nuclear dis-

armament, which is undoubtedly the most urgent task of our time, nor the inalienable right of every sovereign State of self-defence, it should be stressed that maybe the time has come to study this problem thoroughly and to seek feasible ways to formulate international agreements on the transfer of weapons.

Progress towards disarmament, it has been indicated, will require systematic co-ordination and planning with the participation of all States. This points, on the one hand, to the need for more effective means at the international level for information, research and evaluation on questions of disarmament to enable all Members States, not only the largest ones, to obtain effective insight and to take initiatives in questions of disarmament. On the other hand, the United Nations, and first of all its plenary organ, the General Assembly, whose task it is to harmonize the efforts of States in the attainment of their common goals, should be able to fulfil its role of overall guidance in the field of disarmament more effectively than it has been able to do in the past. Of great importance in this respect could be the special session of the General Assembly to be held in 1978. It is also to be noted that consideration has been given by the General Assembly to the convocation of a World Disarmament Conference.[15] There is also a need for expert advice and assistance on a more continuous basis to follow developments closely, to advise the General Assembly, the Sec-retary-General and Member States on questions of disarmament, and to assist in the elaboration, specification and adjustment of targets and programmes. Improvement of the machinery of the United Nations in this direction appears to be necessary if the world Organization is to fulfil its task in the field of disarmament.

ANNEX

General Assembly Resolution 3462 (XXX) of 11 December 1975

Economic and social consequences of the armaments race and its extremely harm-ful effects on world peace and security

The General Assembly,

Having considered the item entitled "Economic and social consequences of the armaments race and its extremely harmful effects on world peace and security",

Recalling its resolutions 2667 (XXV) of 7 December 1970, 2831 (XXVI) of 16 December 1971 and 3075 (XXVIII) of 6 December 1973 on the question,

Deeply concerned that, despite the repeated requests by the General Assembly for the implementation of effective measures aimed at its cessation, the arms race, particularly of nuclear armaments, has continued to increase at an alar-ming speed, absorbing enormous material and human resources from the economic and social development of all countries and constituting a grave danger for world peace and security,

Noting that, since the preparation of the report of the Secretary-General entitled Economic and Social Consequences of the Arms Race and of Military Expenditures,[16] new developments have taken place in the fields covered by the reports that are of particular relevance in the present economic and political conditions of the world,

Considering that the ever-spiralling arms race is not compatible with the efforts aimed at establishing a new international economic order, as defined in the Declaration and the Programme of Action on the Establishment of a new

International Economic Order, contained in General Assembly resolutions 3201 (S-VI) and 3202 (S-VI) of 1 May 1974, in the Charter of Economic Rights and Duties of States, contained in Assembly resolution 3281 (XXIX) of 12 December 1974, as well as in Assembly resolution 3362 (S-VII) of 16 September 1975, and that these efforts imply more than ever the resolute action of all States to achieve the cessation of the arms race and the implementation of effective measures of disarmament particularly in the nuclear field,

Conscious that, disarmament being a matter of grave concern to all States, there is a pressing need for all Governments and peoples to be informed about and understand the situation prevailing in the field of the arms race and disarmament, and that the United Nations has a central role in this connection in keeping with its obligations under the Charter of the United Nations,

Recalling that in its resolution 3075 (XXVIII) the General Assembly requested the Secretary-General to pursue the study of the consequences of the arms race, paying special attention to its effects on the economic and social development of nations, as well as on world peace and security, in order to enable him to submit, upon request by the Assembly, an up-to-date report on that matter, on the basis of the information released by Governments,

1.   Calls again upon all States, as well as the organs concerned with disarmament issues, to place at the centre of their preoccupations the adoption of effective measures for the cessation of the arms race, especially in the nuclear field, and for the reduction of military budgets, particularly of the heavily armed countries, and to make sustained efforts with a view to achieving progress towards general and complete disarmament;

2.   Requests the Secretary-General to bring up to date, with the assistance of qualified consultant experts appointed by him, the report entitled Economic and Social Consequences of the Arms Race and of Military Expenditures, covering the basic topics of that report and taking into account any new developments which he would consider necessary, and to transmit it to the General Assembly in time to permit its consideration at the thirty-second session;

3.   Invites all Governments to extend to the Secretary-General their support and full co-operation to ensure that the study will be carried out in the most effective way;

4.   Calls upon non-governmental organizations and international institutions and organizations to co-operate with the Secretary-General in the preparation of the report;

5.   Decides to include in the provisional agenda of its thirty-second session the item entitled "Economic and social consequences of the armaments race and its extremely harmful effects on world peace and security".

NOTES

1.   Document A/32/88 issued by the United Nations, 12 August 1977.

2.   A/8469/Rev.1 (United Nations publications Sales No. E.72.IX.16) (hereafter referred to as the 1971 report).

3.   The Defense Monitor, vol. 3, No. 7, August 1974 (Centre for Defense

Information, Washington).

4. SIPRI Yearbook of World Armaments and Disarmaments, 1976, pp. 24-25.

5. Ruth Sivard, World Military and Social Expenditures, 1976, pp. 10-11.

6. SIPRI: Disarmament or Destruction, 1975, p. 11.

7. See, among others, The Military Balance, published annually by the International Institute of Strategic Studies. Ruth Sivard, in World Military and Social Expenditures, 1977, cites the following world totals: Tanks: 124,000; combat ships: 12,400; combat aircraft: 35,000.

8. Ronald Huisken, "Naval Forces", Ocean Yearbook, University of Chicago Press, October 1977.

9. This is considered more fully in Ulrich Albrecht, "Armaments and Inflation", Instant Research on Peace and Violence, No. 3, 1974.

10. "Projections of the Post-Vietnam Economy, 1975" by the United States Department of Labor, Bureau of Labor Statistics, 1972.

11. "The Structure of the U.S. Economy in 1980 and 1985", United States Department of Labor, Bureau of Labor Statistics, 1976. The figures cited refer to 1975.

12. See also Marian Anderson, The Empty Pork Barrel, Public Interest Research Group in Michigan (PIRGIM), 1 April 1975.

13. For example, O. Morganstern, The Question of National Defence, New York, 1960.

14. Nuclear power generation was invented before any work started on nuclear weapons, and it is certainly open to question whether the civilian spin-offs from subsequent military nuclear research have outweighed the diversion of entire generations of nuclear scientists and engineers to military pursuits. Supersonic aircraft technology which has absorbed a large part of military R and D funds for decades, has been from the civilian point of view mostly wasted or achieved at an excessive cost, to say nothing of R and D on weapons which have no civilian counterpart at all. Nor is it clear why air transportation should have needed the spur of military applications to develop, when surface transportation did not, and nothing suggests that product innovation in fields such as chemical processes, medical drugs and synthetic materials, where military research has played no major role, has lacked in dynamism.

15. See General Assembly resolutions 2030 (XX) of 29 November 1965, 2833 (XXVI) of 16 December 1971, 2930 (XXVII) of 29 November 1972, 3183 (XXVIII) of 18 December 1973, 3260 (XXIX) of 9 December 1974, 3469 (XXX) of 11 December 1975 and 31/190 of 21 December 1976.

16. A/8469/Rev.1 (United Nations publication, Sales No. E.72.IX.16).

Conclusions for Britain

Brian Johnson

> The Conference at Goldsmiths College included six work-
> shop groups to explore in greater depth the implications
> of the conference themes for policy, especially for that
> of Britain. In this concluding section, Brian Johnson
> presents a consolidated view based on the reports of each
> of these workshops.

The first point to record about the discussions of the conference was the way
they reflected a new convergence of concern. Participants, drawn from a variety of interest groups, were both astonished and appalled as the evidence was
presented of the unrelenting expansion of the arms race, together with its
implications for Third World development. The Conference by its conclusion,
had reached a new and wider recognition of the intimate relationships between
the cancerous phenomenon of ever-increasing production and trade in arms, and
the other major economic problems of British and world society, especially
continuing Third World poverty.

The Conference was left in no doubt that in recent years new forces had been
added to the now familiar coalition of military and industrial interests which
was the legacy of two world wars. The incredible cost and sophistication of
modern weapons production has increased the drive to sell arms abroad in order
to lower unit costs. Meanwhile the terrible effectiveness of such weapons has
made them more destabilizing of military and political balances than earlier,
less powerful military technologies. At the same time, it has greatly increased
the ability of many governments to ride roughshod over their populations which
have become increasingly alienated.

Stock piles of weapons and soaring arms sales to the Third World, for all their
devastating enormity, were seen by members of the Conference as merely a part
of a more general perversion of science and technology. This had led to the
creation of an uncontrolled multiplication of material life-styles involving
waste, pollution in the developed countries and away from the development of a
science and technology relevant to the human needs and aspirations of the
greater part of mankind. This perversion of the means to development is bringing a new unity to groups which were previously separated in their concerns
with social reform: those concerned with world law and order, those concerned
with poverty, those concerned with the environment and the sustainability of
life on earth, and those concerned with mankind's spiritual needs. This convergence was demonstrated by a high degree of consensus among representatives
of these interests as to what must constitute the elements of a new economic
order.

A new order must involve basic structural changes in all societies, including
more equitable distribution of income and access to the means of production
and much greater participation by all groups in the decisions which affect
their future. Only under these conditions, the Conference concluded, can the
scale of technologies and the transfers of resources be such as to satisfy

basic needs everywhere in the world and lay the foundations for sustainable
and harmonious patterns of development.

In contrast to such moves towards a new order, however, the dominant emphasis
in the developed countries in the last few years has been on the resumption of
economic growth on the earlier post-war pattern. At the same time, only weak
and inadequate efforts have been made to restructure economic relationships
with the Third World. Among the most alarming of recent military developments
has been the renewed clamour for further defence increases in the absence of
any particular war threat, a clamour which has involved most Western countries.
The pattern of increase in defence expenditure in the past 30 years had been
one of surges in spending, matching roughly speaking, major international wars
or crises, especially Korea and Vietnam. Between these crises, spending levels
had fallen back slightly but nevertheless sustained a higher level than before:
a step-ladder pattern of growth. The Conference confronted the fact that at
the present time, the world appeared to be braced for yet another move up the
rung — but without the justification of a major increase in tension.

This pattern underlined the dynamic role of the military-industrial-academic
complex. In many countries, the whole echelon of arms-related interests now
included the professional military, a large military dependent sector of industry and of the scientific community. These groups were now widely established
within the logic of a system built on long lead-time, high-technology development which involved massive capital outlays and which, in turn, inevitably
tended towards an escalation of expenditure on armaments.

But the central issue of concern to the Conference was the massive increase in
the arms trade in the Third World of recent years, much of it resulting from
the Arab/Israel conflicts and their aftermath. The enormous transfer of resources to OPEC, and the coalition of interests between the desire of the
wealthiest oil states to import and the need of Western countries to export,
formed the basic dynamic. The prestige value of modern weapons conveniently
matched the West's need to recycle international liquidity. To the purchaser,
armaments were goods available off the shelf, which unlike even motor cars or
hospitals, required no large social infrastructure for their consumption: for
Western governments, arms spending was an alternative to Arab purchase of a
large share of their industry. The result of this convergence of interest was
a quite extraordinary expansion of the arms trade with an important section of
developing countries.

In discussing the connection between arms spending and resource transfers, the
Conference recognized and condemned the failure of the advanced countries to
live up even to the minimal UN aid transfer targets agreed by the General Assembly. Aid transfers would have provided an alternative means for expanding demand and a weapons cut-back could release resources which the rich West claimed
were too scarce to afford for aid. A 1 per cent cut in Britain's arms budget
would represent a 20% increase in UK aid if transferred to this purpose. Meanwhile, worldwide, governments were spending twice the amount on arms as they
spent on health (or roughly the same amount they spent on education). The
obscenity of this distortion was vividly illustrated by the fact that a single
US missile development programme, Sparrow III, represented nearly double the
entire costs of the World Health Organization's successful worldwide Smallpox
Eradication Campaign.

At the same time, the appetite of many Third World countries for arms spending
in the face of their overwhelming poverty indicated an equal perversion of

their own priorities. However, the Conference noted that astronomic increases in defence spending were by no means a universal characteristic of Third World priorities. A relatively small number of developing countries buy most of the arms, and the effect of the enormous Middle East defence spending of the last half decade should not cause people to think that every country in all three developing continents had caught the weapons fever.

At the same time, the Conference accepted that the transfer of sophisticated arms and weapons systems to the Third World was part of the more general problem of high-technology transfers from rich countries which created dependence, distorted development and endangered international peace. For example, another result of the oil price rises of the early 1970's had been a major campaign by the nuclear power industry of the United States and Western Europe to sell nuclear power reactors to the developing countries as an alternative source of supposedly cheap energy. Such nuclear energy investments were not only highly questionable in their economics, but, because their appropriateness was largely limited to large, high income urban complexes and major industrial projects, they often represented a distortion of development priorities. They compounded the dangers of the conventional worldwide arms race by adding incalculable risks of nuclear proliferation.

At the same time, a third effect of the oil crisis held out more hopeful possibilities: namely the increasing recognition among experts and development planners of the immense possibilities in Third World countries for employing alternative energy technologies such as solar power, wind power, geothermal steam and biomass conversion. Such technologies were often highly suitable to stimulating rural development. They were more labour-intensive in construction, operation and maintenance and they offered greater security of supply than did a small number of very large nuclear hydro-power or oil-fired installations located far from load centres which employed very few people and were acutely vulnerable to construction delays, malfunction, and civil unrest.

The Conference was also encouraged by the widespread re-examination in developed as well as developing countries of many other inappropriate technologies and patterns of industrial activity. Even a modest reallocation to development objectives of the current share of world R & D devoted to military purposes could be expected to produce dramatic results in resource conservation and in promoting new patterns of decentralized development better adapted to meeting the basic needs of ordinary people. These could benefit not only developing but also industrial countries faced with their own need for more balanced regional development.

The Conference concluded that the nature of the arms-race-under-development nexus, while requiring further analysis, was already in broad outline. The most urgent priorities now, the Conference believed, were: first, to seek out, and pursue vigorously, the means whereby people in all countries could be alerted to the dangers, distortions and incredible waste of runaway arms competition; second, to find practical measures whereby the conversion possibilities for defence industries could be demonstrated, (despite economic recession and pre-World War II levels of unemployment in Western Europe).

The Conference believed that it was time for a major campaign to challenge governments to test the findings of several authoritative studies which had shown that the conversion of defence industries to peaceful production was in practicable proportions and not the insurmountable problem that defence interests and government officials so often claimed it to be. Almost all of the resources used in defence industries could be rapidly re-employed in civilian production as had been demonstrated in the massive reconversion exercises undertaken in the aftermath of World War II. The post-world war II economic miracles of Germany and Japan had demonstrated that the release of resources from defence claims could generate more economic dynamism than defence-related technologies with all their vaunted spin-off.

In this connection the Conference applauded the efforts of the shop stewards and union members (of Lucas Aerospace) to persuade their company, a major British defence contractor, to adopt an alternative plan to employ their technological capabilities on such non-defence production as medical equipment, public transport and ocean-bed mining technology. The Conference felt that measures to introduce industrial democracy might gain much greater public adherence if people believed that this could alter the priorities and content of production. This was especially true of the weapons and aerospace industries where unemployment was already high and the social and economic cost of make-work programmes costing many hundreds of thousands of pounds per work-place was becoming a national scandal.

Concerning Britain's own defence posture, the Conference concluded that this could not be separated from the type of arms that Britain manufactured and supplied. If Britain stayed in the game of competing for sales of tanks to certain Third World countries and multi-role supersonic fighters to the Middle East this implied that Britain intended to remain at a particular stage of industrial evolution. The only way out would be for Britain to take the lead in evolving a post-industrial role in the world as an increasingly service-based, resource-conserving, participatory democracy. It would then inevitably apply these post-industrial philosophies to its defence industries as well as to other advanced technology sectors of the economy.

Steps towards a measure of unilateral disarmament were seen by the Conference as essential to make a start in a shift to an "alternative life-style" Britain. The Conference was not able to examine in detail the implications of such a defence posture for all aspects of Britain's external relations, e.g. membership of the European Community, the Atlantic Alliance, etc. The Conference was convinced that "the securest defence is a contented citizenry" and that such a citizenry would only result from a calculated reduction of dependence upon violent technologies and a greater emphasis on social justice and equity. The Conference agreed that British defence policy should be based upon a gradual shift from the present posture of a nuclear-armed multi-purpose defence system towards a conventionally armed aggression-resistance defence posture along the lines of the Scandinavian countries.

Finally, the Conference concluded that groups and individuals should "personalize" the issues. Development, disarmament and environmental protection must be linked in the public mind with a consciousness that change can only come about by altered personal values and life-styles.

APPENDIX

At the Thirty-Second Annual General Meeting of the United Nations Association of the United Kingdom in April 1977 the following resolutions relating to disarmament and development were adopted.

1. THE ARMS TRADE

A. The General Council of the United Nations Association,

Concerned that the economic consideration of the arms trade is in danger of exerting an undue influence on the foreign policy of Western states, and that the export of arms to areas of conflict exacerbates the wastage of lives and resources and that developing countries are being influenced to spend on weapons scarce resources that should be used for food and productive industry;

(1) Believes that strict control of important sales from the viewpoint of foreign policy must take precedence over economic considerations;

(2) Urges HM Government to request the United Nations, as a matter of the greatest urgency, to introduce a system of control over the international sale of arms and to create a permanent UN Commission on the international traffic in weapons of war.

B. The General Council of the United Nations Association

(1) Deplores

    (a) that in 1966 the Defence Sales Organization was set up by HM Government to encourage the sale of arms;

    (b) that this organization costs over £1 million to run per year although military equipment contributes only 4% of British exports and balance of payments;

    (c) that there is no control over the ultimate destination of weapons once they are sold and that British weapons and ammunition have been used against British soldiers in Northern Ireland after being sold to New Zealand, Libya and Nigeria;

(2) Notes that, in spite of the present unemployment situation, trade unionists in armament firms have been pressing for diversification away from weaponry;

(3) Urges HM Government

    (a) to disband the Defence Sales Organization and its staff of civil servants and to assist the armament industry to diversify into socially useful products by research and retraining schemes;

    (b) to reinstate the post of Minister of Disarmament;

    (c) to establish effective licensing of the sale of arms and the publications of such licenses prior to sale.

2. DISARMAMENT

The General Council of the United Nations Association

Welcomes the decision of the General Assembly of the UN to set up a special disarmament centre and to hold a special session on disarmament in
1978;

Welcomes President Carter's proposals to limit the world's armaments to
those necessary for each nation's domestic safety, to free all nations
from the threat of nuclear destruction and to establish a lasting peace
not based on weapons of war;

Urges HM Government to give the fullest support to these proposals by
accepting his invitation to join in these initiatives;

Urges HM Government, in consultation with our partners in the European
Community, to formulate a common policy at the UN which will demand as a
matter of extreme urgency the convening of a World Disarmament Conference
and which will continue to press for a meaningful degree of disarmament by

(a) establishing a corps of experienced negotiators who can anticipate
     and resolve problems between states;

(b) strengthening the availability of peace-keeping forces;

(c) greater publicity for the success of existing and earlier peace-keep-
     ing forces;

Requests HM Government immediately to set up an International Disarmament
Council parallel to the recently established International Development
Council so that the Foreign Secretary, the Defence Secretary and non-governmental organizations concerned in that field can regularly consult one
another;

Decides that as a high priority UNA and WFUNA should make a determined
effort to gain political and public support for general and complete disarmament;

Calls upon the Association to make preparations for the special session on
disarmament as follows:

(1) by publishing information on how the manufacture and sale of arms are
     tied up with the British economy, and how and where conversion to
     peaceful purposes is practicable;

(2) by "grass-roots" efforts by UNA branches to co-operate with other
     groups in their area who are working for peace and human rights;

Urges UNA immediately to press for the representation of NGOs both at the
special disarmament centre and at the special session.

3. NUCLEAR PROLIFERATION

The General Council of the United Nations Association,

Viewing with deep concern the danger to world peace inherent in the spread

of nuclear weapons, especially the possibility of states with nuclear capability converting nuclear materials from civil to military use,

Calls upon HM Government

(1)   as a first step to encourage all member states of the United Nations
      to accept the safeguards of the International Atomic Energy Authority
      on all their peaceful nuclear activities;

(2)   to propose, preferably in agreement with our partners in the European
      Community, that the authority of the International Atomic Energy
      Agency be strengthened to prevent indiscriminate proliferation of
      nuclear capability.

4.   HELSINKI CONFERENCE FINAL ACT

The General Council of the United Nations Association,

Believing that building of international confidence is an important precondition for halting the arms race,

Urges HM Government to use its influence within NATO and the EEC

(1)   to ensure that the measures agreed in the Helsinki Declaration are
      taken seriously and are seen as a beginning for continuing negot-
      iations;

(2)   to obtain prior agreement that preliminary stages of the future
      Helsinki-type negotiations may be attended by representatives of
      interested non-governmental organizations, whose attendance should
      be government assisted.

5.   THE ARMS RACE AND DEFENCE EXPENDITURE

The General Council of the United Nations Association

Urges HM Government to withdraw from the super powers arms race and cut
down defence expenditure, thus freeing resources;

Urges the Executive Committee of UNA to initiate talks with the TUC and
the CBI to promote widespread discussion and understanding of alternative
ways in which the present defence industries could be deployed in more
worthwhile ways.

6.   OVERSEAS AID

The General Council of the United Nations Association

(1)   Deplores the Government's decision (made in December 1976) to cut
      overseas aid;

(2)   Urges HM Government to accelerate rather than delay the attainment of
      the 0.7% GNP minimum level of official development assistance;

(3)   Requests that the Minister for Overseas Development be accorded
      cabinet rank as soon as possible;

(4) Welcomes HMG's recent initiative to set up a programme to educate the
     public in the UK on the needs of the developing world and trusts that
     this will include the necessity to increase British contributions to
     a realistic level to combat the present amount of human suffering in
     the world;

(5) Requests HM Government to establish a unit at Cabinet level to ensure
     that the policies of all Departments which affect Overseas Development,
     including those of trade and aid, are fully co-ordinated and mutually
     supportive.

                    *   *   *   *   *

Subsequently the following resolution was submitted to the Plenary Assembly
of the World Federation of United Nations Associations in September 1977.

THE NEW INTERNATIONAL ECONOMIC ORDER AND THE ARMS RACE

The Twenty-sixth Plenary Assembly of the World Federation of United Nations
Associations

(1) Pledged to furthering by all means within its power the realization of
     the new international economic order as agreed by the Sixth and Seventh
     Special Sessions of the General Assembly;

(2) Noting that the Committee for Development Planning has stated (1976) that:

     (a) "Unless there can be a veritable revolution in the political will of
          the world's most favoured countries between now and 1980, the inter-
          national inputs into the Second Development Decade will be grossly
          deficient. Judged by its own standards in respect of such inputs,
          the Development Decade is almost sure to fail";

     (b) The two most powerful blocking factors are national defence budgets
          and "stagflation" in the developed economies and that: "The single
          and most massive obstacle is the world-wide expenditure on national
          defence activity";

(3) Noting also that world defence expenditures presently amount to some $334
     billion annually and are continuing to increase;

(4) Recognizes that the new international economic order and the international
     arms race are mutually incompatible; that disarmament and development are
     interdependent and that neither can achieve their goals without the other;

(5) Calls, therefore, upon the United Nations and all national UN Associations
     in relation to their respective governments, in the preparation of the
     International Development Strategy for the Third Development Decade to be
     declared in 1980, to put forward at the same time proposals for an Inter-
     national Disarmament Strategy, making provision for the specific linking
     together of the two Strategies, which should include:

     (a) a treaty whereby all countries would agree to reduce by stages their
          defence budgets by 50 per cent during the Decade, including the re-
          duction by 50 per cent of the traffic in armaments;

     (b) the utilization of a minimum of 50 per cent of the funds so saved to
          promote the economic and social development of the poorest countries

substantially through agencies of the UN system and to assist for
example

  (i)   the International Fund for Agricultural Development;
 (ii)   a Common Fund for financing an integrated commodity programme;
(iii)   a sustained ten-year programme on behalf of the world's poor-
       est children through UNICEF;
 (iv)   the UN Fund for Population Activities.

Annotated Bibliography

This bibliography contains literature on the military in
development. It includes standard texts on military institutions in the Third World. But it excludes case
studies or less well known analyses of the military in
the Third World, as well as literature about the arms trade
and military assistance which are not directly relevant
to development. Similarly, it includes standard secondary
sources for basic data on the military in the Third World,
but excludes a large number of primary sources.

Adelman, Irma and Morris, Cynthia, Society Politics and Economic Development.
Baltimore, 1967. (Statistical survey of 74 non-communist countries, including
indicators for the political strength of the military.)

Adelman, Irma and Morris, Cynthia, Economic Growth and Social Equity in
Developing Countries. Stanford, Calif.: Stanford University Press, 1973.
(Finding that economic development leads to decreased political participation
based on quantitative analysis that includes indicators for the political
strength of the military.)

Alavi, Hamsa, Army and bureaucracy in Pakistan politics, in Anour Abdel Malek
(ed.), Armées et Nations dans les Trois Continents, forthcoming. (Analysis of
state apparatus as colonial creation and as mediator between different sections
of the international and domestic bourgeoisie.)

Alavi, Hamsa, Bangladesh and the crisis of Pakistan, in Ralph Milliband and
John Saville (eds.), The Socialist Register, 1971. London: Merlin Press, 1971.
(Summarizes some of the argument in Army and bureaucracy in Pakistan politics.)

Albrecht, Ulrich, Ernst, Dieter, Lock, Peter, and Wulf, Herbert, Federation
of German Scientists, Hamburg, Armaments and Underdevelopment, Bulletin of
Peace Proposals, Norway, Vol. 5, 1974. (A Marxist approach to armaments as a
mechanism for extracting surplus product from the periphery in the interests
of metropolitan capitalism.)

Albrecht, Ulrich, et al., New Trends in the Arms Transfer Process to Peripheral
Countries, some hypotheses and research proposals. Hamburg, 1975, mimeo.
(Examines the implications of recent changes in the patterns of transfers,
including the oil crisis, the spread of arms production, new US military doctrines; includes proposals for future research.)

Albrecht, Ulrich, et al., Armaments and Underdevelopment. Rowalt, 1976.
(This is an expansion of their earlier theories expressed in the articles.)

Ansari, Javed and Kaldor, Mary, Military Technology and Conflict Dynamics:

The Bangladesh Crisis of 1971, to be published by the International Peace
Research Association, see below. (Includes some material on the role of military technology and the army in Pakistan's development strategy up to 1968.)

Barber, William F. and Ronning, C. Neale, Internal Security and Military
Power — Counter Insurgency and Civic Action in Latin America. Ohio: Mershon
National Security Program, 1966. (Contains interesting information on the
nature and consequences of American military aid programmes, particularly civic
action, to Latin America in the early 1960s.)

Barnaby, F. and Huisken, R., Arms Uncontrolled, Stockholm International Peace
Research Institute and Harvard University Press, Cambridge (Mass.), 1975.
(This is a description of the current level of the global arms race.)

Benoit, Emile, Defence and Economic Growth in Developing Countries. Lexington,
Mass.: Lexington Books, 1973. (An important statistical analysis of military
spending and economic growth in 44 developing countries during the period
1950-65, from a modernizing perspective. Includes case studies of India,
Mexico, South Korea, Israel and Egypt.)

Berger, Monroe, Military Elite and Social Change: Egypt Since Napoleon.
Princeton University, 1960. Research Monograph No. 6. (Case study of Egyptian
Army as agent for modernization.)

Berglas, E., Defence, the standard of living and the external debt, Israeli
Quarterly Journal of Economics, Spring 1972. (Considers the effect of military
spending, especially the Six-Day War, on the Israeli economy.)

Bienen, Henry (ed.), The Military Intervenes: Case Studies in Political Development. Russell Sage Foundation, 1968. (A collection of "modernizing" case
studies, primarily concerned with political, as opposed to economic and social
change.)

Bienen, Henry (ed.), The Military and Modernization. Chicago: Aldine Atherton,
1971. (A collection of essays, from a modernizing perspective, including a
summary of available literature.)

Daalder, Hans, The Role of the Military in the Emerging Countries. The Hague:
Mouton, 1962. (Argues that the military have important modernizing impact
over and above economic growth effects, e.g. roads, new skills, organization.)

Debray, Regis, Strategy for Revolution, edited and with introduction by Robin
Blackburn. London: Cape, 1970. (Classic on guerilla tactics in Latin America.
Includes material on impact of guerilla movements on ruling class economic
strategy.)

Einaudi, Luigi, Revolution from within? Military rule in Peru since 1968,
Studies in Comparative International Development, Vol. VIII, No. 1, Spring 1973.
(Argues that education and counter-insurgency experience has created a radical
military government.)

Einaudi, Luigi, Heymann, Hans Jr., Ronfeldt, David, and Sereseres, Cesar,
Arms Transfers to Latin America: Toward a Policy of Mutual Respect. Rand
Corporation, R/1173/DOS, June 1973.

Einaudi, Luigi and Stepan, Alfred C., Latin American Institutional Development:

Changing Military Perspectives in Peru and Brazil. Santa Monica: Rand R-586, 1971. (Compares institutional development of Peruvian and Brazilian military and shows how the shift from moderation to intervention in the sixties has different consequences in the two countries.)

Eleazu, Uma O., The role of the army in African politics: a reconsideration of existing theories and practices, Journal of Developing Areas, Vol. 7, No. 2, January 1973. (A criticism of the "modernizing" theories of the army, from an African perspective.)

Engels, Frederick, Origins of family, private property and state, in Marx and Engels, Selected Works. London: Lawrence & Wishart, 1970.

Finer, Samuel, Man on Horseback — The Role of the Military in Politics. Pall Mall Press, 1962. (Standard analysis of military intervention, based on strength or weakness of civilian institutions. Not directly relevant to development.)

First, Ruth, The Barrel of a Gun: Political Power in Africa and the Coup d'Etat. London: Penguin, 1970. (Historical analysis of military intervention and nature of military organization in the context of the colonial heritage and modern imperialism.)

Gilmore, Robert L., Caudillism and Militarism in Venezuela, 1810-1910. Athens, Ohio: University Press, 1964. (Case study of the changing nature of organized violence and relationship to economic and social structure in Venezuela.)

Goody, Jack, Technology, Tradition and the State in Africa. Oxford: Oxford University Press, 1971. (Shows how the type of military technology imported into pre-colonial Africa was related to the structure of the state.)

Gutteridge, William, Armed Forces in New States. Oxford: Oxford University Press, 1962. (Contains material on the organization of armed forces in the Third World, methods of recruitment, etc.)

Gutteridge, William, Military Institutions and Power in the New States. New York and London: Praeger, 1964. (Wider in scope than the above. Includes chapter on "social change and nation-building", based on "modernizing" assumptions.)

Halpern, Manfred, The Politics of Social Change in the Middle East and North Africa. Princeton, 1963. ("Modernizing" argument about Middle Eastern armies based on idea of soldiers as part of a new salaried middle class.)

Halpern, Manfred, Middle Eastern armies and the new middle class, in John J. Johnson (ed.), see below. (Shorter version of above.)

Hanning, Hugh, The Peaceful Uses of Military Forces. New York: Praeger, 1967. (Factual compendium of non-military tasks carried out by armed forces.)

Hawker, Guy J., Canby, Steven, Ross-Johnson, A., and Quant, William B., In Search of Self-Reliance: US Security Assistance to the Third World Under the Nixon Doctrine. Rand Corporation, R/1092/ARPA, June 1973. (This expresses recent American ideas about how to improve the efficiency of Third World Armed Forces in the US interest without a direct American military presence.)

Huntington, Samuel, <u>Political Order in Changing Societies</u>. New Haven: Yale
University Press, 1968. (Primary concern is with stability, rather than with
development. Includes chapter on politicized military — praetorianism — in
conditions of rapid economic and social change with weak political institutions
— political decay.)

Huntington, Samuel, Political development and political decay, in Bienen, H.
(ed.), <u>The Military and Modernisation</u>, op. cit. (Shorter version of the chapter
cited above.)

Huntington, Samuel, <u>The Soldier and the State</u>. New York: Vintage Books, 1957.
(Standard exposition of concept of professionalism in modern military institutions. Not directly relevant to development.)

Hurewitz, J.C., <u>Middle Eastern Politics: The Military Dimension</u>. London: Pall
Mall, 1969. (Contains a good deal on structure of the armed forces in Middle
Eastern countries and their historical relationship to society. Includes a
chapter criticizing "modernizing" arguments.)

Hurewitz, J.C., Soldiers and social change in plural societies: the contemporary
Middle East, in Parry & Yapp (ed.), op. cit.

International Institute for Strategic Studies (IISS), <u>The Military Balance</u>.
London: annual. (Contains data on size, equipment, expenditure and imports of
armed forces in selected Third World countries.)

International Peace Research Association, <u>A Short Research Guide to Arms and
Armed Forces</u>, forthcoming in English. German version in <u>Technologie und
Politik</u>, Vol. 4, March 1976. (Contains a bibliography and a critical assess-
ment of the main sources for empirical research on arms and armed forces.
Particular emphasis on Europe and the Third World.)

International Peace Research Association, <u>Arms, Technology, and the Third
World</u>, forthcoming. (Collection of essays on the transfer of military technology to the Third World, from a radical perspective.)

Jacoby, Neil H., <u>US Aid to Taiwan: A Study of Foreign Aid, Self Help and Dev-
elopment</u>. New York, 1966. (Creates a statistical model showing that Taiwan
grew faster economically than it would have done had its armed forces not
received military aid but slower than if it had had smaller armed forces.)

Janowitz, Morris (ed.), <u>The Military in the Political Development of New States</u>.
Chicago: University of Chicago Press, 1964. (Collection of essays presenting
"modernizing arguments, based on the sociology of organization".)

Janowitz, Morris (ed.), <u>The New Military: Changing Patterns of Organization</u>.
New York: Russell Sage Foundation, 1964. (Essays on changing military organization. Apart from Lissak's essay, there is little directly relevant to
development.)

Janowitz, Morris, Armed forces and society: a world perspective, in Jacques van
Doorn (ed.), <u>Armed Forces and Society: Sociological Essays</u>. The Hague: Mouton,
1968. (Condensed version of Janowitz's own approach to the analysis of military
institutions; contains very little directly relevant to development.)

Johnson, John J., <u>The Role of the Military in Underdeveloped Countries</u>.

Princeton: Rand Corporation, 1962. (Collection of essays on "modernizing" themes.)

Johnson, John J., The Military and Society in Latin America. Stanford, Calif.: Stanford University Press, 1964. ("Modernizing" arguments applied to Latin America.)

Kaldor, Mary, Towards a Theory of the Arms Trade, paper presented to the Conference on Alternative Trade Theories at the Institute of Development Studies, University of Sussex, September 1975. (Contains arguments about the impact of technology on the structure of armed forces.)

Kaldor, Mary, European Defence Industries: National and International Implications, Institute for the Study of International Organizations, Sussex, 1972. (Argues that the momentum of the arms industry has influenced the size and direction of military spending in European countries and has profound implications for the integration of European defence policies.)

Kanovsky, E., The Economic Impact of the Six-Day War: Israel, the Occupied Territories, Egypt, Jordan. New York, 1970. (One of the few studies which deal with the impact of war on development.)

Kennedy, Gavin, The Military in the Third World. London: Duckworth, 1974. (Compendium of various themes on violence and armed forces in the Third World. Includes some arguments about economic aspects.)

Klare, M., War Without End. New York: Vintage Books, 1972. (This is about the techniques of counter-insurgency in the Vietnam war.)

Lefever, Ernst W., Spear and Sceptre — Army, Police and Politics in Tropical Africa. Washington, DC: The Brookings Institution, 1970. (Primarily concerned with the impact of the army on politics. Contains some material on development and "nation-building".)

Leiss, A.O., Kemp, G., Hoagland, J.H., Refson, J.S. and Fischer, H.E. Arms Transfers to Less Developed Countries, C/70-1 to C/70-7. Cambridge, Mass.: Center for International Studies, Massachusetts Institute of Technology, 1970. (Contains a good deal of material on the arms trade. But analysis is mainly directed towards the control of local conflict and the implications for US military and policy.)

Lerner, Daniel and Robinson, Richard D., Swords into ploughshares: the Turkish army as a modernizing force, in H. Bienen (ed.), The Military and Modernization, op. cit. (A "modernizing" case study of the Turkish Army.)

Liebknecht, Karl, Militarism and Anti-militarism. Cambridge: Rivers Press, 1973. (Marxist classic, first published in 1907.)

Liewen, Edwin, Arms and Politics in Latin America. New York: Praeger, 1961. (Anti-military analysis of Latin American military and critique of US policy. Not directly relevant to development.)

Liewen, Edwin, General versus Presidents: Neo-Militarism in Latin America. New York: Praeger, 1968. (Similar to above but more up to date.)

Lissak, M., Modernization and role expansion of the military in developing countries: a comparative analysis, <u>Comparative Studies in Society and History</u>, IX, April 1967.

Lissak, M., Selected literature on revolution and coup d'etat in the developing nations, in Morris Janowitz (ed.), <u>The New Military</u>, op. cit. (Useful bibliography, including a number of case studies that could be relevant for empirical analysis of the military in development.)

Lock, Peter and Wulf, Herbert, <u>A Register on Arms Production in Developing Countries</u>, Study Group on Armaments and Underdevelopment, Hamburg, 1977. (This is a fairly complete list of all arms produced in the Third World together with an introduction which puts forward the thesis that arms imports and arms production have distorted the whole pattern of industrialization in the Third World.)

Luckham, R., <u>The Nigerian Military: A Sociological Analysis of Authority and Revolt 1960-7</u>, African Studies Series 4. Cambridge University Press, 1971. (Case study of the apparent disintegration of an inherited military institution.)

Malek, Anour Abdel, <u>Egypt: Military Society, the Army Regime, the Left, and Social Change under Nasser</u>. New York: Vintage Books, 1968. (Marxist case study of the impact of Nasserism on class structure and economic development in Egypt.)

Mao Tse-Tung, <u>Selected Military Writings of Mao Tse-Tung</u>. Peking: Foreign Languages Press, 1966. (Includes classic texts on guerilla tactics as well as some short relevant pieces on the post-revolutionary role of the People's Liberation Army.)

Marchetti, V., and Marks, J.D., <u>The CIA and the Cult of Intelligence</u>. London: Jonathan Cape, 1974.

Marx, Karl, <u>The Eighteenth Brumaire of Louis Bonaparte</u>, in Marx & Engels, <u>Selected Works</u>. Laurence & Wishart, 1973. (A classic Marxist analysis of militarism. First published in 1852, one year after Bonaparte's coup.)

McAlister, L., <u>Recent Research and Writings on the Role of the Military in Latin America</u>. Latin America Research Review II, Fall 1966. (Bibliographical essay.)

McKinlay, R.D. and Cohan, A.S., A comparative analysis of the political and economic performance of military and civilian regimes, <u>Comparative Politics</u>, October 1975. (This is an attempt to test statistically various hypotheses about the political and economic performance of military and civilian regimes. The main conclusion is that no valid distinction between military and civilian regimes can be made.)

Millikan, Max F. and Blackner, Donald L.M., <u>The Emerging Nations: Their Growth and United States Policy</u>. Boston and Toronto: Little Brown, 1961. (Contains "modernizing" arguments about the impact of the military on economic growth.)

Naya, S., <u>The Vietnam War and Some Aspects of Its Economic Impact on Asian Countries</u>. Tokyo: Developing Economics, 1972. (Empirical study of some of the economic consequences of war.)

Needler, Martin C., <u>Political Development in Latin America: Instability, Violence and Revolutionary Change</u>. New York: Random House, 1968. (Relates the role of the military in politics to the size of the middle class.)

Nelkin, D., The economic and social setting of military take-over in Africa,
Journal of African and Asian Studies, 2, June 1967. (Empirical critique of
modernization theories.)

Nordlinger, Eric A., Soldiers in mufti: the impact of military rule upon the
economic and social change in the non-western states, American Political Science
Review, Vol. LXIV, No. 4, December 1970. (Statistical analysis of the role of
the military in development based on concept of military as middle class.)

Nun, Jose, The middle class coup, in Claudio Veliz (ed.), The Politics of
Conformity. Oxford: Oxford University Press, 1967. Also in Rhodes, J. (ed.),
Imperialism and Underdevelopment. Monthly Review Press, 1970. (Analysis of
military role in politics, based on class analysis of Latin American societies
and idea of military as middle class. Draws on Marx's analysis of Bonapartism.)

Parry, V.J. and Yapp, M.E. (eds.), War Technology and Society in the Middle East.
Oxford, 1975. (Contains relevant essays by Janowitz and Hurewitz on Middle
Eastern military institutions.)

Pauker, Guy J., Southeast Asia as a problem area for the next decade, World
Politics, 11, April 1959. (One of the first "modernizing" articles based on
the military as middle class and anti-feudal.)

Price, Robert M., A theoretical approach to military rule in new states, World
Politics, 23, April 1971. (Based on index group theory. Not directly relevant
to development.)

Putnam, Robert D., Towards explaining military intervention in Latin American
politics, World Politics, 20, October 1967. (Statistical analysis of military
intervention.)

Pye, Lucien W., Armies in the process of political modernization, in John J.
Johnson, op. cit. (Most well-known version of the "modernizing" argument.)

Rockefeller, Nelson D. The Rockefeller Report on the Americas. Chicago:
Quadrangle Books, 1969. (Report commissioned by then President Nixon, recom-
mending less restraint in commercial arms sales to Latin America, on the basis
that armies are opposed to communism and also "the essential force for constructive social change".)

Rosen, S. (ed.), Testing the Theory of Military-Industrial Complex. Lexington:
Lexington Books, D.C. Heath, 1970.

Rouquié, Alain, Military independence and national independence in Latin
America, 1968-71, in Schmitter (ed.), Military Rule in Latin America: Function,
Consequences and Perspective, Sage Research Progress Series on War, Revolution
and Peacekeeping, Vol. 3. Beverly Hills: Sage, 1973. (Interesting analysis
of reformist coups in Panama, Peru and Bolivia.)

Rouquié, Alain, Le role politique des forces armées en Amerique Latin, Revue
Francaise de Science Politique, XIX, August 1969. (Bibliographical essay.)

Schmitter, P.C., Military intervention, political competitiveness and public
policy in Latin America: 1950-67, in Morris Janowitz and Jacques van Doorn

(eds.), <u>On Military Intervention</u>. Belgium: Rotterdam University Press, 1971.
(Statistical analysis of the impact of military rule on public policy and its
consequences.)

Sivard, Ruth, <u>World Military and Social Expenditures 1974</u>. New York: Institute
for World Order, 1974 and 1976. (Contains statistical tables, comparing military expenditures with various economic and social indicators.)

Stepan, Alfred C., <u>The Military in Politics: Changing Patterns in Brazil</u>.
Princeton: Rand Corporation, Princeton University Press, 1971. (Case study of
Brazilian military with emphasis on change and cleavages in internal organiza-
tion. Includes useful appendix on research methods.)

Stepan, Alfred C., <u>Authoritarian Brazil: Origins, Policies and Future</u>. New
Haven and London: Yale University Press, 1973. (Contains important articles
on association of economic growth, military spending, and repression in Brazil
by Marxist Fernando Henrique Cardoso, and critics, Samual A. Morley and Gordon
W. Smith. Also includes article by Philippe Schmitter, explaining Brazilian
economic policy in a Bonapartist analytical framework, and article by Stepan,
on the effects of counter-insurgency techniques on internal military structure.)

Stockholm International Peace Research Institute (SIPRI), <u>The Arms Trade with
the Third World</u>. Stockholm: Almquist and Wicksell, 1971. Abridged version
published by Penguin, 1975. (Detailed compilation of information about the
arms trade with the Third World. Includes a short piece on economic impact of
the arms trade.)

Stockholm International Peace Research Institute (SIPRI), <u>Year Book on Armament
and Disarmament</u>. Stockholm: Almquist and Wicksell, annual. (Contains statistics on Third World military expenditures and trade in major weapons, as well
as details of individual transactions, involving the production or import of
major weapons in Third World countries.)

Stockholm International Peace Research Institute (SIPRI), <u>Arms Trade Registers</u>.
Stockholm: Almquist and Wicksell, MIT Press, 1974. (Contains details of all
individual transactions involving the import or licensed production of major
weapons of all Third World countries since 1950.)

Terray, Emmanuel, Long distance exchange and the formation of the state: the
case of the Abron Kingdom of Gyaman, <u>Economy and Society</u>, Vol. 3, No. 3.
(Analysis of pre-colonial Africa showing how foreign trade, particularly the
import of guns, led to the introduction of slavery and, consequently, the
establishment of a state. Method of analysis can be applied to modern Third
World countries.)

United Nations, <u>Economic and Social Consequences of the Arms Race and of Military Expenditures</u>, Report of the Secretary General, Department of Political and
Security Council Affairs, A/8469/Rev. 1. New York, 1972a. (Estimates the
resources absorbed by world military expenditures and the harmful effect on
development.)

United Nations, <u>Disarmament and Development Report of the Group of Experts on
the Economic and Social Consequences</u>, Department of Economic and Social Affairs,
ST/ECA/174. New York, 1972b. (Estimates the resources released by disarmament,
in general, and by specific measures of disarmament, currently under negotiation, and concludes that these could directly contribute to higher standards
of living.)

UNA-USA National Policy Panel on Conventional Arms Control, Controlling the
Conventional Arms Race. New York, November 1976. (Recommendations for conventional arms control, including arms transfers, by a panel which includes many
important members of the Carter Administration.

United States Arms Control and Disarmament Agency (US ACDA), World Military
Expenditures. Washington, DC: annual up to 1973. (Contains statistics on
world-wide military expenditures, armed forces, GNP, population growth, public
health and education spending.)

United States Arms Control and Disarmament Agency (US ACDA), World Military
Expenditures and Arms Trade, 1963-73. Washington, DC: 1974. To be published
annually. (Contains statistics on world-wide military expenditures, arms trade,
armed forces, GNP and population.)

United States Arms Control and Disarmament Agency (US ACDA), The International
Transfer of Conventional Arms: Report to the Congress. Washington, DC: 1974.
(Contains statistics on the arms trade for the years 1961-71 and chapter on
the impact of conventional arms transfers on the economies of recipient countries.)

United States Congress, Economic Issues in Military Assistance, Hearings before
the Subcommittee on Economy in Government of the Joint Economic Committee,
Washington, DC, January and February 1971. (Contains revelations on the true
size of US military assistance, as well as discussion and information on the
economic impact of US military assistance.)

United States Government, Composite Report of the President's Committee to
Study the Military Assitance Program (Draper Report), Washington, DC, 1959.
(Report which had significant influence on US military assistance programmes,
based on "modernizing" assumptions.)

United States Government, The Scope and Distribution of US Military and Economic Assistance Programmes, Report to the President of the United States from
the Committee to Strengthen the Security of the Free World (Clay Committee),
Washington, DC, 20 March 1963. (Less substantial and influential than the
Draper Report.)

United States Senate, Survey of the Alliance for Progress, the Latin American
Military, a study prepared at the request of the Subcommittee on American Republics Affairs, Foreign Relations Committee, Washington, DC, 1967. (Written
by Edwin Liewen. Brings his earlier works up to date. Contains some arguments
about the harmful economic effects of the Latin American military.)

Wagts, A., A History of Militarism — Civilian and Military, Revised edition.
New York: The Free Press, 1967. (A classic conservative view of militarism as
a feudal hangover, in contrast to "the military way" as the professional
approach typical of capitalism.)

Weaver, J.L., Assessing the impact of military rule: alternative approaches,
in Schmitter, P.C. (ed.), Military Rule in Latin America, op. cit. See Rouquié
(1973). (Radical critique of "modernizing" and "middle class" analyses. Contains interesting case studies of military regimes in Brazil and Bolivia, arguing that they are both reactionary and radical.)

Welch, Claud E. Jr. (ed.), Civilian Control of the Military: Theory and Cases from Developing Countries. New York: State University of New York Press, 1976.

Wolf, Charles Jr., Foreign Aid: Theory and Practice in Southern Asia. Princeton: Princeton University Press, 1960. (Influential book about US foreign aid
policies and methods of assessing cost effectiveness of economic v. military
aid. Contains a lot of material on the impact of US military aid.)

Wolpin, Miles D., Military Aid and Counter Revolution in the Third World.
Lexington, Mass,: Lexington Books, 1973. (This is about the ideological influence on Third World officers of US military training programme.)

Wood, David, The Armed Forces of African States, Adelphi Paper No. 27.
London: Institute for Strategic Studies, 1966. (Contains basic data on armed
forces in Africa, as of 1966.)

Wood, David, The Armed Forces in Central and South America, Adelphi Paper No.
34. London: Institute for Strategic Studies, 1967. (Contains basic data on
armed forces in Central and South America, as of 1967.)

The Contributors

LORD PHILIP NOEL BAKER was for many years a member of Parliament in Britain and after the second world war, Minister of State in the Foreign Office and Secretary of State for Commonwealth Affairs. His long commitment to work for peace and disarmament involved him in the Peace Conference in Paris in 1919, the Disarmament Conference at Geneva in 1932-33 and many subsequent meetings of the League of Nations and the United Nations. His many publications on international law and disarmament include The Arms Race: A Programme for World Disarmament 1958. He was awarded the Nobel Peace Prize in 1959 and in 1977 was made a papal knight.

FRANK BARNABY has been the director of SIPRI (Stockholm International Peace Research Institute) since October 1971. Before that he was the Executive Secretary of the Pugwash Conferences on Science and World Affairs, and a research physicist at University College, London. He is the author of Radionuclides in Medicine and Man and the Atom, and he has written or edited numerous books and articles on disarmament issues.

ROBIN LUCKHAM is a Fellow of the Institute of Development Studies at the University of Sussex. He has previously held teaching or research positions at Ahmadu Bello University, Nigeria, the University of Manchester, the University of Ghana and Harvard University. He is the author of a book on The Nigerian Military (Cambridge University Press, 1971).

MARY KALDOR is a Research Fellow of the Science Policy Research Unit at the University of Sussex, studying arms production and arms trade. Formerly, she worked for the Stockholm International Peace Research Institute where she co-authored The Arms Trade with the Third World, Stockholm, 1971.

ALVA MYRDAL is a former member of the Swedish Cabinet (1966-73) and of the Swedish Senate (1962-70). She was Chief Swedish Delegate to the Geneva Disarmament Committee and the Political (First) Committee of the United Nations (1962-73). Her writings on disarmament have culminated in the 1975 publication of The Game of Disarmament: How the United States and Russia Run the Arms Race, Pantheon, New York. Earlier books in English testify to her contribution to other fields: Nation and Family, second edition, MIT Press, 1968; and Women's Two Roles (with Viola Klein), second edition, 1965. Alva Myrdal has also served as Top-Ranking Director at the U.N. (1948-50) and UNESCO (1951-55) and as the Swedish Ambassador to India (1955-61).

INGA THORSSON is Under-Secretary of State for Foreign Affairs in the Swedish government. She is chairman of the Swedish Disarmament Delegation, and chief negotiator for issues concerning international, technical and scientific co-operation. Previously she has been head of the United Nations Division for Social Development, Swedish Ambassador to Israel and Chairman of the United Nations General Assembly's Committee on strengthening the role of the U.N. in the field of disarmament. Her books include Internationalising Sweden (1971),

<u>The Social Situation in the Developed Countries</u> (1972), and <u>For Sweden in the World</u> (1974).

RICHARD JOLLY is Director of the Institute of Development Studies at the University of Sussex. His professional life as an economist has been spent partly in development research and partly in governmental planning and operational work, particularly in Africa. He was a member of the ILO Missions which reported on employment problems and basic needs in Colombia, Sri Lanka, Kenya and Zambia. His recent writings on development include contributions to <u>Third World Employment</u> and <u>Redistribution with Growth</u>.

ROBERT NEILD is Professor of Economics at the University of Cambridge. He has worked in the economic section of the British Cabinet Office and Treasury, UN Economic Commission for Europe and was Deputy Director of the National Institute of Economic and Social Research in London. From 1967-71 he was Director of the Stockholm International Peace Research Institute.

BRIAN JOHNSON is a Senior Fellow at the International Institute for Environment and Development in London. He was formerly Director of the Institute for the Study of International Organizations at the University of Sussex. His recent work has concerned issues of environment and nuclear energy and includes the publication <u>Whose Power to Choose</u>, 1977.

Index

A-4 Skyhawk aircraft 22
Abu Dhabi, proliferation of sophis-
    ticated weapons 20
Adelman, Irma 73, 161
Aden — see Yemen (Aden)
Aero-engines, production of 12, 13
Afghanistan
  imports of arms 55
  military expenditure 11, 42
  proliferation of sophisticated
      weapons 20
Africa 76, 163
  armed forces 170
  arms imports 54
  arms trade 16
  military expenditure 8, 9, 10, 11,
      12, 55, 120
  pre-colonial 70, 81
Africa, North, weapons imports 17,
      18, 19
Africa, Sub-Saharan 46
  weapons imports 17, 18, 19
Afrika, General 61
Air-to-surface missiles, production
    of 12
Aircraft
  cost 139
  nuclear-capable 22
  numbers supplied to underdeveloped
      countries 21
  production 12, 13, 14
  stocks 139, 149
  supersonic, in Third World coun-
      tries 20
  use of 69, 70
Aircraft carriers 69
  cost 4
  role 69
Alavi, Hamsa 78, 161
Albania 115
  military expenditure 42
Albrecht, Ulrich 65, 66, 149, 161
Algeria 50, 76
  import of arms 50, 55
  military expenditure 11, 43, 55
  proliferation of sophisticated

weapons 20
America, Central 46
  armed forces 170
  military expenditure 8, 10, 11
  weapons imports 17, 18, 19
America, Latin 76, 162, 167
  arms imports 54, 55, 56, 167
  arms trade 16
  de-nationalization 61
  economic statistics 74
  guerilla tactics 162
  military expenditure 120
  military rule 167, 169
  military technology 40
  "modernizing" arguments 165
  political development 166
  role of the military 45, 166
  weapons imports 17
America, South
  armed forces 170
  military expenditure 8, 9, 10, 11,
      12
  weapons imports 16, 17, 18, 19
AMX-30 main battle tank 17
Andean Pact, withdrawal by Chile from
      50
Anderson, Marian 149
Anglo-German naval arms race 68, 81
Angola, arms imports 50
Ansari, Javed 78, 161
Anti-aircraft missiles, use of 39
Anti-ship missiles, production of 12
Anti-submarine detection 69
Anti-tank missiles
  production of 12
  use of 39
Arab-Israeli conflicts 16, 41, 53,
      152, 162, 165
Arab Socialist Union 78
Arab States Military Industrial Organ-
      ization 12
Argentina 48, 76
  defence industry 12, 44
  licensed production of major weapons
      14
  military expenditure 11, 41, 43

173

DISCHARGED

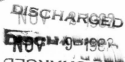

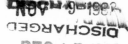

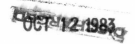

DISCHARGED
NOV
DEC 1 5 1982
DISCHARGED
DISCHARGED

OCT 12 1983

DISCHARGED

NOV
DISCHARGED

DISCHARGED

DISCHARGED